NEAREST THING TO HEAVEN

Nearest

Thing to

Heaven

The Empire State

Building and

American Dreams

MARK KINGWELL

Yale University Press

New Haven and London

Designed by Sonia L. Shannon
Set in Monotype Bulmer type by
Duke & Company, Devon, Pennsylvania.
Printed in the United States of America by
Vail-Ballou Press, Binghamton, New York.

Library of Congress Cataloging-in-Publication Data
Kingwell, Mark, 1963–
Nearest thing to heaven : the Empire State Building
and American dreams / Mark Kingwell.
p.   cm. — (American icons)
Includes bibliographical references and index.
ISBN-13: 978-0-300-10622-0 (cloth : alk. paper)
ISBN-10: 0-300-10622-X (cloth : alk. paper)
1. Empire State Building (New York, N.Y.)
2. New York (N.Y.)—Buildings, structures, etc.
I. Title. II. American icons series.
F128.8.E46K56 2006
974.7′1—dc22   2005035557

A catalogue record for this book is available from
the British Library.

The paper in this book meets the guidelines
for permanence and durability of the Committee
on Production Guidelines for Book Longevity
of the Council on Library Resources.

10 9 8 7 6 5 4 3 2 1

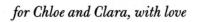

for Chloe and Clara, with love

Contents

Preface

John Updike famously defined a true New Yorker as someone who believes people living anywhere else must be, in some sense, kidding. Anyone who has lived in New York for even a short time can appreciate the profound gravitational pull of the great world capital. I have lived in Manhattan myself at two different times, and close by for another extended period, and like many of us who know the city a bit, I do tend to find life elsewhere, however wonderful, a kind of exile. I always return to the city with a renewed sense of its preciousness, its constant extension of possibility.

This book, like all books, is a complicated expression of love for its subject. Luckily for me, the subject in this case is objectively lovable. The Empire State Building has always been an anchor in my sense of the city, a sturdy peg holding the world of New York, mythic and real alike, firmly in place. I suspect many people feel the same way. But in addition to an accumulated seventy-five years of general admiration, a tribute no less than its due, the Empire State Building has been thrown into greater relief over the past half decade by the terrifying surrenders to violence, and gravity, suffered by its tall siblings downtown.

Since the last days of 2001, the building has assumed a new brightness, a more resonant luster. Affectionate regard, even love, pours toward it from every corner of the five boroughs, indeed from all over the country, and the limestone of its cladding glows with new beauty. If such a thing is possible, it has somehow become more visible than ever before. Or rather, more precisely if also more paradoxically, *it became visible for the first time in decades.* That mysterious dynamic between longing and visibility is the subject of this book.

The building is a symbol of America, to be sure, but it is also far more than that, an embodied cluster of ideas about beauty, technology, politics, and economics. Naturally, my own disappearances from New York condition my thoughts about the building and its meanings, its

iconic status. Much of what follows is concerned with vanishings, failures, deceptions, and distortions—the strange things that swirl around
the building, like windblown paper after a traumatic event. In this vortex
of mislaid messages and dropped signals, there is much to learn, though
not always of the kind we thought to find. Narrative, nostalgia, coincidence, and irony also have their place. You will, I hope, believe me when
I tell you my radio was playing "A New York State of Mind" at the very
moment I sat down to write these words.

This book owes much to the diverse group of people who have, in
their different ways, become essential to its existence. I thank especially
these: my colleague at New York University, Mark Crispin Miller, who
first asked me to consider developing a title for this American Icons
series; our mutual literary agent, Emma Parry, who has been unfailingly
enthusiastic; and Yale University Press, especially Jonathan Brent, Can-
dice Nowlin, and Sarah Miller, for their patience and good will. Three
anonymous readers for the press made many valuable suggestions for
improving the book, and I am grateful for their close attention.

My old friend Maria Mottola allowed me invaluable access to the
day-to-day realities of the Empire State Building from her offices at the
New York Foundation—where, among other things, we looked at the
faded ink record of a $10,000 grant the foundation made to Dr. Albert
Einstein on February 23, 1934. Lydia Ruth, Helmsley-Spear's director of
publicity, is the best ambassador the building could hope for. (She is also,
should you wonder, the person who decides when the building's exterior
lights will change colors to mark a special occasion.) Lydia offered me
her time, her memories, and her incalculable documentation in a way
that would have made the original Empire State visionaries proud. She
forges a powerful link in those shared narratives over time that are the
genius of any great city.

Meanwhile, farther downtown, Leanne Shapton gave me back my
New York neighborhood when I needed a fix. I thank her for her un-
matched generosity and love. Janice Zawerbny and Alicia Hogan collected some pertinent souvenirs for me. I should probably also acknowledge Brian Hahn, of Kansas, who, during a long train ride through what

was then East Germany, argued with me about whether the Sears Tower in Chicago or the CN Tower in Toronto was "the tallest freestanding structure in the world." This debate prompted thoughts of invisible structures, as well as raising the metaphysical conundrum of when, exactly, a structure is not a building.

As my interest in architectural theory has grown over the past decade, I have benefited from discussions with many gifted architects, designers, and teachers. I would like to single out the following: Graham Owen of Tulane University; K. Michael Hays of Harvard University; and George Baird, Robert Levit, Mary Lou Lobsinger, and An Te Liu of the University of Toronto. Karsten Harries, of Yale University's Department of Philosophy, could not have predicted that his intellectual influence on me would only come to light fifteen years late. Nevertheless, I thank him for many illuminating discussions on Heidegger, art, and architecture when I was in graduate school at Yale in the late 1980s and had the pleasure of being his teaching assistant.

My own graduate students at the University of Toronto, especially in recent seminars on architecture and utopia that brought architects and philosophers together, have been important, and challenging, sources of insight. I thank them all for letting me use them as test subjects in this rather peculiar form of theoretical experiment. Jacqueline To, my initial research assistant for this project, stands out from this group as one of those rare architects genuinely given to the pleasures of philosophical debate. Other invaluable research help for both text and images came from the indefatigable and charming Tracy Pryce, to whom I am immensely grateful.

Invitations from various institutions allowed me to work out some of these thoughts in public. I thank colleagues at the Tulane University School of Architecture; the Ontario College of Art and Design; the Nova Scotia College of Art and Design; Concordia University; the Sydney IDEA conference on interior architecture; the London Metropolitan University Department of Design; the University of Toronto Faculty of Architecture, Landscape, and Design; the Royal Architecture Institute of Canada; and Baruch College, City University of New York. Some small portions of this book were previously published in *Adbusters,* the

National Post, and the *Globe and Mail.* The research and writing were supported in part by a grant from the University of Toronto's Connaught Fund.

Finally, and most important, I thank Molly Montgomery for her unwavering support and love. She stands tall, and soars.

1

Palace of Dreams

From the ruins, lonely and inexplicable as the sphinx,

rose the Empire State Building and, just as it had been

a tradition of mine to climb to the Plaza Roof to take

leave of the beautiful city, extending as far as eyes

could reach, so now I went to the roof of the last and

most magnificent of towers. Then I understood—

everything was explained: I had discovered the crown-

ing error of the city, its Pandora's Box. Full of vaunting

pride the New Yorker had climbed here and seen

with dismay what he had never suspected, that the

city was not the endless succession of canyons that he

had supposed, but that *it had limits.* . . . And with

the awful realization that New York was a city

after all and not a universe, the whole shining

edifice that he had reared in his imagination came

crashing to the ground. That was the rash gift

of Alfred E. Smith to the citizens of New York.

F. Scott Fitzgerald, "My Lost City"

A lesser man, an ordinary man, might have retreated into bitterness. But Alfred E. Smith was never ordinary. The charismatic former governor of New York, a firebrand populist of a kind no longer to be found on the American political stage, Big Al Smith first challenged for the presidential nomination in 1924 and lost after being deadlocked with the southern candidate William G. McAdoo. A compromise Democratic nominee then lost the election to Calvin Coolidge—a contest many Democrats, then and later, thought Smith could have won had he been their candidate. Encouraged, Smith tried for the party's nomination again in 1928, and won. In this tilt, he went up against Republican challenger and then commerce secretary Herbert Hoover—who won. Smith tried once more for the nomination in 1932, the year after the Empire State Building was completed, but failed a second time, this time beaten out by Franklin Roosevelt, the man who had nominated him in both 1924 and 1928—and who would go on, decisively, to win the presidency for the Democrats.

Nowadays, and perhaps for most politicians even then, such a series of high-profile setbacks would typically mean a return to semi-obscurity in the Senate or the House, perhaps even a debt-driven slide back to private legal practice. Al Smith—the governor, the Happy Warrior—was a man of larger appetites, and when one grand project failed him, he set about creating another of his own to replace it. He failed to construct a presidency but succeeded in erecting one of the world's enduring architectural wonders, the instantly identifiable soaring tower of limestone and steel that commands the southwest corner of Thirty-fourth and Fifth. He did it, moreover, at a time when the American economy was in a deep trough, and with a command of speed, efficiency, and materials that still astonishes structural engineers and architects. From groundbreaking to completion, the Empire State Building went up in just eighteen months, climbing at a rate of four and a half stories a week—a speed unprecedented and, even in a time of many construction superlatives, almost unthinkable.

To use a word of more recent vintage, it was the world's first megaproject, employing 3,439 workers of all trades, the equivalent of a small

Lewis Hine, "Old-timer, keeping up with the boys. Many structural workers are above middle-age. Empire State [Building]." New York City, New York, 1930. (U.S. National Archives and Records Administration)

industrial town, 104 assorted supervisors, and a general contracting payroll of $250,000 a week. It is a tribute to the Empire State's amalgamated genius of design and construction that the world would not see a building to rival it for almost fifty years. It is a different kind of tribute, this time to the forces of economic depression, cheap materials, and desperate labor, that Smith and his brilliant finance partner, John Jakob Raskob, formerly of General Motors and then chairman of the Democratic National Party, were able to bring the project in under budget and ahead of schedule, reducing the original cost estimates of $43 million to a surprising $24.7 million, mostly as a result of slashed wages and depressed prices for building supplies. In the immediate sense, the Great Depression was very good for the men behind the Empire State Building.

The success of the building would demand more than the perverse good fortune of finding a steady supply of steelworkers and electricians willing to work for pennies an hour, however. It would require rich men to gamble their money at a time when they least inclined to. As early as October 2, 1929, in the volatile weeks just before the Wall Street crash, Raskob held a lunch meeting at which, among various millionaire financiers of his acquaintance, had been William F. Lamb, the architect whose firm had designed the General Motors Building in New York. Raskob knew that the only way to avoid the worst consequences of the looming crash—widespread poverty, riots, maybe even revolution—was immediate reinvestment and rally by those with deep pockets. He also knew, as perhaps only a former stenographer and son of a cigar peddler could, that a grand public achievement would do more to galvanize the American people, and incidentally save the financial markets, than any number of make-work projects or free lunches.

This was a man who, though born into the extreme poverty of the Irish underclass in Lockport, New York, had risen to the pinnacle of American society on a combination of boldness and ability—the American dream made flesh. When his boss at the Worthington Pump Company refused to give him a raise, the young Raskob, on the advice of a friend, wrote to Pierre Samuel du Pont and asked him if he needed a secretary. When du Pont gained control of GM, Raskob went too, rising to a director's chair and eventually financial control of the entire corporation. But his desire to conquer Washington had been, like Smith's, foiled: in the late 1920s, Hooverite opponents blocked his bid to become secretary of the treasury, inventing the pejorative label "Raskobism" for his perceived combination of Catholic conservatism and big business sympathy. He was known to sign his checks, proudly, as "John J. Raskob, capitalist."

Raskob had met Al Smith at the Tiger Club, a smoke, drink, and poker nest on the top floor of construction tycoon William Kenny's Twenty-third Street offices, where the richest men of the city met to socialize and plot. It was a match made, if not in heaven, then in the nearest thing to it: at the pinnacle of human ambition. The two friends, chastened by their respective Washington shutdowns, found themselves looking for something worthy of their talents. And in the idea of the Empire State Building, they found it. Raskob, wealthy and connected as few men were in New York or anywhere, would secure the money. Smith, financially depleted but with boundless charisma, would be the front man. And Lamb, a classically trained perfectionist with an admirable sense of proportion and restraint, would supply the design.

At the October 1929 lunch, Raskob made his pitch. Yes, a big office tower was a major investment, and a major risk. Yes, the markets were going haywire and likely to get worse. But . . . and here Raskob, reports say, broke off the pitch while he and Lamb left the room. They returned moments later with a large model of the Empire State Building. It was, he told the luncheon guests, a building that would represent the United States, "a land which reached for the sky with its feet on the ground." It would, further, be a symbol of "what the poor are able to achieve in America." It was the least the gathered financial geniuses could do to invest in a project that might save the entire economy. "Gentlemen," Raskob told them, "a country which can provide the vision, the resources, the money and the people to build such an edifice as this, surely cannot be allowed to crash through lack of support from the likes of you and me."

Raskob was a persuasive man; also a daring and clever one. He fronted $2.5 million of his own money, got the same amount from Pierre du Pont, and squeezed the financier Louis Kaufman for $5 million more. This $10-million nut paid for the purchase of the real estate, and the Waldorf-Astoria Hotel still standing on it, from Floyd Brown. In December 1929, Raskob persuaded the officers of the Metropolitan Life Insurance Company to give him and Empire State, Inc., a loan for $27.5 million. Just under 30 percent of this sum, $8 million, was immediately paid into the building corporation, with further installments scheduled. The balance, $13.5 million, was to be raised through a bond sale, widening the investment base. But even here Raskob and du Pont took the lead, each buying a quarter of the issue. (The other half was purchased by the Chatham-Phenix group.) Du Pont may have had the coin to take a flyer on the building, but Raskob was not quite that rich. It is fair to say that he bet his bank on the skyscraper he and Smith had dreamed up.

Whatever the other investors thought, and whatever we know with the benefit of hindsight, Raskob had little choice. Ground had been broken on the Empire State Building site two days before, as workers began demolition of the old Waldorf-Astoria Hotel. He was in, for good or ill.

On September 9, 1930, just under a year later, Al Smith wielded a silver trowel to cement in place the 4,500-pound cornerstone of what would become the century's best building. He addressed a crowd of five thousand, many of them workers hoping for jobs on the new project. Journalists dutifully copied down the text of his bland but epoch-making speech. "Eight years ago, a very short time when one stops to think, this land was part of a farm. More recently it was the site of one of the great hotels of the world; and soon it will be the location of the tallest structure ever built by man." In a trademark populist sop, and after some jeering from nearby workers, he added: "So that there will be no mistake or misunderstanding about it, I declare, and firmly, that I have a right to use this trowel as a member of the union. My dues are all paid and I have my card in my office at 200 Madison Avenue."

The Empire State Building opened its doors eight months later, three-quarters of a century ago, on Friday, May 1, 1931. It was a cool, overcast spring day in Manhattan, and Smith, accompanied by his grand-children Mary and Arthur, dressed in their fashionable best, waved his black derby hat at the crowd massed along the avenue. At 11:15 a.m., he leaned down to the children with a pair of ceremonial scissors and said, "Okay, kids, go to it." When their efforts to cut the ribbon failed, he stepped in and finished the job himself, then opened the rather unassuming street-level door of the building at 650 Fifth Avenue: an entrance just thirty feet high. At 11:30, President Herbert Hoover, having excused himself from a cabinet meeting, returned to his desk in the Oval Office and pressed a gold telegraph key wired to the building's lobby, which now glowed with light, spreading throughout the eighty-six stories. The now-familiar marble wall, with its stainless steel inlay of the building's figure and map of the Northeast, was illuminated, light shooting from the summit of the depicted building across the veined surface.

A half hour later, at noon, Franklin Roosevelt, Smith's successor as governor of New York, arrived by limousine and joined the lunch crowd on the eighty-sixth floor. Smith read a telegram from Hoover congratulating him on the building's completion, noting that it would "long remain one of the outstanding glories of a great city." Roosevelt himself opined that the skyscraper, especially in such trying times, was a national treasure: "This building is needed not only by the city, it is needed by the whole nation." The band played "The Star-Spangled Banner," Smith mentioned (but did not read) a telegram he had sent to thank all the workmen responsible for the swift construction, and so the Empire State entered its working life in the usual blast of Smith-generated hot air.

Significantly, amid all the hoopla, it was also May Day, the traditional celebration of international labor, and though probably a coincidence, that fact seems to etch this photo-op moment as the completion of New York itself, not just the building. The familiar skyline, so much the stuff of future cinematic fantasy and youthful ambition, was now substantially done. The city's grid was set, its compression of desire and energy made into a presumptive ideology of constant circulation and exchange —what the architect Rem Koolhaas calls the unspoken urban theory of "Manhattanism."

Money, labor, materials, and largeness of scale all come together in the grid's greatest landmark, a massive vertical column of usable commercial space that obliterates the hotel, and before it the house, that had stood on the same site. The process of the building, its triumphant assembly line, takes over the site, defining a new reality; it becomes automatic, pure construction, swallowing materials, consuming the site, driving always upward with relentless efficiency. Design is smoothly converted into assembly, into process, as if the carefully numbered parts of a scale model were separated, fitted, and glued, one by one, out of the box and according to diagrammatic instructions. Only, in this case, the scale of the model is 1:1!

The building thus becomes, in the process of its own construction, a blind and almost somnambulant servant of an abstract financial idea derived from Manhattanism more generally, the greedy logic of the grid: more rental space, and the faster the better. As Paul Starrett, the building's chief contractor, boldly put it, "Never before in the history of building had there been, and probably never again will there be an architectural design so magnificently adapted to speed in construction."

Thanks to Smith's popularity and seasoned command of publicity, it was already, by that time, famous the world over. On April 29, 1930, Smith and his team began a blanket marketing campaign such as New York, and the world, had never seen. Early ads emphasized New York's trademark combination of history obliterated by novelty, reproducing the 1799 listing by John Thompson of twenty acres of farmland for sale "situated in the heart of New York Island." Follow-up images showed the planned Empire State Building rising from the site over shadows of Thompson's farm and the Waldorf-Astoria Hotel. Smith and Raskob began a relentless series of speeches and articles for the dozen daily newspapers of the pre-television city, plus a host of smaller specialist publications. Soon the architects Richmond Shreve and William Lamb added their own distinctive voices to the barrage of discourse, explaining the design and its construction principles. The building corporation's publicist, Josef Israels, hit on the then novel idea of getting the various manufacturers contributing to the building, including Otis Elevators, Campbell Metal Windows, and Corbin Locks, to publish ads and slick promotional pamphlets highlighting their work for the building.

Newspaper serials tracked the building's gestation from day one, tallying the project's vast appetite for stone, glass, and metal, telling stories of teenage rivet-catchers and fearless Mohawk toppers, lunching casually on steel girders suspended high above the city. Lewis Hine had captured arresting images of this multiethnic workforce of "sky boys" and "poet builders," many of them skilled artisans from Italy and Russia, rescued from breadlines and apple carts by the sudden need of Starrett Brothers and Andrew Eken, principal contractors, for first-rate construction talent—vertiginous images whose own iconic status, often derived from Hine urging workers into spectacularly risky shots, has now become inseparable from the building itself. Radio broadcasts charted the growing height of the steel skeleton and offered predictions of how powerful their own voices would become when broadcast from its summit. When Smith announced his intention to extend the original design from 86 to 102 stories, and add a mooring mast for dirigibles at the new pinnacle, the newspapers could not resist. "Rivalry in Skyscrapers Still Advancing in New York," they said. "Tallest Building to Have Tower Quarter Mile Up."

Story after story chronicled details of the construction process: the hundreds of Pennsylvania steel girders, arriving (according to persistent but probably spurious legend) still warm at the New Jersey side of the Hudson, all shipped over and driven into the concrete foundations where once had stood the Waldorf-Astoria Hotel. The hundred thousand steel rivets heated, tossed, caught, and drilled to stitch together the vast steel frame. The 10,000 tons of metal thrown into the sky each month. Fifty-eight planned elevators; miles of pipe and wiring; thousands of square feet of glass. A forest of 210 steel columns at the base supports the weight of the building, estimated at some 365,000 tons. Ten million bricks were fashioned and laid around the steel skeleton, twenty-seven miles of main and counterweight rails rolled and installed in the central elevator shaft, and 200,000 cubic feet of Indiana limestone cut into ashlar, transported, finished, and installed as the building's distinctive cladding, capable of looking every color from gunmetal to honey, depending on the light and season.

Above all, the awesome *speed* of it all, the vast supply store disappearing into the site and climbing upward as finished work, at one point tallying an incredible fourteen and a half stories in a single ten-day span. The Empire State was designed, planned, and built in less than two years, an astonishing timetable even by today's standards of instant Legoland residential blocks and forests of office towers in Taipei or Berlin. This was the captivating technology of the Ford-hatched assembly line married ingeniously to the old-world appeal of haptic materials such as polished marble and carved granite. Also, on a less triumphant note, the attendant risks and disasters: spilled oil, rain, ice, slips. On January 31, 1931, two Italian day laborers, Luis DeDominichi and Giuseppi Tedeschi, died as the result of a fall. Four others—steelworker Reuben Brown and carpenters Sigus Andreasen, Frank Sullivan, and A. Carlson—would join them before construction was complete.

The city of New York was of course no stranger to high-visibility high-rise construction. In the press of Manhattan's island grid, with space understood to be scarce by definition, the skyscraper form, pioneered in Chicago, had improved and flourished. The Woolworth Building, a humpbacked wedding cake of a structure down at the foot of the island, had opened in 1913. At fifty-seven stories and 750 feet, it was arguably the city's first skyscraper, with twenty-seven acres of floor space and thirty-four Otis elevators, all constructed for a then whopping $10.5 million. The Woolworth surpassed the forty-eight-story, 680-foot tower of the Metropolitan Life Building on Madison Square, tallest at the time, and joined the ranks of distinguished early-century Manhattan peaks that included the Singer, the Equitable, the Park Row, and the Flatiron.

There was more height on the way. At the time the Empire State was just under way, New Yorkers were still reeling from the "Race for the Sky" of 1929, when William Van Alen and A. Craig Severance, former partners turned bitter rivals, vied to design and build the city's, and thus the world's, tallest structure. Van Alen's Chrysler Building, under a heavy cloak of secrecy, had bested Severance's Manhattan Company Building at 40 Wall Street by hoisting its now familiar vertex through the shining, Nirosta-sheathed Art Deco dome. The Manhattan Company tower stretched just under a thousand feet up, with seventy-two stories of office space; but now, though offering only sixty-four functional floors, the Chrysler's "Aztec pinnacle," as the poet Charles Tomlinson has called it, reached to a total height of 1,030 elegant feet. The two buildings had also been erected in record time, in an overheated and unstable economy, and many considered them the last word in skyscraper design.

Sketches show how Van Alen's plan for the Chrysler became sleeker and more spired over time, refining and thinning the steel tower into an elegant arrow. It is still, for many, the most beautiful tall building in the world. Today's admirers may be surprised, except perhaps on general principles that dictate genius shall be disdained by its contemporaries, that the Chrysler was not always considered an aesthetic success. Many people, including William Lamb, thought the vertex design gimmicky and meretricious. The *New Yorker* was especially withering. "It is distinctly a stunt design," their critic said, "evolved to make the man in the street look up. To our mind, however, it has no significance as serious design; and even if it is merely advertising architecture, we regret that

Mr. Van Alen didn't arrange a more subtle and gracious combination for his Pelion-on-Ossa parabolic curves. . . . We cannot help feeling, too, that all this exposed sheet metal is a part of temporary construction to be covered up later with masonry." The same magazine found the Empire State design possessed of "such clean beauty, such purity of line, such subtle uses of material, that we believe it will be studied by many generations of architects." The *New Republic* labeled it "New York's handsomest skyscraper," and William Lamb was named one of *Vanity Fair*'s ten "Poets in Steel"—an honor denied both Severance and Van Alen. In the beauty contest of the day, there was no question who won.

Smith was not to be stopped in the more robust and objective competition, the kind he understood, for brute height. Within a year of the Chrysler victory in November 1929, his Empire State Building was more than halfway to its eventual height of 1,248 feet. A poignant photograph taken from the Chrysler's viewing platform through one of the trademark triangular windows shows the Empire State, just fifteen blocks downtown, stretching its steel frame high into the sky, limestone ashlar already covering the base. Six months later the Empire State would be finished, and so would the race. The Chrysler and the Manhattan Company buildings had gone head to head, neck and neck down the stretch. Now, it was as if a powerful novel breed of animal had rounded the curve behind them and, with a burst of powerful strides, beaten them soundly, going away. No higher building went up anywhere until the Sears Tower in Chicago soared to 1,454 feet, and no skyscraper challenged for the title in New York until the World Trade Center towers were built in the late 1970s.

The World Trade Center never captured the imagination of New Yorkers, and the world, the way the Empire State has. It is not too harsh to say they are mourned more in memory than they were ever liked in fact; and the mourning is surely for loss of life, and innocence, rather than for any architectural or symbolic reason. Except in the pathological imagination of a terrorist, the World Trade Center never really symbolized anything, except the bland face of late-twentieth-century capitalism, with whole floors occupied by traders and brokers, the phone-line and computer-screen workings of spectral wealth. And perhaps that, as much as any idea of America, is what Osama bin Laden was attacking. But he must also have known that attacks on glass-curtain steel frames like the twin towers would be more devastating and final, the steel melting and imploding, than any crash, however finely executed, on the tough stone exterior of the Empire State.

Which is not to say the building has avoided all close encounters with aircraft, planned and otherwise. There has never been a success-ful docking of dirigibles at the top, despite numerous fetching artists' renditions and several wind-blasted attempts in the early 1930s. But on Saturday, July 28, 1945, at 9:49 in the morning, a U.S. Army Air Corps B-25 Mitchell medium bomber, on a routine flight from Bedford, Mas-sachusetts, to Newark, got lost in heavy fog and crashed into the seventy-ninth floor of the building. Fourteen people died in the accident, includ-ing the pilot, Colonel William Smith, his two-man crew, and people both in the building and on the street below. Dozens more were injured and damage to the building was estimated at $1 million—relatively minor, even at the currency value of the day, and with no lasting effect on the tough steel-framed integrity of the building. In the days after September 11, 2001, many eyes looked to the Empire State as a possible next target, but those who worked there knew better, at least in rational moments. The Empire State dates from a period when, however fast they went up, buildings were made to last.

The Empire State is far more dear to the hearts of Americans than the World Trade Center ever was or could be, in part because it is not an obvious warehouse of boomtime capitalism but a symbol of more moving aspiration. Though after all a place of business, it retains the aura of democratic achievement that Smith so clearly wished for it, the concentrated effort across classes and ethnicities that is a key tenet of the American dream. A children's book of recent issue, originally written in German and based on the life of Joe Carbonelli, a young water boy working at the building site, puts the point baldly: "Although there are now numerous buildings that are even taller, this one has remained a symbol for New York and America, and for courage and adventure."

That is not a sentiment confined to children, or children's-book authors. The construction of the building was indeed an astonishing feat of coordinated labor and desire; also of money and political fixing. And it has served a staggering variety of purposes. Businesses large and small have since occupied its eighty floors and 37 million cubic feet of quirky office space, from two-bit garment cutters to shady jewelers and semi-stable insurance companies; even, in fiction anyway, private investigators and shoestring comic-book companies. Many of its offices have also gone empty, sometimes for years at a time, prompting the early nickname that still rises to New Yorkers' lips, the Empty State Building. When the building opened, and was at the height of its fame, just 23 percent of the available space was rented, much of that at a square-footage rate some five dollars below going prices in other Manhattan buildings; the offices from the 45th to the 79th floor, priced higher than those lower down, could not be rented, and Smith ordered the elevators servicing them shut down. By 1936 there were still no tenants in the upper stories, with the notable exception of NBC's fledgling television laboratories on the 85th floor. On the other hand, some 84,000 sightseers paid one dollar each, in the first month alone, to ascend to the observatories on the 86th and 102nd floors. The tourist flow to the building's summit would continue, strong and lucrative, for years, even as its central volume remained ghostly and quiet.

"From the stories," Richmond Shreve commented with grim humor, "the owners might as well lay the building end-for-end, for all the good that rentable area is doing them." This play on the height-comparison rhetoric of the day captures a duality of failure and success that remains in the Empire State to this day. It makes no sense, and yet its absence is unthinkable. Always, whatever the hopes, dreams, and unpaid bills of the tenants in between, thousands of visitors of every nationality and age, princes and paupers alike, have traveled the building's long elevator shafts to rise to the observation deck on 86, even to the smaller eyrie on 102, and take in the foursquare view, gathering together the corners of the greatest American city, the jewel in the nation's crown.

Smith called the building Empire State after New York, and he set up the creative financing of this unlikely venture under the umbrella of the Empire State Corporation, himself in the chair. That sobriquet, so closely allied to the building over the past three-quarters of a century, has a new resonance in the political realities of the twenty-first century. It is worth noting that it is of early vintage, bestowed by George Washington—or so they say—after he toured the fertile farms, advanced harbors, and well-dredged waterways of New York, whereupon he declared the state preeminent in the nation and the "seat of the empire." Sources differ as to whether this alleged proclamation was made in 1778, right after the Revolutionary War, or, more probably, in December 1784, during Washington's presidency. Whenever he said it, it is worth spending a moment to wonder what "empire" he had in mind, especially given that the war had been fought, at least officially, as a resistance to imperial taxation and a violation of Lockean social contract. Perhaps, as a soldier turned politician, Washington simply tended to think in martial terms. Perhaps he was expressing an ambition that was widely shared but mostly kept quiet, the continental ambitions of the new postcolonial Americans. In any event, the name stuck, to the state and then the building, and now that the United States assuredly is an empire, albeit of an unusual postmodern sort, the building has a central place in the economy of meaning centered on the idea of "America."

Even at its inception the building was a strange palace of dreams, a heaven-seeking tower made of solid metal and stone, and serving the needs of business. Standing so firm, technology's latest last word, it appears nevertheless to shimmer and shift before our eyes. "Pure product of process, Empire State can have no content," Koolhaas notes, meaning the building as well as the idea. "The building is sheer *envelope.*" This is not theoretical fancy. The building was, indeed, a total deployment of construction as an idea, as an end in itself. The flex-space innovation of its offices becomes a sort of program of program-free interior volumes. "The skin is all, or almost all," the architect William Lamb wrote, rhapsodically, of his aesthetics-first, outside-in design. "Empire State will gleam in all its pristine beauty, for our children's children to wonder at. This appearance comes from the use of chrome-nickel steel, a new alloy that never tarnishes, never grows dull. The disfiguring shadows which so often come from deeply recessed windows, to mar the simple beauty of line, in Empire State are avoided by setting the windows, in thin metal frames, flush with the outer wall. Thus, not even shadows are allowed to break the upward sweep of the tower."

He concluded with an encomium of startling poetry: "Empire State seemed almost to float, like an enchanted fairy tower, over New York. An edifice so lofty, so serene, so marvelously simple, so luminously beautiful, had never before been imagined. One could look back on a dream well-planned." We fill the empty tower, itself an essay in wish fulfillment, with our own various dreams, and its flex-spaces seem to accommodate them all. Unlike the Chrysler, whose existence was predicated on a prime tenant dedicated to its iconographic program, the Empire State is built in blind hope. Its emptiness is therefore a controversial property, all-embracing but possibly vapid. The building anticipates, we might even say makes possible, the aesthetic and programmatic emptiness of later Manhattan structures—Rockefeller Center, the World Trade Center—which fall into the category Koolhaas labels "the automonument." The automonument is not the monument as described, for example, in Aldo Rossi's structuralist architectural theory: the building that becomes prominent over time, defining a crossroads or arranging an urban fabric around itself via use. Rather, the automonument simply *asserts* its monumentality, makes itself its own argument. No architectural program is necessary, or even desirable. The paradox of the automonument is that, as a building, it is both there and not there; it is dream architecture.

Lamb himself was a dreamer of gifts, a solitary and sometimes somber genius of design, with little of the deal-making talent or financial wizardry of his partners, Richmond Shreve and Arthur Loomis Harmon. Born in Brooklyn and the product of architectural training at Columbia and a de rigueur hitch at the École des Beaux-Arts in Paris, Lamb joined their architecture firm in 1911 and by 1929 was a senior partner of the company, then known as Shreve, Lamb & Harmon. He had lost a leg in a motorcycle crash in Europe and wore a prosthesis that caused him to limp noticeably. Popular legend has it that, after the firm was hired, Raskob—whose own nineteen-year-old son had died in a car crash not long before—called Lamb into his midtown office, held an HB pencil rubber-end on his desk and said, "Bill, how high can you make it so that it won't fall down?" It is tempting to imagine the darker thoughts of the two, poised over that moment of technology and its limits—perhaps pushing the limits.

It is a poignant detail that Lamb, like Raskob—though for quite different reasons—avoided the gala opening of the building by sailing to Europe that very day on the *Île de France*. Three miles out, and so past the Prohibition boundary, he poured two martinis from a chrome shaker, pointed at the building visible in the distance, and said to his wife, "Isn't this marvelous? Here we are and we don't have to go to the party and listen to all those speeches."

Marvelous, indeed. But it is worth pausing to wonder what it could mean to have a "well-planned" dream, a perfectly executed fantasy. Surely the thoughts are categorically incompatible; and yet they seem somehow apt, especially when phrased in Lamb's slightly off-kilter 1930s diction, including the way he, like all the contemporary principals of the project, always refers to the building simply as "Empire State" rather than, as both visitors and native New Yorkers tend to do today, with the full title of "the Empire State Building." That old-school diminutive retains, in our ears, a dreamy quality, a sort of largeness of personality, somehow lost, or maybe tempered, by the tougher and more matter-of-fact address of recent vintage.

Appearances can be deceiving. The truth is, we all wish somehow to enter the dream logic of what I will here call, splitting the difference, either "the building" or "the Empire State." I prefer "building," both for its simplicity and for the fact, buried in its familiar gerundive form, that a building is a process, not a fixed state. We may remember this, and allow deeper insights still to come, when we move from *looking up* at this enchanted tower, and instead *look down* from its summit—perhaps seeing, now, the dream-dashing limits of a merely real city. Enchantment has its costs as well as its rewards. That duality, of imagination and its limits, is the subject of this book.

Our 737 descended from 29,000 feet of clear spring sky and the captain told us what we knew already, that the view was going to be unparalleled. Plowing down to 8,000 feet, the plane drove down the Hudson and the West Side, past the George Washington Bridge and

Riverside Church. Sitting on the left side, I felt like I was slowly entering Manhattan from a dream of cloudless air, decoding its familiar topologies as a three-dimensional map of memory and legend. Not often do we get such a fully realized, magic-carpet-style insertion into the city's streets and avenues, its criss-crossed mesas and canyons built of concrete and steel. The young man next to me, coming to the city for the very first time, leaned over and took his bearings with obvious excitement, finding the landmarks, naming the streets. The Reservoir in Central Park, the Boat Pond, the Zoo. The Plaza and Carnegie Hall. Yes, I assured him, Fifty-ninth and Central Park South are the same street. Madison Square and Madison Square Garden are on opposite sides of the island.

And now, unmistakable in the center, holding it all in place, setting the scale, stood the Empire State Building. It did not flirt and glint in the sun, as the Chrysler did; rather, it stood and waited, so it felt to me, for us to adjust ourselves to its sturdy presence. Slowly, with that illusion of gradualness that airspeed offers, we lowered and braked our way down; and then, the building appearing to loom right outside my porthole, the captain made his approach turn. As it does, the plane seemed to stop dead for a moment in the small g-force of the bank and rudder, a still point in a pivoting landscape, the scene beneath us wheeling and rearranging all the while. The Empire State was right there, filling the window, tall and immobile, another node of stillness momentarily banded to ours. The man next to me, in that moment, before we turned north for Queens and La Guardia, said what I was also thinking. "You feel," he said with what sounded a little like bitterness, "like you could just reach out and touch it."

And we looked at each other and passed a brief moment of understanding, the kind generated by the enforced kinship of economy class, our airless version of the chance railway-compartment encounter of yore. I thought I could detect in him the paradox of vision, the desire to see, to grasp, to *possess* the monumental building, if only for a moment. I could feel, too, the way he felt about the city: its weird gravitational pull, extending in all directions; the way, even if you have never been here before, it seems to exist in order *to make all things seem possible.* Even or especially.

New York is real and imagined all at once, a city of dreams, its myths and meanings too thick to escape. That is a commonplace. But, for all its commonness, it is not a point easy to negotiate; we make an error if we simplify our desires too much here, take the scene, and the action, as one of pure investment and return. For our desires are decidedly not simple, and sometimes aspiration and resentment are close cousins. The hint of bitterness recalled a story another man had told me, of his childhood friend who possessed an Empire State Building snow globe, souvenir of a visit to the city. The man, who had not been to New York, grew to loathe the globe, and somehow by extension the building it modeled. *I hated it,* he told me with a small laugh, *I hated the Empire State Building,* and I was not really surprised by the sting in his voice.

There was, inevitably, another facet, or shard of meaning, in this look of momentary comprehension between the young man and me: a thought of fatal conjunction, airplane and skyscraper surfaces touching farther downtown, destruction of the still-missing towers.

And by that time, we had banked hard over the East River and were beginning to descend along a vector pointing northeast over Queens. The flaps whined to full extension, the landing gear came down with its familiar muffled thump, and now the Empire State was retreating off to the left, an etched image soon lost in the undulating two-dimensional profile of the general skyline. We returned to earth, with only the memory of sight to keep. I watched for the building as we drove in along the Brooklyn-Queens Expressway toward the Midtown Tunnel, and it was there, but not the same way, not as etched and perfect—as fleetingly graspable—as in that short moment somewhere between 8,000 feet and the ground. Then the building disappeared, as it will, back into the forest of New York.

When, and how, is a building visible? When we speak of the Empire State Building as an icon, that visibility, or its possibility, its implicit issue, is the subject of our deepest reflection. What, after all, makes an icon *mean* something, to fire the imagination? And at what point, for what reasons, does it cease to mean, or come crashing down in imagination? In simplest terms, an icon is a religious image, a representation of the holy. But images obscure as well as celebrate, and cultural icons shoulder a heavy burden of metaphysical speculation in the very act of being represented. One dramatic feature of the Empire State Building is its tendency to disappear—that is, as Wittgenstein said of language, to "lie hidden in its obviousness." All icons are more than themselves; it is worth remembering that they are, likewise, less than themselves.

Like the general cultural condition of nostalgia, wherein a notional past is invented and idealized as a magnet of desire, the iconographic positioning of the building as a *past glory* is a symptom we cannot ever escape completely. The Empire State is a powerful symbol of mythic New York, with all the attendant feelings of longing that come naturally when walking New York's thick palimpsest of cultural memory. But that mythic function is never simple, and there are numerous possible ways into the field of meaning that clings to the building, the city, and American society itself. We might say that it is the peculiar function of New York to call us, like Moscow in Anton Chekhov's *Three Sisters* or London in Kingsley Amis's *Lucky Jim,* to the future of our imagined possibilities. I mean that narrative of center and margin that, as we know, embraces both comic and tragic variants.

If the city calls out to all of us, as it surely does, with its siren songs of possible wealth, fame, or recognition—the twinned stories of *arriving* and *moving up*—the Empire State Building is the tower from which the signal is delivered, and the light guiding us back to ourselves. Empire is no longer a term of easy meaning, if it ever was, and that, too, must be part of our reaction to the larger-than-life fact of the Empire State Building. It is both sign and ambassador of New York, capital of the world—or, as we should better say, after Walter Benjamin's characterization of Paris and its epoch, capital of the twentieth century.

A building exists in time as well as space, because we cannot ever see it all at once, sometimes cannot see it at all, only part of it. We must walk around it, enter it, see it from close and far, ignore as well as celebrate it. There is an enduring irony of inside and out, the invitation to the summit being also an invitation to invisibility. Guy de Maupassant was said to have lunched every day at the Eiffel Tower's summit café because it was the only place in Paris where he did not have to look at it. "You must take endless precautions, in Paris, not to see the Eiffel

Tower," Roland Barthes wrote of his city's iconic structure; "whatever the season, through mist and cloud, on overcast days and in sunshine, in rain—wherever you are, whatever the landscape of roofs, domes, or branches separating you from it, *the Tower is there.*" In this sense, the structure becomes so naturalized, so taken for granted, that it disappears. It is, Barthes says, "incorporated into daily life until you can no longer grant it any specific attribute, determined merely to persist, like a rock in a river, it is as literal as a phenomenon of nature whose meaning can be questioned to infinity but whose existence is incontestable."

And yet, the tower does not really disappear; or rather, its disappearance serves to illuminate a larger insight. Not seeing it, but knowing it is there, connects us to all the others who also see it. It becomes a kind of visual lightning rod, a central node in a web of imagined visual connections—a conduit or medium, not of radio signals but of imagination. The Eiffel Tower is more visible to the world's imagination than to a Parisian's. "The Tower is also present to the entire world," Barthes says. "There is no journey to France which isn't made, somehow, in the Tower's name." It symbolizes Paris and France; but also, after its Jules Verne steel-cage fashion, modernity (of a retro kind), communication, science, the optimistic nineteenth century. It is, as we say, richly polysemous. "This pure—virtually empty—sign—is ineluctable, *because it means everything,*" Barthes says in rather plaintive italics. "In order to negate the Eiffel Tower (though the temptation to do so is rare, for this symbol offends nothing in us), you must, like Maupassant, get up on it and, so to speak, identify yourself with it."

What the Eiffel Tower was to Paris and the nineteenth century, so the Empire State Building is to New York and the twentieth. In the dialectic of seeing and not seeing, of being inside and out, down on the street and up at the top, we can find no end of significations that go beyond crude symbolism. Buildings give us back our lost sight, and make visible, in their inside-outness, the things that are unseen. New York without the Empire State Building is unimaginable, far more so than without the World Trade Center; absent its central monument, the city would be broken, incomplete, schizophrenic. *If the Empire State*

Building did not exist, we would have to invent it. And, as we shall see, the iconic life of the building is not merely a collection of facts and images; not a catalogue of souvenirs, a word whose meaning is memory. It is, rather, an exploration of memory itself, the construction and sometimes manipulation of the past, the struggles to remember and make present again. Also—and this too is part of memory's work—the struggle to press forward, to project aspiration into the future just as the architects of our cities and our imaginations project up, and up, always up . . .

Mindful of that, I have not tried, in these pages, to find any final ordered logic in the existence of the Empire State Building. I don't think there is one. Nor have I tried to even out the tendency, I think both natural and illuminating, to amble around this most intractable of subjects. Just as the building cannot be seen in one glance, it cannot be understood in one way. There are architectural and aesthetic appreciations of the building, economic analyses, social histories. I draw to some extent on all of these, but none exclusively, because my concern is the building's iconic function, its cultural role. That role embraces technology, politics, and popular culture, among other features, in a never-stationary system of exchange. We might say that the reason the building remains a living icon is precisely because, like the idea of America itself, it constantly demands renegotiation and revision of its meanings, its significance. The building may appear to stand still, but in reality it is always moving.

The overall argument here concerns the way a landmark can come to express such a layered and rich texture of meanings. I also wanted to convey the profound experience of coming at something again and again, from different angles, with different expectations, at different times of day or with different degrees of thoughtfulness. Indeed, the basic argument is precisely that *nobody sees the building.* Its relation to the coded narratives of Americanness and the dream of liberation are constantly unstable, renewed and upset at every moment. We try to see it, and fail, not least because we are only ever seeing part of it. Even more unsettling, we find that we can only ever see it *as* something, as part of a cognitive frame. These frames of meaning, which structure our *seeing-as,* are themselves invisible; they are what make seeing-as possible. Think of the way a certain kind of drawing may be viewed at one moment as a duck, at another as a rabbit: we whipsaw between frames without (a) seeing the frame or (b) simply seeing the drawing itself. I say "may be viewed" but of course the more accurate formulation is "must be viewed." We have no choice about whether, and when, we see a duck or a rabbit.

The Empire State Building is, you might say, a ramified and extended version of what goes on in that simple drawing. That is, the building supports not just multiple reproductions but multiple *frames,* diverse ways of seeing. The aim of the book, perhaps quixotic, is to draw attention to the variety of these frames as the best way of reading the building—that is, to reveal the building *in terms of* its various invisibilities. From general insights about iconography we move, necessarily, to considerations of height and technology, the inner logic of materials. From there, to closer examination of the relations created between a landmark and its representations, both still and moving. And then, finally, a discussion of the troubling idea of empire, that chance nickname now so unignorable and compromised. Underneath it all, a current of ambition and aspiration runs through the building, a molding of desire and longing, making it a sort of subconscious expression of the American mind, a compression of wishes, an incubator of dreams.

The result is a peripatetic, maybe kaleidoscopic, book—my own kind of dream narrative. I have tried in these pages to replicate that experience whereby, as Roland Barthes remarks, one is "enclosed by a monument and provisionally follows its internal meanders." I hope what follows will answer to that experience of meandering enclosure, perhaps even add to it, without getting lost along the way. This book offers a guided tour of the Empire State Building, then, but from a point of view more idiosyncratic than official; a perspective that is sometimes critical, sometimes celebratory, but always affectionate. To use a metaphor appropriate to the issues of iconic status and nostalgia, the book might be considered a sort of ViewMaster machine. We have in our hands the molded bakelite mechanism, with its squared-off edges and decorative ridging, those peculiar binoculars that look in rather than out. Into this we fit a series of cardboard image-wheels, the store of our representations, and, looking through the eyepieces, press the trigger on the right-hand side to make the machine of seeing function.

Lit from behind, the images now rotate and change, flashing in and out of view, even as our thoughts try to circumnavigate the multifaceted reality of this, the best building in the world. Not the most beautiful, or the tallest, or even the most impressive; just the best, the most perfect, the *superlative* skyscraper. As Deborah Kerr says—twice—in *An Affair to Remember,* the Empire State Building is the nearest thing to heaven we have in New York.

To which one should only add: there or anywhere.

2

Image and Icon

The business of Architecture is to establish

emotional relationships by means of raw materials.

Le Corbusier, *Vers une Architecture*

On a Monday six months after the destruction of the World Trade Center, the crowd at the summit of the Empire State Building, now Manhattan's tallest, is scarce. The longest wait is for security clearance at the base of the tower, and the usually interminable queue to buy tickets, where punters are bombarded with hectoring calls to spend more of their money on package deals and filmshow extras, is mercifully short.

You take the first elevator eighty floors up. Then another one climbs the final six stories and opens on to the clean lines, criss-cross steel fences, and Art Deco details of the observatory. This is as high as you can go now: the final elevator, leading up another fifteen stories to the 102nd floor, is closed.

At its original 1,248 feet, the Empire State Building was the highest structure in the world until 1954, when a guy-wired television tower surpassed it. A 222-foot television antenna mast, which architect William Lamb deplored and opposed, was added in 1950, increasing the building's total height to 1,472 feet—a pinnacle from which it would eventually retreat a smidge, when the old antenna was replaced in 1985 and the overall height was reduced to 1,454 feet. By that time it had been surpassed both by taller buildings—the Sears Tower, the twin towers themselves—and by such tortured-adjective hybrids as Toronto's CN Tower, a telecommunications mast with a revolving restaurant, bar, and observation decks, known as the "tallest freestanding structure in the world."

The Empire State is certainly a building, not merely a structure, in that it was built first, and functionally, as office space. But it is also more than a building; it is an icon. When does a building, or anything, become iconic?

First, via post-facto mythology—mythology that surpasses, and enfolds, the original narrative of its construction. This is a place wrapped in layers of cinematic memory and popular mythology, the ghosts of Cary Grant and Deborah Kerr, of Meg Ryan and Tom Hanks, of Warren Beatty and Annette Bening, even (if you've been paying attention) of Michael J. Fox and a couple of ex-girlfriends to his 1990s television character, the deputy mayor of New York. Not to forget King Kong—in the early versions anyway; in later ones, he scaled a different tower, or one of two

Claudia Esposito Bernasconi, "The Empire State Building," 1983
(Claudia Esposito Bernasconi)

twins, farther downtown. As with so many parts of New York, even if this is your first visit, you know you've been here before.

Or, if you have in fact been here before, maybe when you were young and in love, this time feels different. Of course it does. It is a cold clear day and visibility is superb. Unlike the commanding vista once offered by the twin towers, which made the whole of Manhattan stretch out in front of you like a triangular urban landscape with undulating densities and craggy peaks, including the Empire State itself, this picture is a composite. You must walk around all four ledges to put the city together, piece by piece.

The south side of the viewing space is crowded. People point out to each other what is actually unmistakable, the hole in the sky where the twin towers used to stand. Absence as presence, a kind of retinal after-image whose wavering spectral outlines the mind seems unwilling to accept. A big American flag hangs on the building near City Hall whose height blocks the view of Ground Zero itself. You gaze out as well as down, looking into the bright sky. Airplanes are making their way across the domed air, deceptively stately, even peaceful, at this distance. Visually, they don't give away their terrific speed and power, their coiled kinetic energy and bombloads of jet fuel. Just streaks of lovely silver leaving trails of vaporized fluid behind them, thin straight lines of possibility.

Standing there, cold and alone, you cannot help imagining the converging vectors, the bending flight paths that would connect one wonder of twentieth-century technology with another at the point where you stand.

"The skyscraper and the airplane were born side by side, and ever since then have occupied adjacent rooms in our collective unconscious," the critic Adam Goodheart wrote in the shocked aftermath of September 11. "Before the fire, before the ash, before the bodies tumbling solitary through space, one thin skin of metal and glass met another. Miles apart only moments before, then feet, and then, in an almost inconceivable instant, only a fraction of an inch. Try to imagine them there, suspended: two man-made behemoths joined in a fatal kiss. Fatal, fated: perhaps even long foreseen."

Perhaps, though that sense of precious fatalism misses the wonder, the mechanical joy, of these two quintessential inventions of the passing epoch. Their collision six months ago marks the end of an era and a reminder of the clashing fundamentalism between two world religions (one of which doesn't see itself as a religion), but it cannot diminish the soaring beauty that was turned so heinously to destruction. Technology abused is no argument against technology—not because tools are neutral properties, whatever gun-owners may argue, but because, in violating the beauty of technology in proper use, such abuses highlight the very thing they pass over. Perhaps contrary to intention, they make technology's essential possibilities more evident, not less.

Architects suggested afterward that the era of the skyscraper was over for good, but you cannot believe it. Born in the congested real estate of Manhattan and Chicago, built to new and almost unfathomable heights in Hong Kong and Kuala Lumpur, the skyscraper is, as a nineteenth-century engineer said, the evolution of building from crustacean to vertebrate. Steel beams give us the ability to construct spines and hang floors from them; elevators let us reach beyond the mere six or eight stories allowed by human fatigue.

Sometimes desire rises to mad levels of transcendence. Fantasy skyscrapers of the early modern period show whole country estates lifted into the sky on steel platforms, the transported comforts of home built into thin air where, in fact, only the pressurized, womblike airplane can really go. The human need to rise up, to touch or even inhabit the sky, does not cease. A fatal collision may be implicit in the two beautiful machines, the pillar and messenger, the Atlas and Mercury of our world, but so are the deepest aspirations of human life.

Now, half a year after that sunny black morning, the love of the skyscraper and the airplane is surging back. Long paeans to the chunky Woolworth Building, or the light-absorbing Seagram, appear almost weekly in the press. Habitually jaded New Yorkers, principled opponents of looking up, can be seen gawking openly as late-afternoon sunshine lights up the tough volume of the Empire State, or nighttime mist transforms the Chrysler Building, William Van Alen's unimprovable Art Deco rocketship, into a romantic Tim Burton vision, a peerless symbol of Gotham. You remember, as you have every now and then for years, that the official motto of New York, the empire state, is just one word, an exclamation worthy of the comic-book worlds imagined some floors below you. *Excelsior!*—Higher!

Meanwhile, the forces of memory and money, the public and private interests, try to make sense of that tear in the fabric of Lower Manhattan—so far inconclusively. Memorial or replacement? Building or monument? Building *as* monument? When darkness has fallen on this afternoon, two beams of light will pierce the sky to heights much greater than the lost buildings themselves. And you, because the day's airplanes stayed on course, will be able to watch from the ground, down there with all the other aspirants inhabiting the grid. You have been up inside the invisible, iconic monument-building that still stands, the disappearing wonder that now, for fleet moments, comes back into view. The Empire State.

In the long Thirty-fourth Street lobby gallery of the Empire State Building there is a series of stained-glass panels that illustrate, in garish cartoon colors, the Seven Wonders of the Ancient World. A walk along this rather narrow corridor is like a browse through some long-abandoned textbook or child's encyclopedia of awe. Some of the icons are familiar (the Great Pyramid, the Hanging Garden of Babylon, the Statue of Zeus); others are known more by association than by name (the Tomb of King Mausolus, the Colossus of Rhodes); and a couple arrive as news to those without the benefits of a classical education (the Lighthouse of Pharos, the Temple of Diana). It is an impressive, somewhat campy display of human-made ingenuity and grandiosity, tributes to gods and demigods, to kings and pharaohs. Any child would, in a bygone era, have been expected to know this magic seven intimately, perhaps to recite their names before a Sunday-dinner audience. He or she might not have known, or wanted to, that monumental construction has its human as well as material costs: Chares of Lindus, who designed the massive bronze Colossus of Rhodes in 278 B.C., committed suicide when it far overran its construction budget.

At the end of the row, near the northwest corner of the ground floor, there is an eighth panel, depicting the Eighth Wonder of the World, the building in which you stand, which met its construction budget and prompted no suicides—at least no known ones—among its makers. The explanatory panel speaks of the 16,000 people working in the building stretching into the sky above you, the 35,000 others who will each day visit the observation decks at the summit—numbers more mythological than accurate given that there are just 880 tenants and a staff of 250 in the building right now, and average daily visits run more like 10,000. The panel stands out as the only modern example of constructed wonder offered for consideration: an understanding that the Empire State Building does not merely take its place among some revised list of Seven Modern Wonders but, instead, trumps and even replaces the ancient seven with its awesome presence in Manhattan.

Characteristically, the panel tells us that the building is "as high as all the original Seven Wonders tacked together"—a claim that, in the company of these heroic ancient achievements, might be considered somewhat vulgar. Is height, the sheer brute force of tallness, all you have to offer by way of wonder? In fact, no; but the claim nevertheless expresses the basic form of self-regard that surrounds the Empire State Building. It was for many years, and now is again, the tallest building in a city of remarkable skyline. It has been inhabited and visited by millions, reproduced and modeled hundreds of thousands of times in every imaginable medium from film to butter, starred in more than a hundred films, been deconstructed and rebuilt in Asia (at least via fiction). It has withstood a plane crash as well as the battering weather of seventy-five winters. People have jumped off it, sometimes but not always to their deaths: two rogue BASE jumpers slipped through security, parachuted off the observation deck, and on landing hopped into uptown cabs, folding their parachutes. People have walked, run, and pogo-sticked to its summit. They have walked backward up the same steps. They have, in their millions, taken the still-smooth elevators to experience the splendid view at the top. Radio and television programs have been sent forth from here, businesses started and failed within the solid walls, lives, loves, and deaths all pursued along its thick vertical grid of floors. A giant ape has clambered over its exterior, looking for his own kind of love.

Poems and songs have been offered in tribute to the building. Couples —fourteen of them every Valentine's Day—have been married on its eightieth floor. It has been a yardstick, and fixture, a lodestar of every kind: landmark and comparison, photo opportunity and symbol of human ambition. From almost every part of Manhattan and the other boroughs you can look up and see it. Sometimes it appears monstrously phallic, dense and unyielding; sometimes wispy and ethereal, a dreamscape-scraper. It has inspired and overwhelmed, and has done so while standing there, almost unchanged with the passage of years, apparently impervious to time.

Not that its destruction has not been often anticipated, at least in imagination. In a wry 1997 story, "Mars Attacks," writer Jim Shepard had it topple under the first wave of off-world invaders, broken in half "like a cookie." H. G. Wells and the special-effects artists of *The Day After Tomorrow* both vividly depicted its demise, the second by apocalyptic weather and the first by the inevitable worm in the heart of all twentieth-century technology, obsolescence. In *The Shape of Things to Come* Wells suggests that future generations of city-builders will feel only mockery for the "concrete cavern systems of refuge" typical of the great modernist cities, the crouching midget skyscrapers of the twentieth century. In his version of events, published in 1933 just two years after construction tools were laid down, the Empire State Building, eighth wonder of the world, grows despised and neglected, and is finally torn down in the year 2106.

The Empire State Building was the world's tallest building from its completion in 1931 until the first tower of the World Trade Center surpassed it in 1972, followed quickly by a drop to third when the second twin was finished. From the start it has been an architectural winner, a class star; but it has also become, with the passage of time, a national treasure. William Lamb was awarded the Architectural League's Medal of Honor for the building in 1931, a distinction also bestowed in the same year by the New York chapter of the American Institute of Architects. The Fifth Avenue Association gave the designers their gold medal for design. Billed from the start as a wonder of the world, the building was more practically named, in 1955, as "one of the seven greatest engineering achievements in America's history" by the American Society of Civil Engineers. In 1981, on its golden jubilee, the building was designated a

New York City landmark, and the next year it was listed on the State and National Register of Historic Places. Five years later, in 1986, the National Parks Service named the building a National Historic Landmark.

This catalogue of honors, and there are many more, exhibits a telling arc of change. First appreciated as an architectural and engineering marvel, the Empire State gradually acquires an additional status *as a site,* almost a theme park, of national historical interest. It becomes, indeed, a symbol of the century whose urban fabric it dominates, devotedly visited by more than two million people a year. It never stops being a building, but through the decades it acquires, in addition, its now taken for granted status as a place, a destination, a cathedral not merely of architecture but of Americanness.

The last distinction is worth underlining in a cultural moment, such as our own, where such a thing as architectural tourism has become solidly fashionable and a visit to, say, Frank Gehry's Guggenheim in Bilbao or Daniel Libeskind's Jewish Museum in Berlin are required stops for a certain kind of postmodern sophisticate. These museums, appreciated far more for their design than for any collection they might contain, are nodes in a new cultural economy that begins, perhaps, with the Frank Lloyd Wright Guggenheim in New York, literally inverting the traditional museum design in a swirl of ice-cream-cone concrete but still existing, inside, as a house for art. The new museums are themselves the art; anything else feels superfluous or diminished thereby.

The Empire State belongs to an earlier kind of architectural economy, and offers a different kind of message. In 1924, Ludwig Mies van der Rohe, the genius of modernism in architecture, claimed that, in the twentieth century, "We will build no cathedrals." Buildings, he said, are "mere carriers" of "the will of the age." Since the age was one of drastic functional reduction and utopian simplicity, a postwar urge in literature as well as architecture and social planning, to "make it new," there should be no worshipful buildings, no decoration, nothing overdone or decadent. Adolf Loos famously argued that ornament was *crime,* a judgmental tendency, if not orientation, now mostly preserved in such banal forms as the television makeover program, where fashion crimes are punished, decorating wrongs righted. For Mies and Loos this was never a matter of mere style or fashion; it was a transformative social consciousness, a revolutionary energy.

(It is worth noting that, when it comes to literal cathedrals, Mies was correct: a longstanding project to build a new cathedral in New York has exhibited none of the speed and efficiency of commercial and residential building, and still stands unfinished. Even Washington's National Cathedral, a multidenominational destination site, took decades to build and the result is, as usual when so many competing interests converge, underwhelming. It is an example of that nowadays too-common paradox, the bland monument.)

The resulting early modernist architecture was stripped down, bare, and often lovely; it hovers and rises from the ground. Le Corbusier's celebrated Villa Savoye, for example, built between 1928 and 1931 and arguably the great visionary's best single building, seems to float on thin stilts in an arrangement he liked to call *construction spirituelle*. Even purely utilitarian buildings offered opportunities for this new spirit of material transcendence. Even or especially. Walter Gropius designed a factory in the industrial city of Cologne that features a spiral staircase seen through glass walls, with no visible means of support—a foreshadow, perhaps, of the floating foundation Mies and his partner Philip Johnson themselves used on the midcentury masterpiece of the Seagram Building in Manhattan. The utopian architectural theorist Siegfried Giedion argued strenuously for a pure functionalism in design, almost a functionalism beyond function: a building, he said, is primarily a series of surfaces arranged in three dimensions and designed to stand up. This abstract conception is echoed by today's standard instruction in architecture schools, that buildings are arrangements of intersecting planes and volumes, while Mies's anti-cathedral impulse reaches a kind of apotheosis in Peter Eisenman's idea that buildings are self-organizing systems that exploit us to their own ends.

The Empire State Building stands among these developments in a somewhat unusual, perhaps unique, position. It is an office tower, a place of business. Its central design argument is not style but height: grandness, dimension. It is beautiful, certainly, but not revolutionary in its looks the way buildings by Corbusier, Mies, or Gropius, some of them going up at the very same time, are. Its American solidity contrasts with the European flights of fancy that make the French and German designers into visionaries, social planners, utopian philosophers. Most people, when asked, cannot name the architects of the Empire State, nor do they much care. If the early modern architects of Europe inaugurated what we must now acknowledge as a celebrity economy in architecture, the Empire State resists the movement, swims upstream. It is an icon, to be sure, but not as these other buildings may be—that is, standing as signature works from a celebrated mind, the architect himself (and, very rarely, herself; witness Zaha Hadid) as icon. Rather, the Empire State stands by itself, without support from a famous progenitor or comprehensive vision.

It likewise stands by itself as a focus of national aspiration, an icon of Americanness, a function it could not serve if it were more straightforwardly identified with a particular architectural vision, however compelling. The genius of the Empire State Building as icon is that it appears to offer itself to each one of us equally, the democratic fiction that the wealth of the nation, the pinnacle of its achievements, belongs to everyone. And inside its tallness, its insistent height, what do we find? Business, of course, enterprises large and small, hat companies and lawyers and jewelry wholesalers. A gamut of American dreams, some grandiose and doomed to failure, some quiet and desperate, all accommodated, embraced, by the ninety stories of workmanlike office space. Those enterprises may be invisible to the millions of visitors who have made this building, by their very presence, into a national landmark—indeed, they *have to be* invisible—but the building could not fulfill its iconic role without them. They are the blood that flows in the veins of this Colossus, the light that shines into the American night, a lighthouse of myriad possibility.

The Empire State Building is, at once, always a building and never a building. It is always present, always absent; forever full and empty; unignorable and virtually invisible. When, fifty years into its existence, it passes from being an architectural achievement and becomes historic, a landmark, a site of preservation, it becomes more treasured yet harder to appreciate. Now, a quarter century later still, we may be forgiven for confessing that we sometimes wonder if we have ever really seen it.

We speak and behave as if we understand icons, certainly invoke the term frequently to celebrate or approve a given person, place, or thing, sometimes with the barest distinction to its credit. Iconicity, we note, is a function of desire. But of what desires exactly? They are not simple, and they are not always easily available to view: part of an icon's invisibility concerns the forces that work to fashion it. And we should always recall that "icon," like "commodity," is not another word for *thing* but another word for *relationship*.

To appreciate the nature of iconicity in a mass visual culture such as our own, then—and so to cast some light on the subject standing ready, always standing, at the center of our investigation—let me offer the following excursus in cultural skepticism, a sort of ten-step program for the creation of a modern media icon.

"Icon" is from the Greek *eikon,* which means "image," which (we have been told) is everything: The word for all those little point-and-click pictures on your computer screen. Greek and Roman Orthodox religious objects, little oil paintings of saints with elaborate gold panel coverings. Anybody who represents something to someone somewhere. The image that gives a debased Platonic suggestion of reality without ever being it. So create an image—one the cameras, and therefore we, will love.

The iconic image must be drastically beautiful or else compellingly ugly. It must, for women, show a smooth face of impenetrable maquillage and impeccably "tasteful" clothing (Chanel, Balenciaga, Rykiel; not Versace, not Moschino, definitely not Gauthier), a flat surface of emotional projection, the real-world equivalent of a keyboard emoticon. Icon smiling at the cheering crowds: :-). Icon frowning bravely at diseased child or crippled former soldier in hospital bed: :-(. Icon winking slyly at the crush of press photographers as she steps into the waiting limousine: ;-). There should be only one name, ideally a chummy or faux-intimate diminutive: Jackie, Di, Barbra. Sunglasses are mandatory whenever the ambient light rises above building-code-normal 250 foot-candles. These can be removed or peered over to offer an image of blinking vulnerability.

Or else the image should be, in men, so overwhelmingly tawdry and collapsed, preferably from some high-cheekbone peak of youthful beauty, that it acquires a can't-look-away magnetism, the sick pull of the human car wreck. The only exceptions: (1) athletes—Tiger Woods, Michael Jordan—whose downy smoothness and transcendental physical abilities offer a male counterpoint that is almost female in appeal; they are the contraltos of the icon chorus. And (2), actors or singers, whose malleable faces are so empty of particular meaning as to be innocent of intelligence. Folds of leathery skin, evidence of drug use and chain-smoking, the runes of dissipation etched on the pitted skin of hard living—they all have them. Johnny Cash, Mick Jagger, Leonard Cohen, Kurt Cobain, Chet Baker, late Elvis: the musician in ruins, the iconic face as crumbling stone monument. (One might add W. H. Auden here, in the famous portrait on the cover of his *Collected Poems;* or Samuel Beckett, whose craggy photographed face at eighty excited the sympathy of Jean-François Lyotard: "The network of cracks and furrows," he wrote, "represents so many weak points; misery has entered them, infiltrated them and has been welcomed. Waiting for rain.")

Basic black attire is effective but must be Armani, never Gap. This suggests wisdom and sexual power, deep and bitter knowledge of the world—but with dough. The face need never change, its very stasis a sign of rich inner troubles. Sunglasses are superfluous. They smack of effort.

There must be a narrative structure that bathes the icon in the pure light of the fairy tale or morality play. Beautiful princess beset by ugly siblings or nasty stepmother. Lovely rich girl mistakes the charisma of power for true character. Overweening ambition turns simple boy into gun-toting, pill-popping maniac. Feisty rebel takes on the establishment of (circle one) Hollywood/big business/government/rock music/professional sports. Prodigy singled out for great things at an early age by psycho father.

Indispensable words in the story: "trapped," "betray," "tragic," "love," "promise" (as both verb and noun), "happiness" (always without irony), "fame" (always with venom), and "money" (never spoken). The details of the story may change, but the overarching structure cannot: you can improvise and elaborate, but never deviate. Sometimes a new story (thrill-happy slut consorts with swarthy and disreputable jet-setter) will be temporarily substituted for an old one that no longer applies (virginal bride is unloved by philandering husband). We can't be sure which story will win out until . . .

Death. Already, so soon? Yes, absolutely, for human iconography is very much a post-mortem affair. With monuments, the issue is more ambiguous, as we shall see: not death, but various forms of paradoxical invisibility, the functional equivalent of the human icon's end of mortal life.

The death ends the life but does not quite complete it: that is the business of storytellers and their audience, the cameras and their lights. Death is just the beginning. It should be, if possible, violent, messy, and a bit mysterious. Unwise confrontations with fast-moving industrial machines—sports cars, airplanes, cargo trucks, high-speed trains, bullets. Accidents are good, having as they do an aura of adventitious innocence, followed closely in order of preference by murder, assassination, execution, and suicide. If suicide it must be either a gun or an overdose of illicit drugs, usually in colorful and nasty combination: alcohol and barbiturates, crack and benzedrine, heroin and anything. In all cases, the death is "shocking" and "tragic," though in neither instance literally.

Now, there must be, for a human icon, an outbreak of hysterical mourning, baseless and all the more intense for being so. (Nobody feels quite so strongly, or rather, quite so unambivalently, about someone they actually know.) Extended retrospectives on television. Numerous panel discussions and attempts to "make sense," to "assess the life," to "provide context." Long broadcasts of the funeral or memorial service complete with lingering, loving shots of weeping crowds. Greedy close-ups of the well-known people in attendance, the bizarre fraternity of celebrity which dictates that those famous for being born in a certain family have everything in common with those famous for singing pop tunes or throwing a ball in a designated manner.

News agencies and networks must spend a great deal of money sending a lot of people somewhere distant to cover the death. They must then justify that expense with hours and hours of coverage. We must see images of the iconic face, beautiful or ruined, over and over and over. "Ordinary" people must be shown, on the media, insisting that the media have nothing to do with their deep feelings of loss. They must say that they "felt they knew him (her)," that "she (he) was like a member of the family." This keeps them happy and ensures that no larger form of public participation—say, protesting a tax hike or program cut, resisting a corporate takeover—will ever cross their minds as possible, let alone desirable.

A small backlash must then gather strength, a token gesture of cultural protest that, in pointing out the real faults and shortcomings of the dead icon, unwittingly reinforces the growing "larger-than-life" status of the image. This is the culture's way of injecting itself with a homeopathic inoculation, introducing a few strains of mild virus that actually beef up the dominant media antibodies. Those who have the temerity to suggest that the dead icon was not all he (she) is thought to be will be publicly scorned, accused of cynicism, insulted at dinner parties, but secretly welcomed.

The final storyline of the icon-life will now begin to set, rejecting the foreign elements as dead ends or narrative spurs, or else accepting them as evidence that the icon was "after all" human—a suggestion that, in its very making, implies the opposite. The media coverage will fall into line in telling this story because individual producers and anchors will be unable to imagine doing otherwise. Taglines and feature-story titles will help set the narrative epoxy for good, providing catchy mini-stories for us to hang our thoughts on. Quickie books with the same titles will begin to appear—things like "Icon X: Tragic Ambition" or "Icon Y: Little Girl in Trouble."

The producers and anchors must then claim that they are not creating this tale, simply "giving the people what they want." Most people will accept this because to do otherwise would hurt their brains.

The image will now be so widely reproduced, so ubiquitously mediated on television, at the supermarket, in the bookstore, that it seems a permanent feature of the mediascape, naturalized and indispensable. It will now begin its final divorce from the person depicted. Any actual achievements—touchdowns thrown, elections won, causes championed—fall away like the irrelevancies they are. The face (or rather, The Face) looms outward from glossy paper, T-shirts, fridge magnets, posters, Halloween masks, and coffee mugs. Kitschification of the image is to be welcomed, not feared. It proves that the icon is here to stay. The basic unit of fame measurement is of course, as the critic Cullen Murphy once argued, *the warhol,* a period of celebrity equal to fifteen minutes. Kitsch versions of the image augur well: we're talking at least a megawarhol icon or better (that's 15 million minutes of fame, which is just over 10,400 days, or about 28.5 years—enough to get you to those standard silver-anniversary retrospectives). No kitsch, no staying power: a hundred kilowarhols or less, a minicon.

There follow ponderous academic studies, well-meaning but doomed counter-assessments, sightings, and cameo appearances of the icon on a *Star Trek* spin-off series or as an answer in *Jeopardy.* People begin to claim they can commune with the spirit of the dead icon across vast distances of psychic space. Conspiracy theories refuse to be settled by overwhelming evidence of a boringly predictable chain of events involving a drunk driver, too much speed, and unused seatbelts.

Television retrospectives every decade, with a mid-decade special at twenty-five years. The final triumph of the image: entirely cut off now from its original body, it is free-floating and richly layered. Always more surface than depth, more depiction than reality, the icon now becomes pure zero-degree image, a depicted lifestyle without a life, a face without a person, a spiritual moment without context or meaning. In other words, the pure pervasive triumph of cultural exposure, a sign lacking both sense and referent. In still other words, the everything (and nothing) we sought all along: communion without community.

But is there a rescue? Can an icon genuinely return us to ourselves? Symbolize and crystallize our dreams?

What of a *building* as icon?

One of many counterintuitive claims to be made about the Empire State Building is that *the building itself is not the icon.* The building is surely an example of what the structuralist architectural theorist Aldo Rossi called a monument, that is, "a persistent urban artifact," a part of the city that, through its prolonged relationship to the city as a whole, maintains "a past that we are still experiencing." The Empire State Building is, furthermore, a vivid example of what Rossi labels "vital" (as opposed to "pathological" or depleted) monument. The building's real life in city life continues, forging new experiences of the present and possible future, as well as the contained past. It is a living monument, a working tower. The building establishes a center, an unavoidable orientation. It continually gathers up the city into itself, absorbing the grid by taking its place on the grid; then as it were redeploys those same streets out from itself, setting them in new relation, offering reinforced placement.

All vital monuments, as Rossi suggests, do the same. But I suggest that the Empire State must be understood as iconic as well as monumental. It is more than the automonument described by Koolhaas, the building that presents itself not as a programmed solution to a set of problems in occupation or dwelling but as a simple statement of itself. But it cannot be seen as an early example of the monumental-conceptual architecture so often to be seen practiced in more recent decades, the building (often a museum) as a piece of large-scale sculpture. The Empire State may be, instead, the purest example anywhere of a building that enfolds an entire culture within itself, a perfected sign. What can I mean by that?

The best, indeed only accurate way to understand icons is to see them as relations or nodes within a system of signs, that is, as the subjects of semiotic analysis. We need not be crude structuralists to appreciate that icons, like all elements in a discursive system, function according to accumulated and appreciated meaning. In spoken language, as Ferdinand de Saussure argues, a bundle of phonemes, arbitrary in terms of their relations to meaning, acquire sense in so far as they are conventionally, and usually consistently, associated with a referent. Thus a sign is a conjunction of signifier (the sounds or shapes of, in this case, words) and signified (the intended thing, action, relationship, or concept). The graphic arrangement "bicycle" constitutes a sign because the signifier is obvious to competent users; the closely similar graphic arrangement "bycicle" is not (at the moment anyway) a sign. Meaning is circulated among competent users of the sign system who are able, again usually consistently, to exchange signs with the expectation of understanding. This, as Wittgenstein notes, is much more like a *game* than it is like the mere application of labels to things. That is, things are not preexistent realities picked out by post-facto linguistic assignment; they are what they are as part of the coupled sense/referent bundles circulated by the game via phonemes or letters. We learn to play the game, first, by watching others play.

A referent can of course support more than one kind of sense, and vice versa, and we rely on other features of the system to clarify this feature of the sense-reference economy. "The Morning Star" and "the Evening Star" are arrangements of words that have different senses but the same referent, namely the body in the sky also known by the proper name "Venus." "My favorite meal" is a stable sense with possibly shifting referents. "The present king of France" is a sense without a referent, creating its own logical puzzles for those inclined to play. These cases are not merely marginal slippages but rather highlight the consensual support implied by the whole game. (Sometimes, too, the associated phonemes of a sign are *not* arbitrary: nothing essential connects word/phoneme "cat" to the domesticated feline animal, but "babbling brook" and "bleak broken land" may be, as onomatopoeia, tied phonetically to their meaning.)

If we consider visual signs instead of phonetic ones, we observe similar structures. Visual representation, in a simple case, is a graphic depiction of sense connecting to its referent. The meaning is not merely the referent, however: I may show you a picture of a table meaning not simply to communicate the idea of table but, say, my preference that dinner be eaten, or indeed eaten after a certain fashion. Visual signs are able to support various levels of meaning, and thus, sometimes, to function iconically. Barthes, that master of structuralist analysis of culture, investigated certain examples of visual signs that have what he called a "mythological" significance. That is, these are not mere visual signs in a simple economy of exchanged representations; nor were they even simple symbols in the way that a red rose conventionally symbolizes love. Rather, building on just that kind of symbolic potential in visual signs, they are moves in a highly charged cultural system of layered meanings, telling stories about "how things are" or "what makes sense." In many cases, these "mythologies" were also self-erasing, in that their visual power simultaneously amplified and obscured the clusters of meanings they supported.

Consider one of Barthes's best-known examples. A picture on the cover of *Paris Match,* the French news magazine, depicts a member of the French Foreign Legion in full dress uniform solemnly saluting the *tricouleur.* What is the meaning of this sign? On one level it is merely a photograph of a particular soldier at a certain time and place: a visual representation of a fleeting state of affairs. But the sign is also, clearly, a statement of citizenly commitment, an image of patriotism, even militarism: a coded symbol of Frenchness that functions precisely by conjoining two prior coded symbols of Frenchness, the legionnaire and the tricouleur, in one image.

But now notice what, in the face of the actual image, we see immediately, namely that the legionnaire depicted here is black, and that the date on the magazine places the image in a historical context of struggles over Algerian independence. Now the image is more than either representation or symbol, or both. It is myth—or, to use another word, ideology: it encodes a tendentious political statement that it does not, and need not, fully articulate. A claim about the "true" nature of patriotism, the "transcendent" value of Frenchness, the "devotion" of certain nonwhite Frenchmen, and so on. The image, like all ideology, naturalizes its actually controversial meaning, using the visual power itself to make the disputable seem mere fact. *See, it is simply a magazine photograph!*

As Barthes notes, his reflections were often prompted by a feeling of impatience with this naturalness—a naturalness claimed as much by certain kinds of art as by the more usual suspects of the newspapers, political rhetoric, and that vast space of ideological influence known as "common sense." "I wanted to track down," he says, "in the decorative display of *what-goes-without-saying,* the ideological abuse which, in my view, is hidden." In some cases, the myths explored were things (the standard bistro meal of steak frites, for example, or a new Citroën); sometimes they were images. The special interest of visual mythology, of course, is that the abuse necessarily goes without saying, since the iconic image—to use our own term—is always pre-verbal. It communicates volumes, but not with words.

In this sense, then, an icon is a special kind of visual sign that takes its place within an economy of political meaning. C. S. Peirce's well-known distinction among *indexical, symbolic,* and *iconic* signs is helpful here. Peirce argues that signs are indeed coded bundles of signifier and signified, but that, depending on the example, the *signifiers* could be of quite different kinds. An indexical sign indicates its signified directly, as in the paradigm case by simply pointing to it. A fingerprint or a weather-vane are also indexical signs, however: their meaning is coded by a direct reference, or pointing to the object in question: the person, the wind. A symbolic sign is one that signifies its object without resembling it in any way. Most natural languages are symbolic in this sense, as are, even more clearly, mathematical and logical languages. Here, as with Saussure's arbitrary and different phonemes, there is no need for direct reference in meaning; indeed, a greater range and flexibility in meaning is possible just because there is no relation of resemblances. Twenty-six letters or nine digits and zero suffice to generate a potentially infinite number of meaningful moves.

Iconic signs, finally, are ones that entail some resemblance of signifier to signified. A painting, obviously, is iconic in this sense. So is a graph, whereby growth or velocity is indicated by an upward line or implied volume. A hexagonal stop sign or a green light are symbolic signs in Peirce's sense, but the red hand and walking man used in many pedestrian signals are iconic. The present use of icon is a further extension of this understanding, then, since we will be concerned with images that are visually linked to the Empire State Building but which serve to place the building, and themselves, in a larger ideological field. Icons, like structuralist myths, are both iconic and indexical: they exploit resemblance, and a trace of connection to the "original" object in order to celebrate that object, or reinforce its meanings.

Untangling these meanings is never as simple as following that trace back to the building, for the iconic building—the building that carries meaning in the cultural system—is never merely the building on the street, or even a bearer of obvious signs. The architect Robert Venturi, author of the 1972 study *Learning from Las Vegas,* raised an intriguing possibility during an interview a few years ago with Rem Koolhaas. Discussing the apparent fact that post-postmodern architecture lacked manifestos, and hence a clear direction, Venturi claimed that "the essential element of architecture for our time is no longer space, it's no longer abstract form in industrial drag; the essential architectural element is iconography." Venturi meant not just to denigrate modern formalism—abstract form in industrial drag—but also its late-model cousin, the monumental-conceptual architecture so prevalent today, architecture as sculpture. Architecture is iconographic because it is the communication of meaning, including potential narratives or challenges. These meanings, however, are not simple or reducible to mere propositions, and we make a mistake if we understand iconography as the routine coding of information. To think that way is to succumb to the very naturalization of images we must seek to understand.

We must therefore make one further theoretical distinction, following Erwin Panofsky's provocative work in art history and thus disagreeing with Venturi's still only partial approach. *Iconography,* the reading of subsigns within an icon, is distinct from *iconology,* the reading of iconic meanings, sometimes hidden or encoded, against the cultural and political background. Just as the same topology, or general meaning, can be inscribed on various topographies, so a single iconography can lead to a deeper, and more important iconology. We must, in other words, investigate the icon not simply as a given, or simple, representation of ideas but as a constantly shifting node in a system of cultural self-regard, and self-understanding.

To be sure, "self-understanding" is probably the wrong word, since much of what fascinates here is *not understood,* relegated precisely to the level of taken for granted. Then critical investigation runs the risk of becoming uncritical celebration; done hastily, iconography can, all too easily, become ideology. In consequence, our investigation must entail a special kind of refusal: a refusal to take the taken-for-granted for granted.

It follows that the responsible iconology is the one that makes that refusal necessary, unavoidable, insistent. *That* is the truth in the icon—though perhaps not the truth we thought to find.

Let us begin, however, with the obvious.

The Empire State Building is the clearest single icon of Manhattan's compelling combination of toughness and spirituality, the dream of utopia realized on the grid, and the city as a work of art. The building is a potent icon of Western capitalism and ingenuity, even of modernity itself. It is the spirit of the century, indeed of the American triumph, realized in tempered Pennsylvania steel, Indiana limestone, and the peculiar jazz of homegrown American style, an unimprovable combination of classical proportions and moderne sleekness. Like the unsurpassed popular music of the American Songbook with which it is coeval, the Empire State is a pleasing mix of flowing harmonies, jittery syncopation, and the smart wittiness of lyrics by Lorenz Hart or Cole Porter.

The Empire State's site in the middle of Manhattan makes it, as the architect Robert Stern once said, the lantern of Manhattan, a kind of global lighthouse that focuses and structures the entire city. At the time of construction, the area was an unlikely prospect for commercial development, and indeed the entire project—itself a miracle of early-twentieth-century construction in the immediate wake of the 1929 market crash—bordered on folly. Al Smith had combined money and force of personality to ram the project through. In the architecture firm of Shreve, Lamb & Harmon he found the right mixture of pragmatism and aesthetic simplicity to get a beautiful building up fast.

The politics and economics of the project are an object lesson in American urbanism circa 1930, but also a useful lens for the entire idea of cities: the ordered chaos, the combination of individual and collective aspiration, the forces of greed constrained (and enhanced) by the insistently Cartesian street plan of New York. At the wide corner of Fifth Avenue and Thirty-fourth Street they created a monument to themselves, to the city, to the spirit of the American dream. Like all buildings, the Empire State was constructed in order to effect housing and business—it was, in a modification of Le Corbusier's much-quoted dictum, made suitable for the go-ahead New World, a machine for doing business with. It is thus a potent symbol of enterprise and technology.

But it was also constructed to be consumed as a cultural property, an image. Even as it remains essentially the same through time—its materiality stable, indeed exemplary, just as we would wish from any grand structure—it is nevertheless also a shifting shape, a work in progress. As it is visited and inhabited and remembered by millions of different people through three-quarters of a century, the building's interior spaces alter and its silhouette waves and blurs. The range of appearances it is made to take on, in different lights and through different treatments, swings wildly from the tree-branch utility of the King Kong images to the swaying sub-surrealist distortions and bedded-down kitsch of Empire State images by Madelon Vriesendorp. In the process, it becomes, like all icons, both more and less than itself.

When I was teaching at City University in 2002, I asked my class of political-theory students whether any of them had been to the top of the Empire State Building. It had seemed to me, and still does these few years later, a good time to go, six months after the still-livid memories of the previous September. The aftermath of those events was still, as it were, under construction, just as the site was. There was no clear narrative. The Iraq war and its spectral weapons of mass destruction had not yet come to dominate our thoughts and arguments; both George Bush and Michael Moore had yet to take on their special auras of riven American consciousness. The debates about imperial aggression, the rules of engagement, and the defensibility or otherwise of torture had not begun in earnest.

Likewise, the mass grave at the foot of Manhattan had been cleared but not settled. Daniel Libeskind's short-lived fame as the architect of the World Trade Center reconstruction lay still in the future, just one, as it turns out, of the looping spirals of speculation and ambition that would settle around that chunk of Sixth Avenue. The interested parties, the groups of owners and survivors and politicians and ordinary citizens, had not been offered even the first of the long list of proposals for rebuilding, or memorializing, or celebrating, or mourning the lost towers. Indeed, there is no new building yet, though many have been suggested, and the two shafts of light poking high into the Manhattan night are still the best, the very best, thing we have done and seen to mark that terrible loss.

And so I asked the students whether they would come up to the observation deck with me; whether, indeed, they had ever been there. They were all native New Yorkers but one, a South American transfer student, plus a couple of disgruntled New Jerseyites. None of them lived in Manhattan, as I did. None of them were white. They came from places like Brighton Beach and Astoria and Ozone Park. They sported lots of visible tattoos and athletic gear and wore their ballcaps backwards. They answered their cell phones in class. In a group of fifteen, only one of them had ever been to the top of the building, and she had only done it because her aunt was visiting and wanted to go. None of them showed any interest at all in my idea for a class trip. "You have to understand," the funniest and most outspoken said to me. "We live here."

There is a painting by Charles Sheeler in the Cleveland Museum of Art, an angular arrangement of colors that captures the eye and bounces it around the frame like a tiny metal ball in an old novelty game. The shapes do not resolve into a recognizable pattern or representation until you look and absorb the painting's title: *Church Street El* (1920). It is a view from atop a Manhattan skyscraper—not the Empire State Building, as a tour guide mistakenly suggests, since Church Street is down in Lower Manhattan, near City Hall, and the old elevated railway that ran along its length did not go nearly as far uptown as Thirty-fourth Street. In any event, the Empire State was not completed until more than a decade after the painting. No, the vantage is probably from the tower of the elaborate neoclassical wedding cake of the Municipal Building, a grandiose public edifice in the old style, rather out of place in the press of that neighborhood, perhaps more at home on the Champs-Elysées or Unter den Linden, two sweeping and thronged urban boulevards with bucolic, even heavenly names.

What I love about this painting, though, and especially if we can briefly overlook the mistaken attribution, is the implied presence of the building from which its frame is viewed: an experience of Manhattan, and the urban scene, with the usual polarity reversed. The building is everywhere and nowhere in the image, never seen but always necessary—height experienced from the inside out, presence experienced forcefully by its absence. Most of the images of the Empire State Building—indeed, most images of celebrated buildings of all kinds—work from, as it were, the outside in. There can be no surprise in this, since a building's outward form, its place in the skyline, is its signature, its constant announcement. We watch and gauge its changes, in light and weather, its different shades and shifting volumes when viewed from this vantage or that; but always, always looking at it from the external perspective. We know a building, this kind of building especially, a building of iconic resonance, primarily as a shape, a determinate form.

The form of the Empire State Building is recognizable instantly, almost precognitively, whether in a poster or photograph or bit of kitsch such as a snow globe or part of the compressed skyline of Las Vegas's New York Hotel. It was not just as a result of my own long love affair with the building that I could, wandering through a chaotic junk barn in New Hampshire, a place raftered with old dishes and furniture, signs and medical equipment and fishing rods, clothes and books and magazines of days long passed, see immediately that the small plastic souvenir, the little architectural miniature too light to be a paperweight, gray-painted and with its little square of green baize coming away from the base, was a four-inch version of the most famous skyscraper in New York, probably the world. At any dimension, it self-presents as an immediate whole, a claim about and synecdoche for New York, a sign of New Yorkness. The squat base, the tough but elegant volume of the central shaft, the tapering stages of the top, the familiar shoulders and head—all of these are as unmistakable as the gait of an old friend.

Which is why Sheeler's painting is so unusual. It reminds us of the obvious truth that buildings are also insides, indeed are primarily so when buildings are considered, as they so often are not except by a minority, in terms of their functionality. That truth is so obvious, however, as to become almost invisible, the way anything too long familiar tends to recede into the passed-over as a given: we think we know it, and so very soon we cease to. ("The known," Hegel wrote, "just because it is known, is the unknown.") Such an object is part of the taken-for-granted structure of our shared lifeworld, the unspoken presumptions and concessions—I might say, the compromises and contracts—of existence as we know it. Or rather, as we too often *do not* know it, since these are precisely the things, or features of existence, least often examined or seen. The relation between inside and outside is so basic to human life that we almost cannot see it. Like the threshold itself, it seems to have no dimension and therefore to escape cognitive capture. And yet, without these routine demarcations and liminalities, life as we know it is impossible.

* * *

Any building poses these problems of space, but the tall building, the building as viewing platform, raises still others. We ascend to a summit in order to survey, to take the measure of our surround. This was the function of masts and towers, often in the service of combat, from time immemorial. The earth's curvature, especially on a plain or stretch of open sea, means that even a small ascent expands the visual field, that disc of perception we call the horizon, by an exponential amount. All movements upward work to command more territory, to cover more land or water with the surveillance of my gaze. The desire here may be immediately tactical, to spy the distant galleon or approaching column, but strategically it confesses a deeper wish: for total command, for panoramic vision. The bird's-eye view is the genesis of the transcendental desire in all human thought, the drive to escape circumstance and so, by rising, to achieve true knowledge. Plato's heaven of Forms is merely the most systematic and comprehensive version of this impossible wish, the wish for a final transcendence, a view from nowhere.

The wish starts with a lower-order rising, the achievement of the upright posture: that ascent of the human view to a tower six feet above its emplacement. The exchange of smell for sight as the dominant sense in human perception either drives or derives from this upstanding move— a question of priority that, thankfully, we need not attempt to answer here—and extends itself farther and farther as a result. Having once stood up, we want to stand always higher, and negotiating life becomes a series of ups and downs, not least of which is the resumption of the upright posture after every respite of sleep or, blessedly more rare, fall or tackle. Michel de Certeau, in *The Practice of Everyday Life,* begins his phenomenology of walking in Manhattan by first ascending to the observation level of the World Trade Center and surveying the panorama of New York. The island stretches out before him like a vast triangle of density, toothed and serried in the canyoned streets, populated more by inference than by perception: one cannot distinguish, from this height, the individual humans driving all that energy below; they are present by implication only but necessary for all that.

Here, the urban landscape is seen as a natural landscape, after the manner of the contrived belvedere that, in a semi-wild English garden, offers me a view of water, forest, glade, and valley. A controlled experience of the sublime. The urban ascent is also a controlled experience, but this time of what we might call *the urban sublime.* The natural landscape, even while subject to the forces of growth and decay, is a relatively fixed prospect. The urban landscape, though shaped by buildings, is by definition a scene of motion. We perceive (or perhaps *consume* is better) the presence of humanity not just as space, in other words, but as time. We devour not just the view but the very idea of humanity working within the view, making the view possible. If architecture is, as the critic Peter Conrad put it, "time made manifest as space," a living memorial to its moment, the human overlook of architecture offers a rich temporal palimpsest. We see the movements of time, the living energy, as well as the monuments of time, the buildings that, at some earlier moment, expressed the desires and functions of the builders, and still accommodate the projects and dreams of the inhabitants. Architecture appears sturdy and fixed but in fact it sustains its own kind of movement, a refusal to settle comfortably in space.

We cannot even experience a building except over the course of time, and in this sense, too, it is invisible to us as a totality. At ground level, we must walk around it or enter it. In the sky, with the high view, we try to capture it in the total gaze but have to confess, after a time, the futility of our desire. No view can ever be total. But note the hint of violence here, the surveillance shifting from curiosity to control. The elevated view gives us the world to *read,* not just to perceive. It is the world made map, a chance to transcend sensation and see things in their structure—something impossible for the piecemeal experiences of ground level. The panorama becomes the panopticon, the total surveillance outpost. I take my bearings, finding my own house perhaps—a common preoccupation of those who have risen to a high vantage—and then extend the map of command outward and beyond. I decode the city like a cross-section, or grid plan, or timeline. Barthes, writing of the Eiffel Tower, mentions Victor Hugo's *Hunchback of Notre Dame* and Jules Michelet's *Tableau Chronologique* as imaginative precursors of this act of reading: the one a monstrous ascent, a flight, and the other an act of scientific dominance, time reduced to lines and branches. The same urge is present in an architectural diagram, a blueprint—the sense-making representation of a future or past building, the linear abstraction of a form. In all these cases a constructional logic is revealed to me, to my gaze. I read it, and it is mine.

However high above the city we may rise, we can only see the above-grade levels of that logic. The guts and wires, the piping and phone lines and electric cables—also the subways and tunnels and underground passages—that make the city work, the hidden veins and arteries of urban life, remain concealed. The skin of concrete is largely unbroken, and so the essence of the city's genius invisible. (Surely a large part of the appeal of cross-section books, say of a cruise liner or office building, is the revelation of these layers and layers of functionality, like illustrations in old anatomy books with clear overlays of organs and circulatory systems.) No view, however high, can give us everything we desire.

Even without that consideration, there is no available view that could give us the entire aboveground city in a glance. The view from the Empire State must be composed, accumulated, by the short but demanding walk around its observatory. Like Matteo Pericoli's book of drawings, *Manhattan Unfurled* (2001), which is really one long drawing gatefolded into a case binding, our capture of the city from this vantage is always a work in progress, an achievement. It resists the implicit totalization of the high view even while allowing its pull to be felt: a curious tension, almost poignant. And surely more poignant still in the absence of the downtown alternative. (It was no coincidence, I think, that the Beastie Boys used Pericoli's drawing as the illustration for their heartfelt post-9/11 album, *To the 5 Boroughs,* released in 2004: it is a graphic representation of longing.)

Attempts to read the world from above always fail, then, and not least because we must, at some point, return to the ground. More important, our desires for transcendence cannot ever completely outstrip the material circumstances of their arousal. The tall building points up, inviting us to the sublimity of its summit. But it always stops at some point in the sky, cannot actually reach the heavens it indicates. Moreover, human desire being what it is, every tall building is also an invitation for another, taller one to supplant it at this other summit, the abstract title of "world's tallest building." Tallness strains and collapses in the same moment.

The moment is pregnant with meaning, a paradox that is not a logical tangle to be solved but a moment to set thought free. The Empire State Building was as invisible to my students as any other longstanding—or let us say, *therestanding*—feature of New York life. It had disappeared into the background and become lost. Hence the enduring irony of the cityscape, especially in go-ahead New York, priding itself on sophistication and innovation. The very things that are objectively wondrous, the rising towers and majestic bridges, must go unnoticed in order that the street dweller can maintain his obligatory demeanor of weary cool. It is famously goofy, by local standards, even to look up at the awesome structures stretching away above the sidewalk. This is the act of a rube, one likely to fail at other cognitive imperatives of the real New Yorker, like checking the time, noticing an attractive stranger, and thinking about dinner, even while crossing against the light. The rube, by contrast, notices all the wrong things: he or she is that person likely to take notice of a streetside entreaty, for example, and yet be unable to jaywalk successfully.

The city makes its wonders invisible because it makes its inhabitants unable to notice what they cannot control. Just as the individual struggles, here, to define himself, not against a collective identity but against a roiling background of hyperrealized individual projects emanating from millions of others, so the building struggles to take its place, not so much within the skyline as an architectural landscape as within the vaporous visual space of the citizens' not looking directly at things. As I will suggest, this not looking is, in the case of the handful of superlative buildings, the Empire State in particular, responsible for the iconic fecundity in visual representations. It is, as it were, always more possible to look at an image of the building than at the building itself.

And yet, there are moments, sad and wonderful, when New Yorkers allow themselves to break that basic commandment of city cool, and open up a small space of wonder in the otherwise impregnable carapace of sophistication; to love the building, and all the buildings, for a moment.

3
Scrape the Sky

Skyscrapers, as we all recognize, also express an aspiration towards freedom, a rising above. They may be filled with abominable enterprises, but they do transmit an idea of transcendence. Perhaps they mislead us or betray our hopes by an unsound analogy.

Saul Bellow, *More Die of Heartbreak*

The skyscraper is always, whatever else it might be, a tower; and a tower is always a stairway to heaven.

The very name, initially a mixture of irony and awe, confesses its own transcendent ambition—and awareness of failure. Though we long to scrape it, the sky always retreats from our touch. And the building, once tall, feels its inadequacy. Not least, perhaps, because another building, somewhere else, a few blocks or an ocean away, is ascending just a little bit higher. The tower itself is many things: a military lookout, a security vantage, an escape from flood or disease, a straining for that sense of peace that comes from looking down. An extension of the five-and-a-half-foot physical version we all carry with us, our miniature skyscraper. But it is not a coincidence that rising high, going up, scraping the sky, all imply a stretch for the good, for the Empyrean or Plato's Forms or what you will. The tower joins base with summit, earth with heaven. It is longing made concrete.

There are dangers, too, of course. Perhaps the most famous tower in human thought is the one that tried to reach heaven itself and was sundered into a confusion of languages we still call Babel, a word whose original meaning speaks of the Gate of God. The tower, embodied hope, is also hubris. It is the architecture of dreams. The efficiency of forced architectural precipitates in modern cities, where expensive real estate and small acreages make vertical building and sky-borne square footage merely logical, should not blind us to the poetic and mythic desires forged and elongated in the stone, steel, and glass of the last century. Even with their banal uses, their stock tenants and cookie-cutter designs, each and every one of them speaks of the same human desire, to rise and rise, to soar upward, and finally, perhaps, to fly.

The Eiffel Tower, as noted, offers us the best precursor to understanding the iconic significance of the Empire State Building. That is not because the two structures share any particular functions. The tower houses no tenants while the building, like one of the skyscrapers observed in Saul Bellow's Chicago, teems with an array of humanity widely divided in virtue and interest. It is rather, as we saw, because they assert a meaning beyond their material existence—a meaning that

Titus Paulsel, "Pointed Icon" (Titus Paulsel/Photocorral.com)

extends past the simple suggestion, in all tall structures, of yearning. The Eiffel Tower, or something like it, was imagined as early as 1881, when Pierre-Auguste Eiffel sketched plans for a sun tower a thousand feet tall, with mirrors to illuminate all of Paris, and a sunroom for invalids to take air "as pure as in the mountains." A sort of vertical spa, the tower offers an urban alternative to the anticonsumptive cures of Davos or Yverdon-les-Bains, those havens for Nietzsche and Thomas Mann. Lacking steel, the plan called for this tower to be made of masonry, a structural impossibility.

Eight years later, the material conditions had changed drastically. The Exposition Universelle, celebrating the centenary of the French Revolution, offered Eiffel the chance to create a version of his dream, artifact of this second iron age, the one of mass-produced I-beams and rivets. Originally meant to be disassembled after the exposition, the tower survived through second use. Roland Barthes may see the tower as a zero-degree sign—"for all lovers of signification, it plays a glamorous part, that of pure signifier"—but Eiffel himself defended it as useful. The tower offers, he suggested, a testbed for extreme science, otherwise impossible forays in aerodynamic measurement, the physiology of the climber, resistance of substances, radio-electric research, optics, meteorology, and telecommunications. In this last respect, the Eiffel Tower foreshadows the construction of later engineering marvels such as Toronto's CN Tower, now rarely included on lists of tall edifices, and Shanghai's sublimely hideous Oriental Pearl Tower, a cartoonish concrete excrescence dominating the Pudong district of China's monstrous architectural wonderland.

As with so many other aspects of iconicity, the dialectic between meaning and use carries over to the Empire State Building. The more we see it as significant, a conjunction of seeing and being seen—a completion of the two verbs, a transcendence of position itself—the more insistent are claims that it simply offers a scientific testbed or efficient experimental site. In an age overwhelmed by science and its instrumental application, technology, we somehow find it unacceptable to emphasize anything *other than* the use-value of even so obvious an illustration of human desire. Al Smith, singing the transcendental pleasures of the

Empire State Building in his 1934 souvenir pamphlet, *Above the Clouds,* could not resist doing the very same thing. "The Tower has served many purposes besides that of a platform to look out on the world beneath," he said of the building's summit. "Aviation authorities, many times each week, telephone to learn the wind velocity and the height of the ceiling above its pinnacle. Scientists have used it as a laboratory for the study of radio transmission; for the study of wind velocity and pressure; and for the study of electrical action."

Sufferers from hay fever and sinus afflictions, he adds, sought relief in its vast elevator shafts. "One dear old lady rose up and down for hours on the fast-moving elevators in an effort to cure or reduce the intensity of approaching density"—whatever that means. These seekers after cure are no longer to be found haunting the building, but their place has been taken by an invisible crew of stunt-masters, pranksters, and hobbyists who desire, as it might be, to pogo or walk backward up the stairs, rappel or BASE jump off the building, or otherwise subvert its businesslike efficiency, its stolid *buildingness,* into something more playful, and human. Building officials report that, with some exceptions such as charity stair-climbs, these incursions are resisted. The building is there for all to see, but only for some to use, and only in the prescribed ways. As so often, the triumph of use-value is a victory of constraint, an extended legislation organized around the "proper" or "appropriate" uses of a thing, the sanctioned consumption of its energy and nothing else.

The organized violence of speed, as Paul Virilio called it, is here embodied and implied in the organized logic of the building, born as a stop-action essay in swift construction and now a series of possibilities at once raised and closed off. The observation deck becomes, on this view, a kind of safety valve or ritual space of avoidance. Visitors are herded (sometimes, alas, literally) along vertical chutes of permitted access, deposited into the controlled space of the uppermost view, a platform far smaller than most people usually imagine, and then ushered back down to the street from which they have come. The building beckons with every inch of its height, a beacon of suggestion; but the reality is far more restricted and surveilled than we have been led to believe. Thus, perhaps, the persistence of perverse desire here: to leap the barrier, penetrate the boundary, exit or overturn the edifice to my own tune or liking. We all harbor a wish to parachute off the Empire State Building after pogo-sticking our way to the top. At the same time—and thankfully, too, for us—the building itself refuses to be bound by its own use-value fetishes, its culture of restriction. It bursts out of its own limits, shifting and shimmering in the changing light or distance, never presenting precisely the same image twice, even while calling us, again and again, to its top, promising something, we're never quite sure what.

The Eiffel Tower is a structure of the nineteenth century, still interested in harmonizing old and new, bridging medieval with modern Paris. Jean Cocteau called it "the Notre-Dame of the Left Bank," and that is about right: it is a cathedral of early modern aspiration, a temple of Progress. No wonder that it inspired so much image-making and poetry, from Georges Seurat's multiple paintings and Robert Delaunay's fractured photographic views to Henri Rivière's best-selling series of lithographs, *Les Trente-six Vues de la Tour Eifel.* V. V. Mayakovsky and Guillaume Apollinaire were both inspired to write poems in its honor, and its sight lifted Cocteau to one of his more obviously strained metaphors. The tower, he said, is "a beautiful young woman in mittens, whose sole former employment was that of reigning over Paris and who today is simply the telegraph lady."

The Empire State has, as a Manhattan building, little interest in forging a link between past and present. If anything, it is a bridge from present to future, a gateway to what the critic Jed Perl once described as "the adolescent city," the city of big dreams and unquenched ambition. The right building for New York, for the New World, for the empire state, for the American empire itself. Joyful but tough, a place to think big thoughts and survey worlds to conquer. From here, I look down at the city, and the world, I will overcome. Poems are not written for this building, though they might be for others that are less central, less plentiful in their significance. In the Everyman's Library volume *Poems of New York,* published in 2002, there are tributes to the Chrysler and Mies van der Rohe's Seagram, but not a line directly addressed to the godfather of skyscrapers, the pinnacle, the Empire State. It is as if the building is its own poetry, and needs no other. And yet—wisely, aptly—the book's designers have made the only possible choice for the cover: on the front, a daytime lithographed view of the Empire State, reminiscent of an old picture postcard, and on the back a nighttime shot of the same, the chrome-plated communications tower glowing red and yellow like a lantern of hope in a dark world.

"The Tower can live on itself," Barthes said of Eiffel's creation. "One can dream there, eat there, observe there, understand there, marvel there, shop there; as on an ocean liner (another mythic object that sets children dreaming), one can feel oneself cut off from the world and yet the owner of the world." But that is not quite right, and we must correct a Frenchman's forgivable error, even as his insight resonates. The world surveyed from the Eiffel Tower is no longer the world to be owned. That site has shifted, and its new coordinates, from 1931 on, for better and worse, are Thirty-fourth and Fifth.

The skyscraper's appeal is closely linked to modernity itself, especially the high point of aspiration realized during the early part of the twentieth century, but it is also, we might say, universal. American skyscrapers are architecture's clearest standing utopian gestures, more realistic than the celestial City of Towers of Le Corbusier, with its sixty-story office towers and sprawling parks, or the layered futuropolis of Antonio Sant'Elia but nevertheless transcendental, sky-catching, awesome.

The skyscraper also carves a breach in traditional architectural logic, separating space from programming in a single building. Rem Koolhaas, decoding the dreamscape of 1920s Manhattan, notes that the skyscraper functions as a "utopian device for the production of unlimited numbers of virgin sites on a single metropolitan location." Each floor, each office, may house any kind of business or home, all unrelated to each other except in occupying the same vertical column of steel and glass: a phenomenon Koolhaas calls "vertical schism." The skyscraper may mislead us, as Bellow's narrator says—a point well worth making in the novelist's adopted home of Chicago, site also of that novel. Inside their sleek cladding and vertical beauty may lie a multitude of sins large and small, of evil corporations and dastardly deeds. And yet, the analogy of scraping the sky, and so getting closer to heaven, resists dismissal, renews its hold on us, every time we stop, and forget, and look up, and see the sheer wall of stone or glass and metal climbing its defiant way into heaven.

Skyscrapers, like airplanes, offer a concrete expression of human ambition, an ambition to transcend the mundane, dirty, or slow. If the airplane or racing car was the era's purest expression of speed, the desire to overwhelm and annihilate space, the skyscraper was a materialization of pure direction. The Olympic motto revived for the modern movement, *citius altius fortius*—faster higher stronger—is, for all the well-meaning rhetoric about sportsmanship and competitive ideals, really a form of technological manifesto. This point is not lost on viewers of the current Olympic Games, who notice not only that performance enhancements of various kinds, legal and otherwise, are crucial to success at the far end of the human research program (which is after all what physical competition is); but also that assessment of success is now inextricable from technology, such that victory is measured in first hundredths, then thousandths, perhaps soon ten-thousandths of a second. A version, albeit a compelling one still, of Zeno's famous contest between Achilles and the tortoise.

Often enough now, such imperatives are buried or obscured by hazy thoughts of purity and fairness, by the second-guesses of ambivalence about technology's value and impact. The early twentieth century, the skyscraper's birthplace, was more straightforward, or perhaps we should say more confidently deluded by the liberating promise of speed and height. Filippo Tommaso Marinetti's first Futurist Manifesto, published in *Le Figaro* in 1909 with the appropriate motto *Velocita,* is only the most extreme and vivid articulation of a desire surely widespread then and after, even considering the mechanical horrors of the First World War. It is now impossible to imagine Marinetti's feverish advocacy without the specters of tank battle and machine guns, of aerial bombardment and dogfight. Indeed, his arc as an intellectual provocateur spans the war years, not as cause to effect, certainly, but perhaps as symptom to disease.

The manifesto seems to come as a natural literary form of those who design, create, and build—especially if they feel the need to destroy first.

It is, we might say, the rhetorical strategy best suited, indeed necessary, to utopian thought, and in the early twentieth century utopian energies, especially in Europe, swirled and collected around artists, architects, and illustrators: the aesthete-warriors of a new age. Le Corbusier's *Vers une Architecture,* for example, brims with breathless imperatives and commands, and frequent use of disease metaphors and the verb "demand." The manifesto form, with its blasts of empty declarative energy, comes naturally to Futurism, and there are Futurist manifestos on everything from art to sex to clothes. They embrace the desire Evelyn Waugh attributes to a disdainful modernist in *Put Out More Flags* who, we are told, "had always rather specialized in manifestos. He had written one at school; he had written a dozen at the University; once, in the late twenties, he and his friends Hat and Malpractice had even issued the invitation to a party in the form of a manifesto. It was one of his many reasons for shunning communism that its manifesto had been written for it, once and for all, by somebody else." Not the best reason for a political affiliation, or lack thereof; but you can see his point. Where is the fun if someone else has made all the declarations, set all the rules?

These days, manifestos are most likely to be issued by designers or architects eager for what they imagine is intellectual cachet. Tibor Kalman's "First Things First" manifesto, which called graphic designers to social accountability in 1964, was revised and updated by the editors of *Adbusters* magazine in 1995. Bruce Mau's "Incomplete Manifesto for Growth" let them off that hook in 1999. In between, the subtitle of Koolhaas's 1978 analysis of the dreams that live in the congested culture of the city grid, *Delirious New York,* carries a subtitle that seems both meant and ironic: "a retroactive manifesto for Manhattan." Meanwhile, the anti-technocracy extremist known as the Unabomber issued his own manifesto, a garble of social science and paranoia published by the *New York Times* and the *Washington Post* in an effort to forestall further mailbomb terrorist attacks from the man eventually identified as the schizophrenic mathematician Ted Kaczynski. There are even anti-manifesto manifestos, often from nihilists or skeptics such as graphic designer Jessica Helfand, whose stated "goal is to debunk the exalted claims of wannabe philosophers and soap-box proselytizers, to critique the posturing and the pretense, the lofty promises, the loose-cannon platitudes." But not even these tangles approach the full nihilism of the later "Manifesto of Negativity," which includes such dicta as "Nihil obstat everything," "Our only chance is total denial," and of course "All previous manifestos are hereby declared null and void."

The Futurists were just as comprehensive, if also more robust. "Hoorah!" Marinetti wrote of the speedy machines he loved so much, the race cars and biplanes and swift war machines. "No more contact with the vile earth!" But the vile earth could mean, as he would come to see, not just the slow road that holds me back or the airstrip that falls away in the heart-lifting sweep of takeoff—or the distant street, home to ants and taxis, viewed from the top of the Woolworth Building—but also the bogs of Ypres. Marinetti's happy paean to "dynamism," his love of machine speed, reached its apotheosis, its own terminal velocity, only when he declared himself a fascist another decade later, in 1919. "We intend to exalt aggression, a feverish insomnia," he wrote then. "We will glorify war—the world's only hygiene—militarism, patriotism, the destructive gesture of the freedom-bringers. . . . We will destroy the museums, the libraries, academies of every kind. . . . We will sing of great crowds excited by work."

The excitement of those crowds was already in the air, in the fast machines Marinetti and his acolytes so admired. Futurism, he said, is about the "acceleration of life to today's swift pace." It held a "dread of the old and the known . . . of quiet living." The future required a "negation of distances and nostalgic solitudes." It would entail "a heroic idealization of the commercial, industrial, and artistic solidarity of people" and "a modification of the idea of war" into "the necessary and bloody test of a people's force."

The Futurists were also fascists, and Marinetti's position would become ever more strident and violent as the years passed from the time his first manifesto was published in *Le Figaro* in 1909 and claimed that space and time had perished. From that moment, he said, narratives and spaces themselves could no longer exhibit linear coherence or compositional harmony—illusions from a more naive age. The Futurists would sweep them aside, and offer the hygiene of war. Also cocktails, though not the martinis and manhattans that we associate with the fast-living New Yorkers of the time, enjoying the benefits of the moments just before the First World War and the Prohibition that lasted from 1920 to 1933, two years after the Empire State Building was opened. Instead, the Futurist cocktail, as described and sketched by Marinetti, combined honey and hot sauce with a huge dollop of brandy—fiery, sweet, and intoxicating all at once—that will give you a feverish insomnia all right!

Thus runs a familiar narrative of our relationship with technology and transcendence. We fall headlong in love with it, with the speed and smoothness and grace of those vehicles and buildings and aircraft, and then we see, or are forced to confront, the other side, the false promise of salvation: the bondage and violence and ugliness, crashes and attacks and rent bodies. Every act of transcendence hides a condemnation, every call to liberation shrouds a new form of slavery. Marinetti's fascism makes sense, as perhaps all fascism makes sense, as an extreme, even pathological response to a broken promise. Technology itself does not liberate. And it leads to a specific form of false syllogism, what we might call the fallacy of selective transcendence. Not all technology liberates; therefore, technology is not for all, it is only for the strong; and so, only the strong shall be free. Everyone else belongs to the earth, and may stay there.

The truth coiled within this dark vision—a vision, let it be said, that would offer the world much technological innovation first developed in the service of evil, not least the jet engine and the mass media—is that transcendence of this worldly kind, aided and abetted by machines, sits uneasily with a democratic vision of politics. If everyone transcends, then no one does. If all of us are fastest, none of us are.

The Olympic analogue is once more instructive: whatever we may say about the pure value of participation and the joy in competition as an end in itself, winning a race or besting your rivals is a positional good, the very type of such goods. There can only be one gold medal winner—unless there is some technological glitch, that is, and the judges are sometimes forced to award two because of a three-decimal-point calculation error. Even those cases serve to remind us of the basic logic of winning, however, since they sit oddly in our minds, and we wonder what value a gold medal could possibly be to someone who knew he or she had won it on the basis of an error—as opposed, importantly, to winning it on the basis of a judgment call, which is part of most sports' accepted set of contingencies. (I mean such things as an umpire's strike zone or a referee's discretion, as distinct from a straight error in calculation or a mechanical malfunction; but of course in some sports, witness the slow-motion replay, this distinction is not as obvious, or as sharp, as it used to be: here again technology pervades our contests of struggle and transcendence.)

No, the value of the gold medal lies neither in its material, itself merely a metonym (gold = value) since there need be no real gold in such a medal at all; nor in its simple possession, since a medal may be stolen or even given away at any time without transferring value to its new holder; but, rather, in its just conferral. The gold medal is coveted, in other words, simply because its possession, when legitimately assigned and carried out, represents peak achievement. Or, more precisely, peak position, a weaker but more accurate word for what is implied, namely, that on that particular day, in that particular competition, against those particular opponents, I was first and therefore best. Absent the chain of causal connection between position and possession, absent the value. A gold medal I did not justly win is as nothing, and its continued possession worse than nothing, a reminder of the falseness of my position.

Positional goods are everywhere in human affairs but rarely as obviously so as in games of physical skill, where after all, notwithstanding the marginal complexities I have already mentioned (what hell, surely, to lose the gold over a matter of a few thousandths of a second, a span of time without any everyday meaning), the winners and losers are obvious. For the two always arise twinned in positional goods: there can be no winner without a loser, no first place without a second. Positional goods are just any goods that run according to the same logic, where what is desired is desired not for its material value, if any, or for its mere possession, whatever that may be, but for the conspicuous conferral of status it demonstrates.

And yet, in democratic societies, though such goods, and the general quest for the status they offer, are everywhere rife, there is an abiding confusion about what precisely is going on in our rush to acquire them.

One reason we are so drawn to games of physical contest is surely that here, for once, our democratic illusions may be set aside and an avowedly elitist scene take their place. Sports do not tolerate democracy, indeed make no sense when conceived so. They are without illusion and even, sometimes, cruel. That is why we love them.

Matters are more contested elsewhere. Democratic politics cannot openly admit elite aspiration even if we know, in our hearts, that it is nevertheless omnipresent in democratic societies. True democracy (at least, that is, on the egalitarian model fashioned by most of the early modern social theorists, including Thomas Jefferson) aims to elimi- nate, or at least minimize, the impact of differences in social status. But the craving for status does not easily submit, not least because it is so deeply encoded in our primate behaviors. Human males may talk sports instead of grooming each other, as bonobos do, or create military rank and social classes instead of simply battling for sexual predominance, but our more primitive roots are never that far under the social surface. The trouble with egalitarian democracy, as the old saw has it, is that in the land where everybody's somebody, nobody's anybody. The disease of democratic envy is iatrogenic: in trying to make everybody somebody, we at once acknowledge and thwart the human aspiration to acquire position. This problem is unsolvable in its own terms. The goods of status cannot be distributed more widely than they are without losing their status as goods. That is what position means.

Such aspiration must therefore be deflected into various kinds of cultural and rhetorical cowling, such as taste or style or cool, where we think we are seeking a piece of art, clothing, or music (or experience, feeling, or memory) rather than the position such a thing (or non-thing) confers. It must, furthermore, be accompanied by a pervasive ideol- ogy of social mobility, suggesting that the goods of position are in prin- ciple available to everyone—a bare contradiction, but one it is seldom profitable to acknowledge.

Thus the almost always meretricious notion of the meritocracy, whereby those with talent (superiority in "natural" differences) are al- lowed to rise to the top of the social order and enjoy the fruits of their status with a clear conscience and a glad heart. That sounds good, except that what counts as such a difference is always a matter of social negotiation, and nothing is natural until we make it so. Why is a gift for making jump shots or arguing points of law translatable into a very great deal of the fungible status-marker called money, while a gift for baking bread or paving roads is correspondingly less so? Since money is translatable into status via the acquisition of many, though not all, positional goods, this is the central question of all democratic politics. We may answer that the goods created by the basketball player or the lawyer are themselves highly valued, or stand out in a market of choices regarding goods and services, but this just begs the question. Naturalizing the market, together with the economy of desire it both answers and creates, merely kicks the problem upstairs. Why do we value what we value? Every democratic society that is not egalitarian poses that challenge to itself.

Fascist politics suffers from no such restriction: fascism is, if you like, the Olympics (or perhaps the pro football) of social organization. Not for fascists the myth of the democratic consumer market, in reality often a frenzied race to the bottom in search of elusive status and cool markers. Once upon a time, elegant clothes and art were the positional goods of choice; nowadays, mutatis mutandis, it is elegant clothes and gargantuan sport utility vehicles. The fascist has no need to cloak elitism in a rhetoric of equal opportunity, or to confuse positional goods with the status they confer. For here, position is its own argument and power its own justification. The strong rule and therefore are meant to rule. Those who rule delight in the benefits of their position without qualm or apology. In this way, the very best things in the world may be both created and enjoyed.

According to all logic of desire, power, and technology, the skyscraper is a fascist form. It manifests transcendence in an aggressive, costly, and exclusive way. It sets itself apart, asserts a bold independence, speaks with the clear voice of power and height and grandiosity. Today, a century after the birth of the form, the most stunning examples are found rising not from the cultivated squares of Paris or London or even New York but from the forcibly cleared slums of Shanghai and Kuala Lumpur, places where labor and life are cheap, politics authoritarian and overwhelming, money concentrated and fast-flowing. Here, in the twenty-first century, the skyscraper appears to find its natural setting, the new medievalism of emergent Asia.

And yet, it flourished first and best in a democracy.

One of the lesser-known tourist attractions of summer in New York is a series of midtown walking tours that view the city through the eyes of Ayn Rand. The controversial author of *The Fountainhead* and *Atlas Shrugged* lived in Manhattan for many years, and its magnificent skyscrapers and railway terminals inspired her to pen huge swaths of her rambling, breathless prose. Along the way she mistook a cramped sense of personal grievance for a coherent philosophy: a common error. But the buildings and tracks remain, a testament to human ambition and folly, if not divinity.

On a rainy Sunday not long ago, fifteen assorted visitors and residents gathered at the corner of Park Avenue and Fiftieth Street, near the entrance of the Waldorf-Astoria Hotel, to walk through what the ads excitedly labeled "Randland!" Rand or no Rand, this is a great corner in a great city. The Waldorf is a superb example of Art Deco, now joined by the wonderful but often overlooked gothic-inspired weirdness of the GE Building, and Johnson and Mies van der Rohe's Seagram Building, that trademark matte-black peg like one-third of Toronto's Toronto-Dominion Centre. Van Alen's beautiful Chrysler, still and always the superlative *aesthetic* skyscraper, is just a few blocks downtown.

The little group huddled on the northwest corner of the intersection, trying to avoid the shin-kicking pedestrians while simultaneously listening to Fred, the lumpy Rand disciple from Jersey City who was our Virgil. We all gazed up at the battery of towers, their different styles and densities structuring the gray sky. It's a wonderful thing, to be able to gawk unabashedly in New York, because most of the time the thronging commuters demand constant eyes-front vigilance, and anyway you don't want to look like a tourist geek.

It started to rain harder, and suddenly all the tourist geeks, in their windbreakers, baseball hats, and running shoes, produced colorful anoraks and portable umbrellas from their fanny packs, deftly unfolding them like Batman drawing matériel from his utility belt. Their Japanese camera equipment snapped and whirred. The native New Yorkers huddled deeper into their T-shirts and got wetter.

Rand had a vocal appreciation for architecture, especially the organic style pioneered by Frank Lloyd Wright, model for her own architect-hero, Howard Roark. *The Fountainhead,* her novel about Roark, is Rand's best work—which is not to say it is good. Made into a 1949 King Vidor film starring Gary Cooper and Patricia Neal, the book has drawn generations of rebellious youngsters, including unlikely ones like Art Garfunkel, to the profession. That is not surprising: Roark's decision to dynamite his own housing project rather than suffer compromise is, after all, pretty compelling to the adolescent mind, rock-and-roll before the fact.

Not that Rand would favor the comparison. Her architects are less rock stars than otherworldly beings, who possess a vision and aptitude denied mere mortals. In Vidor's film version, the squat red-headed Roark is transformed into a gaunt, wiry Cooper, a sort of exquisite scarecrow, man of few words but many opinions.

"The man who works for others without payment is a slave," he tells the all-too-slavish Peter Keating, a hapless contemporary who has come to him with a plan to design, in secret, a humanitarian public housing project. (It's worth noting, perhaps, that an architect acquaintance of mine said she spent all of architecture school thinking *everyone else* was Peter Keating.) "I do not believe that slavery is noble. Not in any form, nor for any purpose whatsoever!" Roark lectures the successful, vapid Keating. "I'll be glad if men who need it find a better manner of living in a house I build. But that's not the motive of my work, nor my reason, nor my reward. My reward is the work itself. My work, done my way!" It's not done his way, in the event, hence the dynamiting and subsequent trial for public menace—not your average architect, obviously. After an impassioned speech against mob rule and runaway collectivism, the gathered mob cheers for Roark and he is released in time to complete the Wynand Building, "the tallest structure in the city."

"This will be the last skyscraper built in New York, the last great achievement of man before he destroys himself," Gail Wynand says to Roark, his sense of doom showing rather too obviously. Wynand, the

Hell's Kitchen orphan played here by Raymond Massey, self-made and cynical, has risen on a tide of populism fed by his scurrilous newspaper, the *Banner,* "paper of the people." Now, having met the unbendable Roark, a man of the very integrity he yearned for but lacked, he is disconsolate. "Build it as a monument to that spirit which is yours, and could have been mine." When Roark leaves his office, Wynand, shamed into despair over his lost virtue, shoots himself—incidentally freeing Dominique Francon, his reluctant wife, to marry Roark, the man she really loves. At least, that is, since the night he came to her room and practically raped her while working in a quarry near her father's Connecticut estate: Rand's sexual politics, like her politics more generally, are more than a little dubious by contemporary standards.

Of course, Dominique is just the sort of beautiful nutjob likely to fall for that approach, not to mention Roark's skillful wielding of a pneumatic drill. Willowy and slightly deranged as played by Neal, given to ecstatic embraces and tragic overplay, her face becomes an Expressionist mask among the angles and shadows of William Kuehl's weird chiaroscuro set design. The funniest scene in the film is the one where she throws a beautiful statue down the airshaft in her apartment building. "I think I am in love with it," she tells Wynand. "But I broke it. I wanted to destroy it rather than let it be part of a world where beauty, genius, and greatness have no chance, the world of the mob." The swelled-strings closing sequence of the film consists of Dominique ascending in a fast elevator at the site of the Wynand Building, in the Hell's Kitchen streets from which Wynand crawled. As the lift soars past the summit of the Empire State Building across town, higher and higher, the camera follows her rapturous gaze toward the human heaven; and there he is, sturdy in the wind, fists on hips, tie and hair flapping: Howard Roark, genius of original style.

The real skyline of New York plays, as so often, a central unbilled role in *The Fountainhead.* Mostly it is abused, however: when Roark's buildings are finally built, rendered here as glowing, science-fictional versions of trademark Frank Lloyd Wright cantilevers and central-spine high-rises, they are made to look intentionally bizarre in a context of bankrupt classicism. Such abuse by association is a running theme of the film, which begins with Roark being thrown out of what looks very much like the Yale School of Architecture for refusing to learn "accepted styles," and where "that modern architecture" is repeatedly disdained by fusty old men in high collars, who keep trying to add superfluous friezes and useless columns to Roark's sleek designs. Just as Le Corbusier mocked American architects for knowing how to build high but not how to design appropriately, *The Fountainhead* pits modern progress against classical stodginess as a matter of warring architectural styles. (The young Corbusier, concerned with democratizing modernism and matching progress with populism, would have had little time for Rand's politics—though a later flirtation with the Vichy regime complicates the issue.)

Notice specific buildings that appear in the film but are not explicitly foregrounded. Gail Wynand's spare, expansive newspaper office, for example, which resembles a sort of James Bond supervillain's lair, a place to plot world domination, looks out on a vista of lower Manhattan, the Woolworth Building and the Municipal Building office complex clearly visible in two scenes. Roark, by contrast, occupies a smaller lair uptown: outside his window, revealed in two separate scenes, is a superb view of the Empire State Building. A central irony of the film, difficult to judge if intentional or not, is that Roark's impassioned speech that altruism is slavery—his longest dialogue barring a wordy harangue of the jury in the trial—is delivered with a clear view of the Empire State Building behind him.

"Peter," he explains, sounding rather plausible for a Rand character, "before you can do things for people you must be the sort of man who gets things done. But to get things done, you must love the doing, not the people. Your own work, not any possible object of charity." Compelling, yes; but also ironic because, whatever might be said of the genesis of the Empire State design, it is neither pointlessly classical nor, for that matter, the result of a single exalted genius. William Lamb's solitary genius aside, if the Shreve, Lamb & Harmon architects had any scrap of the sort of take-it-or-leave-it attitude that Roark raises to the level of categorical imperative, their building probably would not be there—or anyway, they would not have built it. In 1949, the tallest building in New

York was not the individualistic fantasy of the Wynand Building (whose construction hoarding anyway shows, in the film, the necessary range of cooperative professionals, from structural engineers to glass specialists) but, in fact, a triumph of original style that had emerged from a collective design-and-build frenzy, a coordinated group achievement.

Rand's concern wasn't really with architecture, of course. It was a practice she did not really understand, and her grasp of its midcentury politics is all wrong: there are stories that suggest she disliked the film's Frank Lloyd Wright designs because, though she had championed his form-follows-function organicism, and used a version of his life story as a model for Roark, he was unimpressed with her reactionary libertarian ideas. In *Atlas Shrugged,* a novel of even greater length and prolixity, Rand chose a legendary early-industrial pioneer as her namesake, a man safely dead. Celebrating her character John Galt, she went even further in linking the fact of urban infrastructure to extreme libertarian ideology. Galt, a mysterious stranger who so impresses the headstrong young railway heiress Dagny Taggart, is another one of Rand's impossibly Olympian industrialist champions. He rules the massive web of Grand Central Terminal's tracks with shadowy energy, and he meets Dagny in the cafeteria of the subterranean Oyster Bar to discuss his conspiracy to disrupt the world's flow of trains, capital, and energy.

Park Avenue is the channel beneath which the tracks run north out of the terminal, and the street itself is actually a platform set atop the massive wide tunnel. You can see the metal joints of the street's slabs at Fiftieth Street, and you must walk up one floor in the Waldorf before boarding an elevator because the machinery cannot be housed belowground. In the newly renovated Grand Central, the Oyster Bar is returned to its former glory as part of a new food concourse, and the ceiling of the main hall has been cleaned and restored to reveal the zodiacal patterns of decades gone by. It's awesome.

Rand's obsessions cannot obscure that awe. Ironically, Randland's lesson is not the one she taught. The infrastructure that humans have built for themselves is indeed amazing. New York and other spectacular human creations are evidence of our transcendent desires, our wish to go beyond the given. And so we become capable of daily miracles, unlikely successes: the New York subway system and the global airline schedule, the skyscraper and the airplane, those disastrously twinned icons of century's end.

These machines, like the twisted conviction that chooses to turn them to evil, are human creations, not divine inventions. Buildings are ongoing negotiations among millions of human voices, not gifts from above. They are also immensely fragile. It was Rem Koolhaas, himself the owner of a considerable ego, who documented over and over the crucial fact that infrastructural success comes only with a constant threat of failure. Gridlock always looms, breakdown ever impends; this is the dream logic of the utopian scheme made real on the grid.

Such are the limits of human ambition. Unfettered by justice or wonder, Rand's position becomes a particularly virulent brand of anti-humanism: in praise of excellence, she forgets balance. The basic awe of cities is not that they function well, but that they function at all. And for this we must thank not just the daring architects and high-flying railway executives of the libertarian imagination, but each and every citizen who navigates the crowded streets.

Height is, we might say, the ultimate positional good, not least in conferring literal position, but also in its metaphorical reach, such that higher most often equals better, and standings are recorded spatially, seating charts pictured likewise, and lists begin at the top and move down, all working to confirm the preeminence of above over below. Olympic contests, like many competitions, double position by making medalists stand on a podium arranged in steps from gold to bronze. High ground, moral or otherwise, is occupied to one's advantage; judgments delivered from on high arrive with force and authority; high rank and high tone make their unignorable claims; and when we're stepping high, or coming it a bit high, or getting high, we are, not always wisely or for long, living large and feeling good. A tall man is more likely to get elected president than a short one, and a short man, if he succeeds, will always remain open to the charge of Napoleonism, as if ambition were a natural property only of the tall, and therefore in everyone else to be considered a pathology.

The race for height in buildings is not all position, to be sure. There are good reasons, in Manhattan and Chicago—and now Kuala Lumpur and Shanghai—to build up rather than out, to stretch rather than sprawl. The population density of Manhattan, its squeezing millions moving through the foursquare grid, naturally finds release in the vertical. An island is, after all, no place for sprawling; so many people, so little space. The wonder, really, is that there are any low buildings at all in Manhattan. Many of them were restricted not by desire but by material constraint. The six or eight stories of many residential blocks in Lower Manhattan is a function of human fatigue, since a walk-up—the casual-sounding name, as if everything to do with it were a sort of stroll, for a building without an elevator—cannot demand too much from its tenants' legs and lungs. For a time I dated someone living on the sixth floor of a West Village walk-up and was reminded almost daily of a scene in the 1973 film *The Way We Were,* the first film I ever saw in a cinema, where the boho activist played by Barbra Streisand, living somewhere similar, rescues the young naval officer, Robert Redford, with an oxygen bottle kept handy for the purpose.

Otis is thus one great deity of the skyscraper form and the race for height it allowed. Even here, the properties of tensile cable introduced another materials-science constraint, since tempered steel cable, necessary to run the elevator cars up and down, can be safely stretched only to about a thousand feet, or eighty stories—even less with the high-speed units the Empire State engineers opted for, which traveled a maximum twelve hundred feet per minute versus the seven hundred feet that was the standard at the time. It takes two legs to reach the top of the Empire State Building, and though modern cable can do wonders, the world's tallest buildings still demand several elevator rides, a herky-jerky progress to the summit of Jin Mao in Shanghai or the Petronas Towers in Kuala Lumpur.

The other divine enablers of the skyscraper, of course, are even more fundamental: the metal frame and its early devotees, especially James Bogardus, J. I. Hittorf, and Henri Labrouste. As the architect Harvey Wiley Corbett argued, the skyscraper is America's signal architectural innovation, on the scale of jazz or the Hollywood movie, in that it manifested the first structural innovation since the Romans invented the arch. Masonry arches freed the world of what had held back even the brilliant Egyptians, post-and-lintel construction, where the height of a structure and the clear space beneath a roof were limited by the height of the supporting column, which ever adds mass as it grows, and the length of the stone lintel, which does likewise. Greek temples, even with their massive, and beautiful, triangular lintels and refinements of the column from Doric to Ionian to Corinthian, do not advance the basic principles.

The Roman arch does, lifting the horizontal lintel into a new shape and creating expanses of airy space underneath—an innovation itself refined by the Gothic arch, which can sustain greater height with equal mass on the principle of countervailing force, thus lifting the world of habitation even higher into the air. The two sides of the arch press their weight against each other, pushing the point up, as it were, in their static strength. Hence the feeling we often have that a Gothic arch is striving, urging itself upward toward the heavens. The Roman arch completes itself, dimensionalizes its line, in the dome, the rounded smoothness of civilized proportion best realized, perhaps, in the Pantheon in Rome, that vast geometric wonder of cube and half-sphere, with its coffered dome and wonders of wandering sunlight. The Gothic arch completes itself, rather, in a mass of spiky folds and spines, the ribbed, groined, and cross-hatched archways and naves of the cathedral churches at Chartres, Aix, or Notre-Dame de Paris—the biggest buildings the world had yet seen.

Even here, the great weight of the massive roof, supported by tree-trunk columns within and massive walls without, always threatened to tip the building out of the equilibrium, to bring itself down. And so the added refinement of flying buttresses, those stone precursors to the guy wire or pegged tent standing alongside the walls, props and struts for the huge weight of stone and glass hovering overhead. With stone and wood, and to a lesser extent glass, as the primary building materials, even the Gothic arch soon reached its limit, and it was not merely for theological reasons that the church spire was typically the highest point in any town or city. Buildings could be more massive, as the Bank of England building was, a neoclassical stone pile swallowing whole blocks, but they could not be higher. Not, that is, until the perfection of cast iron in the middle of the nineteenth century, and the superperfection of steel in the twentieth.

It would be hard to overestimate the importance of rigid metal forms to modern architecture, not least in the skyscraper. Metal had not been much available as a building material before, when it required labor-intensive hand-turning and expensive finish. It was a detail material only. But with casting a new world opened up, and cheap, well-formed iron allowed buildings for the first time to reconceive their structural principles. Even the arch, seen as a stretched lintel, does not equal this revolution. Until cast iron came along, the weight of buildings had to be supported by their walls, which are really just rows of columns with the spaces between them filled up with masonry. The notion of walls as separating spaces is secondary. (This is of course still the case in your house or mine.) The larger, and so heavier, the building, the thicker, and so heavier, the walls had to be. Even buttressing does not eliminate the constraint, merely distributes its load over more ground, and so allows the Gothic cathedral to achieve its wonderful appearance of inner light-ness, and empyrean openness, by way of what is, in fact, an incredible tonnage of limestone or marble.

With the advent of reliable cast-iron, and later steel, construction together with the invention of ferroconcrete—thin layers of concrete laced with iron rebar—the weight of a building could be supported not by the walls but by an inner frame, the skeleton. With structural strength realized within, they no longer needed it without. And now walls could return to meeting just their secondary purpose, namely, establishing a threshold between inside and out. The glass-curtain windows of twentieth-century modernist architecture, that sleek all-over cladding of transparency so beautifully realized by Mies and his imitators, is possible only because the building is holding itself up from the central shaft out, its floors hanging from supports ranged along a rigid spine of metal. The walls do not hold, they only shelter. Discussing his glass-curtain plan for the National Life Insurance Company in Chicago, Wright remarked that "the exterior walls, as such, disappear. . . . The walls themselves cease to exist as either weight or thickness."

But that lay in the future. The philosopher T. E. Hulme noted with disgust that "the superb steel structures which form the skeletons of modern buildings" were still subject to a "gradual envelopment in a parasitic covering of stone." This sight, he said, offered "one of the daily tragedies to be witnessed in London streets." And indeed the first tall buildings of the new epoch were really only semi-vertebrates, still wedded to their overall coverings of stone and, for a long time, the rigid derivative styles of Greco-Roman architecture, the neoclassical norms laid down, most prominently, by the École des Beaux-Arts in Paris. Pierre-François-Henri Labrouste, born in 1801, had studied there from the age of eighteen under Antoine Vaudoyer and Louis-Hippolyte Lebas. In 1824, still a very young man, he won the Prix de Rome for his Tribunal de Cassation (Supreme Court) building and soon began specializing in grand-scale public buildings. But, though classical in inspiration, Labrouste did not ignore new technical innovations, and between 1842 and 1850, building the Bibliothèque Sainte-Geneviève, he became the first architect—earlier even than James Bogardus in 1848—to use a skeleton of cast-iron posts and beams to support a building from within. He followed this marvel in 1854 with the reading room of the Bibliothèque Nationale, another cast-iron structure that pushed neo-classical norms in a new direction. Charles Garnier's Opera House and Hittorf's magnificent Gare du Nord, where architecture students can still be found sketching the intricate lattices of ironwork, date from the same extraordinary period of innovation.

Indeed, though Labrouste was trained in the tradition, he was more influenced by currents of thought peculiar to his own time, especially various kinds of Romantic reaction to the stiff regard for antiquity—a veneration for history that becomes, over time, ahistorical. Neoclassi-cism was ossifying, forever insisting on the forms of the past in a time when the demands and possibilities of building had moved well beyond them. Labrouste's "engineer's aesthetic," as Siegfried Giedion called it, struck a chord with the more radical anti-traditional social and aesthetic movements of nineteenth-century France; not for the first or last time, a particular way of building became emblematic of a social upheaval. Le Corbusier was to do the same with utopian internationalism a century later, and some would argue that Frank Gehry and Rem Koolhaas have achieved a similar symbiosis of structure and mood for the globalized post-postmodernism of the centerless twenty-first century. It is worth noting that the best-known buildings by the latter two—the Bilbao Guggenheim and the CCTV Building in Beijing, respectively—are deliberate anti-skyscrapers. One is a mound of titanium-clad curves, as if melted; the other is a knocked-over Moebius strip of a building, provocatively labeled by a Koolhaas associate as an "iconic exosymbiont" and (maybe less obscurely) a "built organism."

The Romantic thrust was often undisciplined and self-contradictory, but its position on architecture, circa 1850, was clear. Victor Hugo argued in *Ceci Tuera Cela* that building had lost its way, so constrained by old forms that it was unable to find new ones suitable to the age. César Daly, writing in the *Revue Générale de l'Architecture et des Travaux Publics*, expressed a common frustration: "Modern society," he said, "powerless to express through art a harmony among souls that no longer exists, and powerless to attribute a fixed meaning, the same for everyone, to the fundamental forms of architecture . . . is without the power to create, and is constrained to borrow." Thus was neoclassicism indicted on two related counts: that it was borrowed, not created anew; and that, in any event, its celebrated harmony of form was meretricious, out of sync with the fractured times.

The Romantics—also known, in architecture, as Saint-Simonists, Comtians, and Rationalists, after the great philosophers and social theorists who inspired them—were not nihilists, and they were not postmodernists *avant la lettre.* They did not aim to destroy or to destabilize merely; they were interested in finding new harmonies, ones suitable to the time and place. Labrouste himself read architectural history as a procession of "structural organisms"—not mere styles to be copied but organic responses to the linked factors of material, function, and social conditions. In this, he does indeed anticipate by a hundred years the postmodern sociology of Michel Foucault, who argued that architecture was best conceived not as a baseline material fact but as "an element of support, to ensure a certain allocation of people in space, a canalization of their circulation, as well as the coding of their reciprocal relations."

Such a coding is always reciprocal: buildings create spaces, but buildings are also expressions of aspiration—or, indeed, repression, as in the grand urban plan of Baron Georges Haussmann following the violence of 1848, the creation of Paris's now familiar wide boulevards and spiraling arrondissements, not coincidentally accommodating of cavalry charge and resistant to barricade.

Labrouste also anticipates another current of thought, one habitually misidentified with a much later American architect, Frank Lloyd Wright. In a letter of 1830, to his brother Theodore, he outlined his architectural theory: "I would like to try and compose with certain simple notions, 1) see clearly the end or purpose of the work and the importance it will have for each party. 2) the solidity of the building depends more on the combination of materials than on their mass. 3) give the construction itself ornamentation that is rational and expressive. 4) the form must always be appropriate to the function." *Form follows function,* in other words, and the great byword of postclassical architecture is born.

It was, to be sure, really a restatement of a different classical nostrum, namely the function argument of Aristotelian causality: in a fourfold causal scheme—that is, material, efficient, formal, and final—a fully realized or perfect substance is one in which there is immediate and perceptible identity of formal cause, or outward shape, and final cause, or purpose. Here, as in a well-formed chair or, indeed, swept-back wings of a jet aircraft, the form is an expression of the ends that the object serves.

Just such a union of form and function was realized, powerfully, in the grand space of the Bibliothèque Sainte-Geneviève, where the occupant is ever aware that the books themselves are, as Labrouste put it, "the most beautiful ornament of the interior," while the exterior is dominated by the names of the authors whose works, within the walls, occupy the same space. "This monumental catalogue is the principal decoration of the façade," he noted, a list of 801 famous names running from Moses to the contemporary Swedish physicist Berzelius. Embodying the Romantic regard for progress, the building itself reads like a series of historical references, moving from a Greco-Roman vestibule through a Renaissance "ascending knowledge" staircase, to the upper reading room itself, the vast space of iron-built modernity.

Labrouste's work is transitional, laying bare the early stages of a conflict between emergent modernism and Greco-Roman traditionalism. This historical conflict, as we have seen, is given graphic expression in *The Fountainhead,* where Roark, portrayed as a sort of Wright disciple, is forced to fend off attempts by teams of Beaux-Arts cronies to add classical columns and lintels to his sleek modernist designs. Now we can see that this is an anachronism, as well as rather silly, since it was International Style modernism, not neoclassicism, that Wright's organic forms repudiated. And the International Style was all about form following function: tall buildings should be spare and clean-lined, like posts or daggers, because they were, after all, knifing their way toward a better future where we all might live in the sky! But we should not suppose that the battle is finally over, since it is possible still to see new buildings rising four dozen stories into the air in Shanghai, clearly structures of the modern age, nevertheless adorned with absurd Greek temples on their summits, with fake Doric columns, fountains, and statuary below—the architectural equivalents of a tacky wedding cake.

It happens that *form follows function* was the very sentiment that motivated the designers of the Empire State Building too, though that can be hard to credit if we accept too readily a simple dichotomy—encouraged by Rand and her followers—between classicism and modernism. The proposed building would knife into the sky like the pencil Raskob had wielded in his famous conversation with Lamb.

In truth, the Empire State Building, though taller than all its Manhattan relatives, is not very pencil-like. It has a squat base and broad low shoulders, and its thick central volume, inlet on the east and west sides with setback runnels that create the unmistakable silhouette, sits solidly atop the cunning arrangement of half-slabs and height-varied blocks that boldly possess the limited site. In this way, the building offers a superb example of how to negotiate the strict setback restrictions of the 1916 Manhattan zoning bylaw, as illustrated by Hugh Ferriss in the utopian study called *Metropolis of Tomorrow.* The plan was designed to maximize density without blocking out the sky and casting the streets below into permanent shadow. The low base and compact arrangement of volumes mean that the building begins to rise in a grand tower, large for the time, only at the thirtieth floor. Its central arrangement then runs upward for fifty-five stories—an impressive volume of office space—and then sets back, in three proportional grades, to the familiar summit, later topped with the Deco-winged broadcast tower. The form is exceedingly well shaped, but it is not slim or lithe, one consequence of which is the fact that the Chrysler, actually not much shorter, looks far smaller. The Empire State is not a stylus; if anything, it is more like a pillar-box or a jackhammer.

Nevertheless, in this escalating scale of escalation, the Empire State Building would take a big step forward—big enough, Lamb hoped, to silence rivals for some time. It was no longer the heat of the sky race; a depression was already dragging the country down, and this was decidedly not the time to embark on a megaproject of this or any other kind. As Lewis Mumford, then writing as the architecture critic for the *New Yorker*, remarked acidly: "There is not an office building in the city, according to the best business and architectural advice I have been able to gather, that is anything except an extravagance and a non-negotiable jewel when it pushes beyond the fortieth story; the losses may be written off as advertisement, or, with the large margin of safety under which these investments are made, they may be covered up by the general success of the building, but still the upper stories are an extravagance." This was written of the new Radio City Music Hall, which opened in June 1931, but Mumford was generally withering about the magnificence of the Manhattan skyline.

"The architects who have put forth vertical transportation as a remedy for street congestion—which in turn is caused by this very overcrowding of the land—are only having their little joke," he said. "The tall skyscraper is the businessman's toy, his plaything, his gewgaw; in an expansive mood, he calls it alternatively a temple or a cathedral, and he looks upon the romantic altitudinous disorder of a modern city with the same blissful feeling that the Victorian industrialist had for his factory chimneys, belching forth soot and foul gases. The skyscraper makes him feel prosperous even when he is losing money on it. In the interests of congestion, the businessman is willing to make the streets impassable, lose thousands of dollars a day in lost motion and delay, waste millions in building more subways to promote more congestion, and in general to put up with any and every sort of nuisance, so long as he can feed his inflated romantic dream."

But such aspiration dies hard in New York, then as now; the backers of the Empire State did not quail. Nor did the architects. If the function was efficient, bright, and above all impressive office space—office space, to be sure, at a time when more businesses than ever were going belly up—then they would build tall. Never mind the Wall Street crash that was just a month away, or the unpleasant irony of erecting a high building when some ruined investors were using existing ones to end their woes. Never mind, too, that, as Saul Bellow reminds us, the structure of transcendence does not much guide the business conducted within its elevated walls; abominable enterprises are as readily housed as divine ones, provided they can make the rent. Function, after all, is a flexible concept, and maybe sometimes the function of a building—certainly *this* building—is simply to exist, to be there.

The skyscraper as such rarely makes economic sense, of course; its meaning is never primarily practical. In this sense, once more the Empire State is paradigmatic. It was, and is, an expression of ideas more than a business venture. Skyscrapers are not office buildings, they are concrete realizations of thought, and the occasion for thought. In Don DeLillo's novel *Cosmopolis,* a character's thoughts run this way: "He went outside and crossed the avenue, then turned and faced the building where he lived. He felt contiguous with it. It was eighty-nine stories, a prime number, in an undistinguished sheath of hazy bronze glass. They shared an edge or a boundary, skyscraper and man. It was nine hundred feet high, the tallest residential tower in the world, a commonplace oblong whose only statement was its size. It had the kind of banality that reveals itself over time as being truly brutal. He liked it for this reason. He liked to stand and look at it when he felt this way. He felt wary, drowsy and insubstantial."

Neither brutal nor banal, from the moment of its completion in 1931 the Empire State nevertheless set a gold standard in skyscrapers, outpacing its midtown rivals and anything Chicago had to offer at the time. It enacted a superlative, being the World's Tallest Building, a title it would retain for four decades. That span of dominance is itself a thing of the past, like those athletic records that held for unimaginable midcentury years only to be surpassed four or five times more in the 1970s or '80s. Nowadays, the world's tallest building is in Asia—that much can be safely claimed—but only a foolhardy writer would actually try to name it with certainty. Here, architecture outstrips the mechanics of the printed word, and leaves such a claim open to swift falsification.

In Shanghai, the eighty-eight-story, 1,380-foot-high Jin Mao Tower, including the vertiginous Grand Hyatt Hotel that occupies floors fifty-four to eighty-seven, was briefly the world's tallest building and the glory of China. Now it is merely the world's third highest, bested by both Taiwan's Taipei 101 (1,671 feet) and the 1,483-foot Petronas Towers in Malaysia, perhaps best known as a standard backdrop in high-octane adventure films with exotic locales. The Petronas building is an unappealing spindle of two circular columns joined by terrifying skyward bridges. Jin Mao and Taipei 101, meanwhile, are, unlike the Empire State, true realizations of the pencil held vertically by Lamb or Raskob back in New York in 1928. Jin Mao is the more beautiful, a slim glass-and-steel shaft with pagoda-style cornices; it occupies a wide-open site big enough to support its height, like an open book to its vertical stylus—though this will change when two taller buildings, already modeled at the Shanghai Urban Planning Center, rise up next to it. That will move Jin Mao into the bizarre status of being merely the third tallest building *in Shanghai*. One of these new rivals, the $750-million, ninety-story Shanghai World Finance Building, a sort of elongated glass spinnaker, like a knife blade embedded in the ground, will rise 1,518 feet high and thus surpass Petronas by 35 feet, which would have made it the tallest building in the world—in 2003.

Things were different in architecture's equivalent of the dead-ball era, and a building of 1,454 feet (albeit with the last 200 an uninhabitable spire) could hope to hold on to the laurels for longer than five minutes or until next season. So it was not until 1972 that the Empire State found its crown slipping, and the rival was only some fifty blocks downtown. The first tower of Minoru Yamasaki's World Trade Center design was completed that year and put its uptown forebear, though not literally, in the shade. The completion of the second tower two years later completed the rout: the once indomitable Empire State was now the third tallest building in Manhattan, and at the time, that meant the globe. The future challengers, and titleholders, would be from a tough midwestern city, the birthplace of the skyscraper but for decades overshadowed by New York's swagger. The Sears Tower and the John Hancock Building once again confirmed Chicago as the broad-shouldered city of Sandburg or Bellow, exemplars of a 1970s new order of tapering black slabs, with their cowlings of communications technology. Still later challengers dwarfed even these marvels, the spun-sugar confections of the supermodern Far East, the gossamer glass and titanium tubes of warmer climes in Malaysia, Indonesia, Dubai, and China. Up to the 1970s, the action was all in New York, still the capital of the world, of the century.

The aesthetics of the World Trade Center—rather, the lack of them —are again significant here. Yamasaki was notoriously afraid of heights, and perhaps as a result the twin towers exhibited none of the soaring quality found even in the earliest skyscrapers, those hybrids of stone and steel that stretch themselves upward as pure gaze responds to mass. The towers were a lesson in anti-aesthetics, tall buildings that actually refused tallness, abjured their own height. That is partly why there were two of them.

We must not be misled by misplaced or simplistic notions of function. It was not the function of the twin towers to respond to a congested island site with a vertical volume of office space; that is by the way. Rather, it was the function of the World Trade Center *to deny tallness in its tallness.* Hence the absolute refusal not only of decoration—a standard architectural imperative of modernism—but of any suggestion of grace or style. The towers were designed to resemble square plugs, like wooden pieces slotted ham-fistedly into the playground sand of Manhattan. The second tower completed the idea with a resounding gesture of affirmation. It added nothing in terms of design; it was, necessarily, identical to the first. This was no mere duplication; instead it realized a necessary redoubling of the anti-aesthetic argument, an essential underlining. The first tower said: I am deliberately ugly in order to reverse the standard logic of scraping the sky; I refuse to play your game. The second tower said: I am here to make sure you get the point, that this has not been done idly or by chance. *Its only statement was its size.*

Taller buildings have followed, framing the short lifespan of the doomed World Trade Center through a fusion of capitalist energy and old-fashioned adolescent competitiveness, the locus shifting ever eastward. The aesthetics of the skyscraper shift along with it. Chicago's Sears Tower is, in some ways, the final possible American skyscraper, a stretching mass of slablike volumes arranged elegantly around a central upright spindle rising from its small downtown footprint. Jin Mao or Taipei 101 finally realize the skyscraper's arrowed ambition, even while showing their local Asian influences melded to the drive for height. Jin Mao rises like an attenuated temple, isolated on its patch of land in a nighttime dead zone of financial Shanghai, Pudong-side. The linked Petronas Towers resemble a twinned assembly of two corncobs or machined gear-bolts silently struggling into the yonder side by side.

Other, still taller buildings are planned and they too will surely arise, but perhaps nothing in the offing quite matches the astonishing plans of a group of four engineers and designers for what they call Psilopolis, "the future of tall building." Expanding on the bundled-tube structure used in the Sears Building, for example, whereby the site actually accommodates several separate cores, or spines, each supporting the others with their weight, like a house of cards or, maybe better, the flying buttresses of a cathedral, the Psilopolis designers envision a stack or tube of twelve circular levels. Each of the levels resembles a city block, with tubular support all around its circumference, together able to support an overall structure that will rise to 4,700 feet, or more than three times the height of the Petronas Towers, and accommodate about 100,000 people with just under 10.5 million square feet of usable floor space.

Images of Psilopolis show the designers taking inspiration from Chinese pagoda towers, and situating this bizarre ziggurat of circular density in the skyline of Shanghai's Pudong, dwarfing Jin Mao and the Oriental Pearl Tower. Or, even more unnerving, placing it in a kind of crawl-walk-run evolutionary diagram that runs left to right from cathedral spires and tall office blocks to the Met Life, the Woolworth, the

Chrysler, the Empire State, the World Trade Center, the Sears, and the Petronas buildings. Next to the tiny scalar advances of former races to go higher, Psilopolis is a giant among men, a monstrous vertical city on the order of the most unbridled gargantuan imagination. It will be clad in aluminum and laminated glass. "The aluminum cladding will give the structure an ultra-flat and modern look," the designers write. "While the glass will provide the beautiful views."

Psilopolis may well be the future of tall building; it is certainly the future of architectural arrogance (though on that score we can take leave to wonder if the designers were mostly kidding). Regardless of that, there was a time when the language of buildings was more romantic, less brutalist and matter-of-fact—or maybe just more naively spiritual, in the way that adolescent seekers can be, virgin and astringent. DeLillo again: "The wind came cutting off the river. He took out his hand organizer and poked a note to himself about the anachronistic quality of the word skyscraper. No recent structure ought to bear this word. It belonged to the olden soul of awe, to the arrowed towers that were a narrative long before he was born." The Empire State retains within its midcentury beauty that olden soul of awe. It is, whatever else we might want and need to say, a skyscraper. It reaches out and runs its fingers through the clouds, scores the firmament, asks the sky for more room, and then more.

4
System and Structure

Manhattan, as they neared it from the north,

looked like the coda to the urban-erotic, the garter

and stocking-top patterning of its loops and

bridges now doing service as supports and braces,

hernia frames. Above it all, the poised

hypodermic of the Empire State.

Martin Amis, *The Information*

T o say that the construction of the Empire State Building was a miracle of modern technology is to indulge either understatement or, perhaps more to the point, an outdated vocabulary. We do not invoke the miraculous with the same blitheness and simple confidence of a century ago, the era of undiluted faith in technology. But let us invoke the phrase anyway, not least to capture something of the spirit that still and always clings to the building. The Empire State is so much a miracle of modern technology, in fact, that its first and perhaps most lasting iconic achievement is its mere existence. That is, though there are many images and appropriations of the building floating through the culture at large—images and appropriations we will examine in the two following chapters, and confirming its transformation from mere material edifice into larger-than-real symbol—the building itself remains its own central argument, a physical testament to the wonders of twentieth-century technology.

It certainly boosted the image of the architectural profession. The design, with its solid-shouldered base and rising thick column with channels set into the east and west sides, was not particularly adventurous but, instead, cautiously incorporated Art Deco detailing into a more or less plain adaptation of the Ferriss setback style. The chrome-nickel mullions that run from the sixth to the eighty-fifth floors, the red lining of the window facades, and the soaring wings of the radio antenna and projected dirigible moor are the most obvious external details that follow the quintessential Jazz Age style, but they are hardly obtrusive.

Indeed, you could say that the style of the Empire State Building is almost sui generis, or anyway transitional in a manner unique to itself. It is neither the shiny Deco perfection of the Chrysler, so reminiscent of a lair for some world-dominating supervillain in silver-screen melodrama, nor the neo-gothic box-plus-tower of the Woolworth or the Singer buildings. These last two are amalgamations of what Rem Koolhaas calls "three distinct mutations," previously visible individually, for example, in the competing layout of Madison Square at Broadway and Twenty-third Street, circa 1909: the tower of the Metropolitan Life Building ("the lighthouse"), the space-filling efficiency of the Flatiron Building ("the

Photographer unknown, Albert Einstein atop the Empire State Building, circa 1955
(Hannah Fantova Collection, Princeton University Library)

multiplication"), and the ground-level oasis of Madison Square Garden ("the island"). Separately, they enact a "triple impasse," but when combined "their weaknesses become strengths," and the Woolworth, designed by architect Cass Gilbert and completed in 1913, offers "the first built amalgamation of the three mutations," the first true skyscraper. This new "Cathedral of Commerce" climbs sixty stories in total, half of them a solid block, the rest a tower: a sort of swan or, better, Trojan horse shape dominating the reaches of Lower Manhattan.

The Empire State refines and alters the proportions dramatically, following the lead of the more elegant Chrysler and offering a new amalgamation, centering the cityscape. It is both decisively of its period and unique unto itself, even in its apparent classicism a presage of the explicit functionalism already emerging in the ideas and sketches of Le Corbusier, whose glass-curtain slabs would influence so much of undistinguished midcentury modernism.

When we think, then, of the form-follows-function dictum in its regard, we have to think past any simple exercise in office-space creation and apply the lessons of the future to the past. Or rather, of the past to the present, because the key to understanding the Empire State Building may be found in an unlikely place, the theory that a building may be, even more than its design or program, *a gesture,* an ongoing enactment of thought's play.

The notion of the gestural building may seem fanciful, but it is impossible to understand modern architecture without it. The Seagram Building in midtown, designed by Mies van der Rohe and completed by Philip Johnson and Phyllis Lambert, is a case in point. Its matte-black surfaces and floating base, themselves apparently developments of earlier Mies ideas about the integrity of the flat surface, elevate the building to a kind of commentary on its urban context, not least the nearby Chrysler Building and the new Waldorf-Astoria Hotel right across the street. The flat-sided, dull-finished Seagram creates a dead space in the midst of midtown light, blots out the sky in a manner more complete and decisive than any other building could hope to do. It is, in its way and in this context, the anti-building. It is also an attempt, as Mies himself said, to realize in the building the "zero degree writing" attempted by Stéphane Mallarmé and the other ascetic literary modernists. A gesture is not a claim, a normative proposition demanding rational assessment; it is a move or gambit in a scene of play, an ongoing aesthetic performance. And here, the gesture is one of negation.

The refusal of decoration should lead, finally, to the building that is pure manifest functionality, an exercise in verticality (the smooth flat surfaces of the elegant foursquare slab) that is also a negation of it (the dark finish now making a blank screen, absorbing light rather than reflecting it). In its way, the Seagram Building is the architectural equivalent of an Ad Reinhardt painting, a rectangle of pure black pigment that simultaneously celebrates and destroys the blank canvas. That is why any variation or duplication, in contrast to the World Trade Center's aggressive twinned argument, has the effect of lessening the impact. Toronto's downtown TD Centre, for example, places several cousins of the Seagram Building in close conjunction, the familiar Mies-Johnson design repeated at different heights and volumes, creating blustery courtyards and wind tunnels at street level. Here, on a site almost wholly lacking in Manhattan's layered architectural history, a New World location, the same elements show forth only their elegance and purity of line. There is no critical gesture because there is nothing to be critical about, or against, and the energy of resistance is tamed into a hum of domesticity. A now lost setback building in the old Manhattan style offered a brief moment of struggle that was soon depleted, the skyline mostly conforming to this new glass-curtain norm. And though initially reviled as creating, in its plaza, mass private space rather than true public space, these are now among the Canadian city's most beloved buildings.

That might be the eventual fate of all spirited modernism. "Machines will lead to a new order both of work and of leisure," Corbusier enthuses in *Vers une Architecture*, breathlessly outlining his massive City of Towers, with its vast parkland dotted by sixty-story ferroconcrete cruciform blocks. "Entire cities have to be constructed, or reconstructed in order to provide a minimum of comfort." But in practice the utopian idealism freezes into banal progressions of cereal-box towers marching witlessly away to the horizon. The soaring dreams of futurist social change are merely assimilated, per tradition, to the forces of a money economy and middle-class approval. (The TD Centre is headquarters to one of Canada's four massive chartered banks, which together control most of the country's assets.) Even the towering optimism of the Hancock and Sears towers suffers a certain gestural collapse because it exhibits a confusion of means typical of the era: the buildings seek both height and negation, a soaring blackness that is neither fully one thing nor the other.

Such failures in the project of modernism, whether perceived or real, are frequently cited as causal factors in the excesses of late-century postmodern architecture and, by extension, the more recent confusions of what is sometimes called "supermodernism," as designed by Jean Nouvel or Dominique Perrault. Whatever the precise etiology, it is fair to say that these latter trends are vividly exhibited in the protracted, and still-continuing, dispute over reconstruction of the World Trade Center site. The sudden elevation, followed by the swift demise, of the Berlin-based architect Daniel Libeskind has become a piece of cultural detritus in its own right, a cultural narrative on the subject of mediation and fame. More than a dozen designs have been mooted, more if one counts early public competitions that were undertaken before the multi-form site controls had been established. Donald Trump even entered the fray in 2005, pushing a taller-than-before twin tower conception that would have replaced the square originals with tapered Sears-style towers. David Childs, of Skidmore, Owings & Merrill, has produced at least two different skyscraper designs for the site, even as he and his powerful firm moved Libeskind to one side. A design has apparently been finalized, incorporating (at least in public statements) some of Libeskind's ideas along with Childs's revisions. But no one, it seems, really expects the ground of Ground Zero to be broken anytime soon.

The Empire State Building, too, can be understood as embodying a gesture, in this case *a gesture about the materials themselves.* The finished building is a sign, a representation in built form, of the logic of construction. Indeed, in this case, because the gesture is so positive, so optimistic—so adolescent and joyful—it acquires the force of a claim, an argument about the tough, interlocked beauty of technology.

Functionalism in architecture is like consciousness in philosophy, a flawed but necessary category with no fixed meaning and so a cause of endless dispute. In both cases, we seek the very same zero degree that alike marked modernist literary ambition and the utopian desires of modernist architects. If only we could scrape away the distractions and empty condolences of style, the criminal superfluities of decoration, we could, as it were, expose the pure essence of the building, building *as such.* Thus would we confront, at last, the essential fact of spatial existence, the unalloyed function realizing itself without mediation in its appropriate form.

The desire has a long pedigree, even if the particular discourse varies. In some part, there is a Platonic residue here, of course, a foundationalist hangover that suggests all actual things, however perfect, are still shadows of some more nearly perfect thing existing elsewhere and otherwise. The difficulty then becomes one of constant dissatisfaction and deferment, since the actually experienced thing not only fails to measure up to its formal counterpart but also goes on teasing us with its reflection thereof, a simultaneous beckoning and refusal. Thus are beautiful things so mesmerizing and so unsettling: they attract our attention only to suggest that possibility of a larger beauty beyond them. We get stuck with a beautiful token both because and despite the fact that, according to Plato, our desire is really for the type.

Because architecture belongs, as the philosopher Arthur Danto has noted, to the "third realm" of beauty—the realm, that is, of applied beauty like fashion, design, craft, and cosmetics, neither natural beauty nor so-called fine art—it is an especially acute version of this problem. We encounter architecture whether we like it or not, simply by inhabiting a place, walking the streets of our cities or towns. Very little of it is good architecture, perhaps, but that is no solution to our entanglements with the beautiful, since the relative absence is arguably the only thing as tantalizing as the relative presence. We find ourselves longing for the sustenance we think beauty will provide, and every disappointment is just another reminder of what we do not yet have. Transcendental desire results, inevitably, in immanent failure.

Functionalism is at once a response to this conundrum and a continuation of it, as Le Corbusier himself grapples with the idea of "the natural." A functionalist architecture cannot help but borrow some of Aristotle's anti-Platonic naturalism, hoping to find standards of flourishing or success not in a timeless, unchanging plane of Forms or Ideas, but in the bottom-up causality of form, matter, purpose, and construction. And yet, there always lurks, in "the natural," a hint of a form, or pattern, that transcends the human plane, proportions that are not merely human scaled, but divine, like the simple perfection of the Pythagorean Theorem, one of Le Corbusier's touchstones of excellence. Furthermore, functionalism must cope with desire by scraping away all the unnecessary and insincere elements thereof, trying to find a state of formal perfection so pure that it would, in and of itself, settle the question of the building's nature. We would no longer have to penetrate so transcendental a veil, or exit some imagined epistemological cave-prison, to view the truth of the building, for it would be realized before us in its operation.

The trouble is that, even here, we cannot be so sanguine about what a function is, and what form we believe should appropriately materialize it. That is, we could argue for the functional beauty of the swept-back aircraft wing or the sturdy grace of the suspension bridge, but (a) these examples already admit of variation, since there is more than one way to create an airfoil or span a distance over water; and (b) even so, such instances of fairly obvious form-function alliance are rare, especially when it comes to such a complex practice as architecture. Creating spaces for work and leisure—for toil, play, rest, thought, and death—is no simple engineering project. Even a simple engineering project is no simple engineering project, in fact. Erect a bridge. Create an airfoil. Build a house. Well, yes; but there are ways, and ways. We may say, in other words, *form follows function* and we would not have said much. Or rather, we would have a great deal that now has to be unpacked and, like a large-denomination banknote, cashed out. Function is an abstraction, not an obvious or simple fact; and like all abstractions, it invites ambiguity apparently by necessity.

The phenomenologist Edmund Husserl says we are all "absolute beginners" when it comes to understanding the texture of human experience, always needing to clear thought of presuppositions in order to perceive thought's basics—a project closely akin, in its way, to the anti-ornamental modernisms of writing and building. But Husserl also demonstrated, in a familiar paradox, that the notion of absolutes is itself the reigning philosophical fiction to be dethroned. "No thought can lead to an absolute beginning," Theodor Adorno said of this doubled Husserlian insight. "Such absolutes are the product of abstraction."

Adorno's particular concern at the moment of making that point is, coincidentally, architecture. Speaking of functionalism's challenge to "spurious" or "degenerate" eclecticism—the challenge issued by Loos and others, that form should follow function merely as the technical solution to technical problems—Adorno reminds us of a deeper wisdom, which is that neither function, nor form, nor materials, nor even meaning itself is *fundamental* in the sense of providing a baseline or *telos* to order and govern the others. Moreover, beauty is never a mere decorative super-addition to utility, though the functionalists were right to see that, in the modern division of aesthetic and technological realms, this becomes a practical danger. But to insist on that division between beauty and utility—whether pro or con—is merely to perpetuate it. Failing to see that beauty and utility are inseparable is to commit another error of abstraction, violating the true nature of lived experience by trying to derive the whole from a part, an Ur-phenomenon that grounds the rest.

"[Great] architecture asks how a specific purpose can become space, through which forms and materials," Adorno says; "all these moments are reciprocally related to each other. Architectural fantasy would thus be the ability to articulate space through the sense of function, and let the sense of function become space; to translate purposes into formal structures." Nothing is fundamentally given, guiding all the rest; building, like life more generally, is not a project of sovereignty but of mediation: of functions and purposes as well as materials and forms. Building is a project of finding our way, not solving a problem or decorating a shed. The key concept in that mediation is, notably, one that derives from the lived experience of an embodied person: *Raumgefühl,* or the feeling of space. "The feeling of space has grown together with the purposes and functions," Adorno adds. "Whenever in architecture this feeling of space asserts itself by surpassing mere functionality, it is at the same time immanent to the sense of function." A valid functionalism does not reduce to mere functionality; it is not a one-sided rejection of "style" that becomes a style of its own. It is—or rather, would be—a practice of building ever mindful of the inseparability of form, function, materials, and purpose, the four-sided causality typical of Aristotelian metaphysics.

The Empire State Building, as the quintessential skyscraper, opens up this world of smoothly executed causality. It does so not only in generating a host of enduring images, but also in the simple fact of the building, its material realization. Smith's grandiose plan becomes, in the event, a limestone and steel hymn to industrialization and the logic of materials. The Empire State Building rose so fast it seemed to appear by magic, downloaded from the ether of technological possibility.

We should not neglect the site, itself invisible and necessary. It is a rectangle marked out by the orderly grid of Manhattan's 1811 Commissioners' Plan. The 155 parallel streets resulting from the plan, each 200 feet apart, and the dozen 100-foot-wide north–south avenues, carved the city into saleable lots, each 25 by 100 feet. "As an aid to speculation the commissioners' plan was perhaps unequaled," John W. Reps says in his study *The Making of Urban America*, "but only on this ground can it be justifiably called a great achievement." That judgment, though widely shared, is perhaps too harsh, however, since the genius of the Manhattan grid is precisely its multiform flexibility, an ability to realize numerous kinds of spaces and environments within itself—to set the urban scene without determining the play. Like every square foot of Manhattan, the site of the Empire State Building is layered with history and mixed use, a palimpsest of American life.

In 1827 it was farmland, and William Backhouse Astor was able to acquire it for $20,500, a rather tidy sum given the value of the dollar at the time. By 1856 his daughter-in-law, Caroline Schermerhorn Astor, had inherited the land and moved there with her husband, William, and built a freestanding brownstone house; her cousin John Jacob Astor III also moved to the site, building a separate house. Thirty-five years later, William Waldorf Astor, son of John Jacob, inherited his father's house, and the land, but found it uncongenial as a residence. To spite his relatives, especially his conservative aunt on the Astor side, William contemplated demolishing the house and building a hotel on the site, a vulgar move in the Knickerbocker ethos, not least because the American Golden Age offered numerous benefits to the landholding rich, including low property taxes and no income tax at all—something the flat-taxers and the low-corporate-rate and capital-gains-cuts advocates of today can view only in their wildest dreams. In 1893, the Waldorf Hotel opened its doors to an enthusiastic market of well-to-do customers.

William and his Aunt Caroline were not to feud forever, though, despite the hotel now crowding her gracious home. Indeed, she gave in, albeit reluctantly, to the logic of converting the land to use. Between 1894 and 1897 they together planned an addition to the Waldorf, the Astoria, which would be joined to the original hotel by an ornate corridor. And so the luxurious Waldorf-Astoria Hotel opened three years before the century's turn and stayed there for almost thirty years, becoming a byword in urban sophistication, creating, among other things, an eponymous salad and claims for the invention of more than a few cocktails. In 1925 the hotel was bought by the real estate speculator Coleman du Pont and its days were numbered, at least as a lower midtown institution. In 1928 du Pont sold the site to the Bethlehem Engineering Corporation for a sum rumored to be between $14 million and $16 million—a geometric gain over the original asking price of a century before—and the linked hotel buildings were demolished and the Waldorf-Astoria relocated, indeed reinvented, in entirely new surroundings on the other side of Grand Central Terminal.

A Waldorf-Astoria Office Building was planned but no one associated with the site was, in 1929, able to appreciate the expansive breadth of Alfred Smith's ambition. The Empire State Building Corporation was created early in the year of the great Wall Street crash, and Smith immediately set about creating the kind of consortium of financial interest, combined with what we would today call media buzz, that typified his energetic and vivid, if ultimately unsuccessful, brand of populist electioneering. There had been no buildings of such a scale since the completion of the Chrysler; indeed there was good reason to doubt whether another Manhattan skyscraper would ever be feasible. As so often, foolish ambition was the engine of greatness and New York was novelty's fertile soil.

The flipping of the Thirty-fourth Street site marked—or marked again—a change in attitude that had gripped Manhattan and was, by this point, beyond reversal. In her 1913 novel *The Custom of the Country*, Edith Wharton depicts an impassioned opponent of what was then known as "Fifth Avenue" architecture, the emergent practice of building for speed and change. This relentless spate of fast construction was obliterating the fabric of Wharton's own New York, the society of comfortable ambition and observance so brilliantly portrayed by the supple ironies of *The Age of Innocence* and *The Buccaneers*. The novel is prophetic, the character tragicomic. The hotel at Fifth Avenue and Thirty-fourth Street represents a transitional moment, regrettable commercial enterprise corrupting, however luxuriously, a venerable Manhattan site. When it, in turn, made way for a skyscraper, and moreover a skyscraper explicitly organized around ideals of speed and efficiency, clearly the past world of New York was gone forever. Manhattan is finally, and irreversibly, what most of us now consider it, a thick palimpsest of newness and sometimes greatness, a city forever erected anew on the bones and dust of the past.

In a sense, Smith was himself the servant of an even larger force, the inner logic of applied instrumental reason, otherwise known as technology. Nowadays—by which one might mean, roughly, in the decades since the atomic-bomb explosions of 1945, to choose one handy terrible example—we are accustomed to view technology with an eye both skeptical and optimistic, wondering, for example, whether biomedical advancements constitute desirable goals of human ingenuity or ethical quagmires best avoided. Our attitude is often, paradoxically, that when it comes to risk, technology got us in and it can get us out: science may have created the airborne toxic particles or background radiation that are killing us, but science can also invent the medical techniques and psychopharmaceuticals that will render us healthy and happy. Technology is, as a Don DeLillo character says, "lust removed from nature . . . what we invented to conceal the terrible secret of our decaying bodies. But it's also life, isn't it? It prolongs life."

Technology may prolong life but it does so while it also threatens life; we cannot avoid the general knowledge that more often than not, and despite our best efforts, the drive to innovate is more powerful than any humanistic or skeptical desire to wed innovation to benign purposes. Rarely is it driven by the sort of standards of human flourishing the ancient Greek philosophers claimed to find buried in the natural functions of humans and their crafts, the original *logos* of *techné*.

Instead, a sense of technology *as instrumentality* is the inevitable outcome of a Western philosophical tradition driven by satisfying desire, exerting will, and pursuing a metaphysics of presence. An overreliance on an uncritical version of Aristotle's scheme of formal, material, efficient, and final causality has resulted in distortions. First, the sense of final cause as telos or guiding principle of flourishing has been truncated to mere purpose, in the sense of a job to do, rather than a sense of the work's web of relation to a larger truth. Second, most assessments of causality are now limited to efficient cause anyway, understanding efficient cause as mere making or wielding of tools. Thus is a rich human account of causality mangled by a procrustean modernism to become crude ends-means reasoning, the use of tools to solve problems, rather than the profound revelation Aristotle offered. Technology, which the Greeks saw as the gesture of all creativity, here becomes, pejoratively, the merely instrumental: tool-based problem-solving, pursued as if free of any consideration about ends themselves.

"Everywhere we remain unfree and chained to technology, whether we passionately affirm it or deny it," Martin Heidegger says. "But we are delivered over to it in the worst possible way when we regard it as something neutral; for this conception of it, to which today we particularly like to do homage, makes us utterly blind to the essence of technology." In one sense, instrumental technology is the ultimate human arrogance, a belief that all desires are good desires, all effective solutions valid regardless of the assumed problem; at the same time, it conceals its essence by successful invocation of what we might call the *neutrality defense,* which obscures the project of world-mastery nestled in technology's heart. Cut loose from any deeper concerns, human thought issues in the liberal-scientific worldview characteristic of modernity: success-oriented, licentious, potentially decadent.

At the same time, the urge to flee technology results in projects of voluntary simplicity or off-grid living that are themselves doomed to likely failure. You cannot run far enough or fast enough to outpace the machine world, written into your very garments and body. They are also self-contradictory. A flight from technology is another attempt at mastery, and therefore another failure to understand technology. We have elevated human tendency to the status of a divinity, allowing the inner logic of techné to outstrip any concerns for authenticity, situatedness, or care. Speedy modern life becomes a playground of value-relativism, nihilism, subjectivism, and a host of other dangers diagnosed by critics of liberal modernity from Hegel to Nietzsche. The freedom offered here is no freedom at all, just the empty choices of a quick-time marketplace of unbridled desire.

Speed, as Paul Virilio reminds us, offers the dominant trope of the technological cast of mind, the logic of war, as well as the background presupposition of all efficiency-driven undertaking, namely that anything is done better if done faster. Speed annihilates distance between locations, rendering them closer; it also, by necessary extension, annihilates time, the duration formerly needed in order to effect traversal. It is no coincidence that so many of the most powerful technological innovations of the modern era (but not just the modern) result from military need—from tactical to practical, as the catchphrase now has it. Here, under conditions of violence, obliterating space and time are particularly urgent projects. I need to deliver my ordnance or troop strength before my enemy can respond with full awareness. I need, furthermore, to do so from long range, to maximize effectiveness and minimize risk to the decision-making apparatus and, ultimately, the homeland. Speed is the ideal means to the end of conquest.

It is also, to be sure, the prevailing theme of urban life, the sense of excitement that comes from a constant surplus of stimuli. At the level of human experience, speed is really nothing except a perceived increase in stimulus flow. That is why getting on and off a busy freeway, for example, constitutes a cognitive challenge, however routine: in each case, I need to adjust my reaction times and internal flow monitors to the new rate of stimulus. The city of the twenty-first century may be similarly defined as the central site of speed, speed understood now as constant sensory excitement. This constant and sometimes overwhelming volume of excitation, a fact of urban existence captured rather blandly by the idea of "the pace of life," in turn creates the need for various coping mechanisms. As Georg Simmel suggests in his classic analysis of "The Metropolis and Mental Life" (1903), this need to cope is largely responsible for what we know as the big-city attitude, the alleged rudeness and violence of the urban street, which is revealed as, instead, a form of individualism holding out against the onslaught of demand and sensory excitation. It is worth noting in passing that Simmel was prominent among a generation of anticapitalist German philosophers, just older than Heidegger, who fell decisively out of favor with the ascension of the Nazis in the early 1930s.

"The metropolitan type—which naturally takes on a thousand individual modifications—creates a protective organ for itself against the profound disruption with which the fluctuations and discontinuities of the external milieu threaten it," Simmel writes. And "there is perhaps no psychic phenomenon which is so unconditionally reserved to the city as the blasé outlook. It is the consequence of those rapidly shifting stimulations of the nerves which are thrown together in all their contrasts and from which it seems to us the intensification of metropolitan intellectuality seems to be derived." Quick on the uptake, not easily fooled, street-smart—these are the prized features of the metropolitan psyche, a psyche which, moreover, performs the great bulk of its transactions in the impersonal, quantified space of the money economy, where dollar values and duration are alike precisely calibrated. Time is, literally, money because time, exactly and minutely allotted, is a necessary presupposition of the city; absent its precise measurement and the city would descend into chaos. But time's precision always contains an imperative of speed—the common sense in which time is money—and the fast-moving, appointment-keeping, transactional beings of the urban scene have no time to spend being impressed by anything.

We seek the essence of a building, its solidity and relative permanence suggesting a tangible being. But where does this lie? In the uses to which the building is put? The space it occupies? The space it *creates*? The sum total of its materials, intersected planes, architectural details? No such answer seems adequate, and any focus on versions derived therefrom—form follows function, for example—will prove misleading. We are driven, as it were, inside the building to find an experience—not the literal inside, the interior, but the conceptual heart of its endurance, the presence of the building felt by all those who dwell in it, ascend to its summit, or walk along its street.

First, of course, the building must *be there*, and here Smith's energy and the moment's love of technology come decisively together. The Deco grace notes of the Empire State are the traces of its deep kinship with the style of design best suited to deep belief in technology's gifts: the speeding locomotives, gleaming aircraft, and long-hooded cars of the era, the very armchairs and teapots, elevators and cocktail trays, that seem to suggest loose-kneed Charleston movement and, in their fluted edges and back-leaning lines, a desire to fly. They are material expressions, in familiar and domesticated form, of the Futurists' perfervid desire to lift free of the earth and soar; or what Heidegger calls "the standing reserve" of speed visibly present, ready to be unloaded down the runway, in a momentarily stationary airplane. Le Corbusier, too, was fetched by the airplane's beauty, its engineering perfection; he was moved, likewise, by the economical success of the automobile, the ocean liner, the typewriter, the telephone, and the Eversharp mechanical pencil (and, maybe less obviously, the briar pipe, the bowler hat, and the well-cut suit).

These are all, for Le Corbusier, examples of functionalist triumph, where necessity has generated a beautiful material solution to a well-articulated problem. "The creations of mechanical technique are organisms tending to a pure functionalism," he says in a very optimistic statement of technological naturalism, "and obey the same evolutionary laws as those objects in nature which excite our admiration." This can also be a painful process, however. Indeed, as he adds, the problem of the airplane, for example, was pressing because linked to war: here, when it comes to design, "death followed a mistake remorselessly." For him, the tragedy of architecture is that the house remains a set of needs lacking in clear articulation. Sounding more than a little like Marinetti, he laments, "The problem has not been stated as regards architecture. There has been no salutary war as in the case of the airplane." (An enduring irony is that his own building designs, especially when combined with the ubiquity of functional automobiles, generate the architectural dead zones so typical of late-century suburban development.)

The skyscraper is, we might say, a perfect gesture of the standing reserve, of evolutionary functionalist beauty. The upward movement is always potential and implied, the beauty of verticality offering, at a glance, all the necessarily presupposed achievements of commodity, construction, conveyance, and capital. There is a resonant boyishness, the techno-happy exuberance of hugely popular dime-novel fictions of the day (themselves the product of a literary assembly line, interchangeable items manufactured by the Stratemeyer writers' syndicate), which saw the Bobbsey Twins, Nancy Drew, and Tom Swift—"Swift by name and swift by nature"—dashing around in six-cylinder racing cars, jets, or balloons. Speed, speed, and more speed! Not for these juvenile heroes the handmade appurtenances of Jules Verne's lushly furnished Victorian technotopia, with its damask wall covers and leather upholstery; not for them the elaborate steampunk machinery of moving parts and old-fashioned difference-engine calculations.

Instead we find the clean young lines of the New World, the swift efficiency of invisible power and smooth surfaces: what we might call *cultural syncopation.* This is James Bond gadgetry fetishism before the fact, a prescient Deco version thereof, whose exemplars run from the evil-fighter Doc Savage, with his improbable turbocharged gyrocopter and sinew-strained jodhpurs, to the comic-book antifascists of the period, who have globe-trotting airplanes and tactical atomic weapons. The Old World's celebrated utopian architects, Le Corbusier and Antonio Sant'Elia and their followers in the Bauhaus, Walter Gropius and Bruno Tout, had bequeathed to the New World a vision of futuristic cityscapes and luminous technology that was, wonder of wonders, actually coming to be.

Though clad in stone and, thus, a falling short of the characteristic glass tower of this dream, the Empire State Building is distinguished in this trend as the last and arguably greatest piece of Art Deco technology ever produced, certain of its absolute expression of the wonders nestled within instrumental reason. It is, after its fashion, an expression of the very same desires for fast and inevitable progress that had been expressed by the Futurists two decades before. To look at a drawing by Sant'Elia, Virgilio Marchi, or Umberto Boccioni is to see, in full flower, the kind of optimism and cheerful immersion in materials that New York promised—never as a complete transformation, as they imagined, but as upthrust dream-constructions in the layered palimpsest that is Manhattan's force-fed grid.

Futurist architecture found its strongest voice in Sant'Elia, a gifted visionary whose 1914 Città Nuova designs included such science-fictional elements as a railway station overlaid with an airport and tower blocks with exterior elevators. Futurist architectural thinking was not, perhaps, as bloodthirsty as the program more generally; it nevertheless maintained a characteristic violent streak, and a fondness for what we could call the uppercase utopian declarative: "The fundamental characteristics of Futurist architecture will be impermanence and transience," Sant'Elia wrote. "THINGS WILL ENDURE LESS THAN US." Like his less intoxicated contemporaries, Sant'Elia's clean-sweeping vision was structured by changes in materials, which offered, he said, "surrogates for wood, stone, and brick" in the up-to-date forms of "reinforced concrete, iron, glass, cardboard, fibre"—sentiments that would not have been considered at all out of place in the boardroom of Shreve, Lamb & Harmon a decade later.

As we have seen, Futurism's vibrant but often incoherent views, urging us to speed up to a frenzy of transcendent annihilation, express a destructive strain of technology worship that Heidegger despised but understood very well. For Heidegger, as for us, it is the endurance of the building through time that arouses awe and prompts the question of being. The setting of the building on the earth grounds its presence and structures its field of meaning—its world. The unfettered modernist desire to float free of the earth, expressed architecturally in the massive cantilevers, hidden foundations, and extensive glass curtaining of Le Corbusier's cubist houses or the inverted proportions of Wright's anti-gravitational buildings, can be wonderful; but these features can also obscure the profound truth of architecture's connection to the earth. The result of disconnection of that sort can only be a confusion of means with end, a desire that is, like speed itself, direction without destination.

These less profound but more dangerous strains would come to dominate much of the modern imagination, proving how tragically apt were Heidegger's concerns about attempts to realize the transcendent via the instrumental. Philip Johnson, the wizard of self-promotion who dominated the American architectural imagination for most of the twentieth century, offers a depressing case in point. In 1932, the year after the Empire State Building opened, Johnson, who died early in 2005, organized a landmark show at the Museum of Modern Art celebrating the architecture pioneered by Le Corbusier and others. The show established the sleek glass-curtain skyscraper as a central modernist ideal, offering along the way a decisive—and somewhat ironic—rejection of the bankrupt "style" Le Corbusier had condemned in his *Vers une Architecture* essays of the previous half decade. The exhibition title,

"The International Style," highlights the irony: even as Johnson's curation gathered up the utopian possibilities of this new modernism, it swiftly nullified them by replacing one style with another. Johnson's own famous creation, the Glass House in New Canaan, Connecticut, is at once his best building and the purest expression of an ironic commitment to this notion of modernism, an unadorned box of windows boldly asserting its transparency and unforgiving right angles in a generous natural site.

These early gestures at self-reflexive knowingness—acknowledging that architecture is about style, no matter how much architects protest —now seem prophetic. It is now very much the received view that the utopian possibilities of modernist architecture were overestimated. Actual realizations of the International Style, everywhere from Brasília's planned high-rise neighborhoods to the eye-filling banality of the Potsdamer Platz reconstruction in Berlin, where glass-clad sheds march witlessly away to the horizon, seem to bear this out; they have been anything but emancipatory. The intellectual rejection of antique style, meanwhile, has proven far from revolutionary; it has not produced a trickle-down of either thought or deed in the public sphere, and now appears little more than a brief stylistic interlude spanning the confused middle of the last century. "The new buildings of Le Corbusier and Wright did not finally change the world, nor even modify the junk space of late capitalism," the critic Fredric Jameson has written, "while the Mallarmean 'zero degree' of Mies's towers quite unexpectedly began to generate a whole overpopulation of the shoddiest glass boxes in all the major urban centers of the world." When the rubber met the road, the judgment on modernist architecture was that—Jameson again—"its Utopian ambitions were unrealizable and its formal innovations exhausted."

The story is more nuanced than this standard narrative would suggest, not least because of the way utopian aspiration continues to inform architectural practice; but there is nevertheless an important truth in this assessment. Utopian architectural ideals did not translate into political liberation, still less the transformation of humankind. Johnson himself unsettles the conjunction, not only because, after the Second World War, he rejected the modernism he had championed and became a self-described corporate "whore." The gestural collaborations with Mies, such as the Seagram Building, were indeed superseded by a string of prosaic glass-shed towers, and the mix-and-match postmodern style Johnson favored latterly has been reduced, in places such as Shanghai, Taipei, and Kuala Lumpur, to an oppressive hypermodernism, dominating and unjust, casting futuristic shadows over cities otherwise mired in medievalism.

But in addition to these failures—the routine effects of history, one might argue—Johnson has a special personal blot in his youthful embrace of Nazism in the 1930s, a biographical fact that was detailed in Franz Schulze's 1994 biography but emerged with force only after his death. (This post-mortem drama of adolescent taint is itself the standard narrative sequence of the obituary, of course: the truly shocking thing today would be to hear that some long-established cultural figure, recently dead, had never even flirted with the Nazis.) Johnson later called his ideological infatuation "stupidity" and apologized, but it was far from a glancing affair, occupying most of his young adulthood—including the years spent creating and installing the MoMA show. He tried to start a fascist party in the United States in the 1920s, worked for Huey Long and Father Charles Coughlin, and was a guest of the Nazi Party at the Polish front in 1938. "The German green uniforms made the place look gay and happy," he reported in a letter. "There were not many Jews to be seen. We saw Warsaw burn and Modlin being bombed. It was a stirring spectacle." He was promoting the Nazis as late as 1940, but desisted when an FBI investigation was threatened.

Johnson thereafter withdrew from political life, but more important he decided that he, and by extension architecture itself, was not part of the political. "I mean, I'm not interested in politics," he said in a 1973 interview, claiming that forms of government had no bearing on aesthetic success. "I don't see any sense to it. About Hitler—if he'd only been a good architect!" It is no coincidence that Johnson's aesthetic sensibilities become unmoored just at the time he decides, maybe unwillingly, that he must give up politics. Aesthetic independence may argue for its own kind of narrow utopian ideal—the Kantian "disinterest" that alone sets beauty free to realize itself—but Johnson's story is also one of what Jürgen Habermas calls "the exhaustion of utopian energies." In the wake of the Second World War, just as theorists began to discuss a "post-ideological" condition, architecture's leading voice, and much of architecture itself, simply abandoned any kind of political commitment. Johnson's demeanor of aggressive playfulness and cheerful cynicism in the following decades of architectural self-conception are, alas, the dominant model. (Less significant but maybe more annoying, his trademark owlish black glasses have also been widely imitated.)

The trouble with this stance is that architecture, as an inescapable feature of the public sphere, what Hannah Arendt called "the space of appearance," is through and through political. Unlike the conceptual art that it has increasingly attempted to imitate in monumental form, it cannot be avoided and will last far longer. Johnson's own Glass House provides the insight: a dream space, a stage set, it blurs the distinction between inside and outside, private and public—and so thematizes, unsettlingly, the very things all buildings work to establish, the boundaries of shared existence. The Glass House thus suggests the very thing Johnson should always have remembered, and confronted. When it comes to politics, you can run but you cannot hide; because your private is always dependent on someone else's public; which, like it or not, is your public too.

Even at the moment of its birth, leftist utopianism was, in a familiar twinning, subject to a parallel dystopian critique. Yevgeny Zamyatin's novel *We*, for decades circulating in Russian samizdat editions and translated into English in the 1930s, is perhaps the earliest example of a genre that would find expression in Aldous Huxley and George Orwell, and futuristic films of the early twentieth century tended to depict grand urban plans as liberal-technological optimism run amok, with Charlie Chaplin crushed by relentless clocks, ubiquitous surveillance, and massive machine gears in *Modern Times* (1936), or underground city workers rendered robotically zomboid in the year 2000 in Fritz Lang's *Metropolis* (1926), a man unable to cope with the pace of 1980s life in *Just Imagine* (1930), and the world at war in *The Shape of Things* (1933), the film version of H. G. Wells's bestselling novel.

And yet, the literary-filmic dystopians were mistaken about the real form the danger of instrumentalism would assume. Reactionary pre-modernists were likewise off the mark in their diagnosis of scientific liberalism's evil tendencies. The twentieth century's truly vile realization of dark technology was not an excess of liberal technotopia, with its anything-goes optimism and Big Science cheerfulness; it was, rather, the mercifully short-lived fascist techno-tyranny, with its elimination of the slow or unfit amid hymns to blood and earth: the Nazi Third Reich.

However beloved and apparently innocent, the Empire State stands poised on the cusp between these declensions. Given its date of birth, as well as its essential relation to Lamb's totalizing principles of design and construction, it could hardly do otherwise.

Fed by spooling assembly lines and thrusting upward in the middle of exurban Manhattan, a megaproject motivated by equal parts grandiose rhetoric and profit motive, it is a great machine work that sweeps away its surroundings, obliterating in a moment not just the previous occupants of its site but all previous conceptions of Manhattan, New York, and America. Product of all those converging materials conduits, including the massive tonnage of limestone and steel, the building is, though constructed exactly according to the schemes once imagined by Le Corbusier after Henry Ford's Model T construction, unique and untranslatable but also implacable and domineering. "Stone of this size will be used all the way to the top of the building, in keeping with its massiveness," Lamb told reporters a month before steelwork began on the building, celebrating the keynote of his design. Massiveness abounded. The four central columns of the structure, mounted in concrete, would support a load of 10 million pounds; the columns themselves, ranged among a small forest of pile-driven secondary support piers, weighed between 73,000 and 103,000 pounds. The Empire State is not a modernist creation in architectural style, hovering uncertainly between Lamb's French-taught classicism and the clean lines of Deco, but it is a pure excrescence of modern technocratic success, a triumph of coordination: not just one Fordist rationalization, in other words, but multiple ones gathering together the entire economy of the Northeast into one upthrust point.

This was no mere practical result; rather, it was the thin edge of a massive theoretical wedge that dramatically changed American social thinking. Thorstein Veblen, for example, the man who had exposed the inner logic of conspicuous consumption, was also America's most outspoken advocate of social engineering on the Saint-Simonist model. In New World soil, the nineteenth-century utopian positivism of France mutated into a strain of liberal-capitalist management science. The irony is one that Veblen ought to have appreciated. The Empire State, that sweeping gesture in the positional-goods race of height, is also an expression of coordinated technocratic ambition, a foreshadow of American megaprojects to come, from the Hoover Dam to the space program. The central-command progressivism of the 1930s morphed, over the course of the Second World War, into what used to be called the military-industrial complex.

The building also reminds us, however, that any theory of technology so overarching—it's all good, or it's all bad—is likely to be both wrong and misleading. Wrong because insensitive to the genuine wonders of modernity. Misleading because a belief in the metaphysical dominance of technology, like belief in any overwhelming system of thought, divests us of responsibility, rendering individual choice and action meaningless.

Every building is an implied hymn to what lies beneath its surface, the plumbing and electricity and telephone lines, but none more so than the implausible Empire State, erected on the very cusp of capitalism's worst ever spasm, what economists like to call a market correction and other people call, simply, a crash. The building goes up just as the market goes precipitately down, a living challenge, in its very uprightness, its physical assertion of height created and maintained, against the possibility of downfall.

The building's design communicates this message, but it is delivered even more tellingly in accounts of the building that emphasize its gargantuan appetite for materials, like those still distributed by its in-house publicity department. It is, in this way as in so many others, a fitting synecdoche for New York itself, the city of self-conscious massiveness in consumption and production. Unlike the signature buildings of a more recent architectural moment, the Empire State makes itself a kind of organic genius of destruction (of raw materials and money) and creation (of office space and . . . money). In this way, it utterly fulfills the structural and commercial drives of its creators, realizing along the way the inner logic of all hyper-technological modernism.

Not for the Empire State, or New York, the historically conditioned grandiosity of Albert Speer's almost exactly contemporary structures. Speer famously advised Hitler to construct massive buildings with traditional load-bearing masonry rather than steel or concrete frames. Such edifices would be longstanding but noble, such that when they eventually crumbled, a thousand years hence, their broken columns and tumbled-down stone walls would convey a message of glorious achievement followed by decay. Steel frames would simply topple and tangle, breaking into a refuse pile of rusted beams and glass shards—the very images we now associate with the chaotic scenes of the postwar imagination. Speer instinctively sensed that the Nazi desire for ostentatious posterity, the dreams of a new Roman imperium and millennial Reich, would be served better by classicism than by the sleek modernism of the architectural moment. The architect Otto March had designed for the 1936 Olympiad what Speer called "a concrete structure with glass partition walls"—a scheme Hitler furiously rejected, calling for the cancellation of the games. Hitler, Speer wrote, angrily vowed "never [to] set foot inside a modern glass box like that," a perverse endorsement of at least some of the revolutionary ideas of architectural modernism.

The Nazis were dedicated to exterminating modernism, not to following its grand logic of transformation; looking back instead of forward, they abjured the soaring towers and heavenward spires of the decadent New World, opting instead for the pediments, columns, and lintels of ancient Greece and Rome, monumental stadiums and vast open squares suitable to arrayed ranks of soldiery and matériel. And if these structures should fall, no depressing mass of twisted metal and shattered windows would litter the ground. Instead they would leave an elegant pile of suggestive ruins, like something from a painting by Poussin. Speer saved the Olympics by altering March's plan such that "the steel skeleton already built could be clad in natural stone and have more massive cornices added." We might have expected very tall towers, for the first time architecturally possible, to figure prominently in fascist architecture, and yet, with some exceptions, they do not. We see, rather, Speer's vast domes and large volumes, or the parabolic arches offered to Mussolini by Giuseppe Terragni and Marcello Piacentini.

Indeed, only in the Stalinist Eastern bloc do we observe anything like the grandiose "wedding-cake" skyscrapers of the kind imagined by the Futurists. These buildings—Moscow University, the Palace of Culture in Warsaw—sprawl wide as well as rise high. They are out-of-scale implants, inhuman and brutal, which enter the urban landscape and dominate it by reordering the very sense of proportion. Stalin's projected Palace of the Soviets, for example, never built, is a gargantuan plan of columned setbacks and staggered shafts, oddly reminiscent of Manhattan style, capped with a ten-story-tall statue of a torch-wielding Lenin: a statue of liberty in supraterrestrial scale, a collective building achievement to dwarf the pyramids and cathedrals. Pythagoras was wrong; man is the measure not of all things, but of just one, namely, his own insignificance. These buildings are the steroidal cousins of the Empire State, in style as well as scale.

Such designs were not acceptable to the Nazis, however. Though scale certainly mattered to them, towers as such did not appeal, nor did the hyped-up violations of proportion so typical of Soviet Suprematism. Grandeur would be achieved, instead, with massiveness wrought according to the classical orders. The height and scale of Roman temples could be observed, respected, then multiplied many times over, fashioning vast slabs of building at once familiar and strange. Thus the peculiar "classical futurism" of the fascist style—a combination in thought as well as in material culture.

"Today, not only in peasant homes but also in the city sky-scrapers, there lives alongside the twentieth century the tenth or the thirteenth," Leon Trotsky observed in one of a series of prescient articles written in the 1930s. "A hundred million people use electricity and still believe in the magic power of signs and exorcism. . . . Despair has raised them to their feet; fascism has given them the banner. . . . [C]apitalist society is puking up the undigested barbarism. Such is the physiology of National

Socialism." The vertiginous nausea of observing this process, whereby a form of political time travel, or time collapse, is effected by mixing technical marvels and cultural darkness, can be seen again anywhere skyscrapers cast their long shadows over peasant homes occupied by the very people who clambered over the rickety bamboo scaffolds of the towers.

The Empire State embodies its own kind of technotopian dream: not the genocidal Nazi fantasy, of course, but an extended celebration of machine logic and the forces of capital. The building achieves, in its smooth and hygienic Huxleyan fashion, a totalitarian ideal of command and control, the inexorable logic of assembly line and social engineering. The building is all about vertical space, and in Manhattan's force-grown grid, space is money: upward is not upward for its own sake, but for the sake of possibility and profit. On the cramped Manhattan street plan, there is nowhere else to go, and so the skyscraper was born. The Empire State's relation to the grid is therefore symbiotic, born of its pressures but also exploiting its conduits, the streets and pipes and gaslines that tangle beneath its surface. It is a node growing, massing, developing in the entire network of power and commodity, rising like a magic tower from sheer force of energy concentrated below.

While older stone-clad buildings typically had one vertical foot of exterior stone for every 45 to 50 cubic feet of interior space, the Empire State's hybrid metal-stone structure—a steel skeleton fleshed in polished ashlar—produced 200 cubic feet inside for every foot of stone. It sits on just 197.5 feet of Fifth Avenue frontage, site of the 30-foot-high main entrance and ornate lobby, but runs longer east–west, 425 feet on Thirty-third and Thirty-fourth streets, an efficient footprint of 84,000 square feet. The lower part of the building, the pedestal or base, extends upward 350 feet, or twenty-nine stories.

The rising extension, or tower, occupies approximately 25 percent of the original plot volume, accounting for the assertive but elegant outline. From the thirtieth to the eighty-fifth floors, the east and west sides are 135 feet long, the north and south 185 feet, forming a grooved rectangle sitting atop the shouldered base. The five topmost floors start 1,050 feet above the distant sidewalk and the roof is a flat staged cap 180 feet by 130 feet. The top observation deck, naturally the highest in the world at the time, is 150 feet higher than the Eiffel Tower and 250 feet higher than the observatory in the Chrysler Building. Banks of sixty-four elevators, moving at speeds as high as 700 feet a minute, could shuttle people or freight up and down the central shaft of the building, also the site of mail chutes, staircases, and electrical wiring. Surrounding this lifeshaft are some 3 million square feet of rental space, 6,400 windows, radiators hidden under window sills, and, outside, hundreds of ornate spandrels, cast aluminum, fashioned after a design first employed by Raymond Hood for a 1928 apartment house at 3 East Eighty-fourth Street. Measuring 4½ by 5 feet, these shiny doodads weigh 130 pounds each.

The designers conceived the building not only as an exercise in materials but as an experiment in flex-space. With its unprecedented height, the Empire State could have created another 300,000 square feet of space and still remained within the zoning laws, but Raskob and Lamb wanted occupants to at least entertain the possibility of shared window frontage and open-plan offices, then luxuries still in their infancy. The usable stories were offered unfinished, with modular office units that could be as small as 600 square feet or as large as 3,600. The big open floors, suspended from the central core and the virtually invisible steel frame, were a revelation, a sign of things to come—though neither the building's creators nor their potential clients could have predicted the lifeless declension of the open-plan office, the carpet-covered cubicles and dead-air, glass-curtain prisons of the modern work world, rabbit warrens of alienation.

The revelatory beauty of the Empire State Building emerges precisely, almost despite itself, from within a technological dream. It confronts, and penetrates, the "extreme danger" Heidegger identifies in the technological, the overpowering reduction of everything to mastery, to consumption in the standing reserve. When we question technology, seek its essence beyond mere instrumentalism, we restore both it and the other neglected part of making, *poésis* or art, to a condition of wonder.

The Empire State Building's relation to technology is a mixture of faith and doubt. It offers a useful antidote to metaphysical conundrums, and becomes, along the way, its own work of art.

The building is an extended essay in materials-based problem solving, a cross between architectural design and a realized theorem in the fields of manufacture, transport, and construction. Listen to William Lamb as he describes the almost transcendent success of the Fordist, beauty-through-efficiency dream: "So perfect was the planning, so exact the fulfillment of the schedule that workmen scarcely had to reach out for what they next required. As if by magic, their supplies appeared at their elbows." The general construction even created systems within systems, enclosed economies of movement and overarching structures of time—reminding us, among other things, of Lewis Mumford's claim that the most influential invention in human history was the clock, for only then could action be completely coordinated. "On each floor," Lamb continues, "as the steel frame climbed higher, a miniature railroad was built, with switches and cars, to carry supplies. A perfect timetable was published each morning. At every minute of the day the builders knew what was going up on each of the elevators, to which height it would rise and which gang of workers would use it."

The perfect system spreads in all directions from the site of precise placement, the moment of laying of brick or riveting of girder. "Down below, in the streets, the drivers of the motor trucks worked on similar schedules. They knew, each hour of every day, whether they were to bring steel beams or bricks, window frames or blocks of stone, to Empire State. The moment of departure from a strange place, the length of time allowed for moving through traffic and the precise moment of arrival were calculated, scheduled and fulfilled with absolute precision. Trucks did not wait, derricks and elevators did not swing idle, men did not wait. With perfect teamwork, Empire State was built."

As if by magic. There is obvious joy—even the trace of mystical awe—contained in every yard of steel, every square foot of stone, every strip of chrome-nickel plating laid down "with absolute precision," according to the "perfect schedule." The dark worries of technology's nighttime are here set aside in this perpetual morning of belief, the refined assembly lines stretching from New Jersey and Connecticut to central Manhattan, the lone arterial conduits of raw material drawing life into the heart of the city.

This magnificent edifice, standing so firmly on its rectangular block of earth carved from the foursquare grid, thrusting upward in its serried slabs and runnels, is a living, beating monument to the interconnectedness of things—a continuous celebration, we might say, to the *thingliness* of things, the world conceived and experienced as equipment. This is a dream building, but not via the bucolic vision of interwoven nature found in the Thoreauvian imagination, that residue of pure adolescent romanticism; rather, this dream embraces the grown-up urban awareness that pipes and lines and wire, hidden but necessary, sustain the spaces and sites of our aspiration. The building argues that technology is redeemed through itself; it opens up a world, a revelation—perhaps even a kind of salvation.

5
Still Life

Like man himself, who is the only one not to know

his own glance, the Tower is the only blind point of

the total optical system of which it is the centre. . . .

The Tower is an object which is a complete verb,

both active and passive.

Roland Barthes, "The Eiffel Tower"

In Don DeLillo's 1985 novel *White Noise,* two main characters—a professor of "Hitler Studies" who is the book's first-person narrator, and his colleague, a cultural-studies lecturer from New York—drive into the countryside near their unnamed college town to visit a tourist attraction, "The Most Photographed Barn in America." As they approach the site, roadside billboards announce their destination every few miles. When they arrive, the hillside is scattered with people photographing the Most Photographed Barn in America, some forty cars and a tour bus.

Murray, the New Yorker, looks at them for a long moment and then finally says, "No one sees the barn." And: "Once you've seen the signs about the barn, it becomes impossible to see the barn." And: "We're not here to capture an image, we're here to maintain one. Every photograph reinforces the aura."

The barn exists, we might say, only in its multiple representations and so becomes invisible, no longer present for ordinary experience. Or rather, it is present precisely by being absent from any direct experience of itself, available only as the subject of all future possible photographs. It is no longer a barn; it is no longer anything at all. This point extends beyond the important but rather more routine insights that (a) the barn embodies a self-fulfilling prophecy by billing itself, and so then becoming, the most photographed barn in America; that (b) in becoming its own self-description, the barn ceases to be a real barn—that is, a barn dedicated to the usual uses of barns such as storing equipment or housing livestock; or even that (c) the real energy in play here is the medium's mediation, its power to deflect experience, resulting in the banal paradox of having a present experience only through the lens of something intended to capture an image for some future experience. Which experience, in the event, rarely happens, since no one wants to look at the photos or, still less, video.

These are all true; but the disappearance of the barn is a deeper phenomenon, a function of the simulacral culture of tourism itself, and the strange transcendence, the auratic collection, of the experience. In taking its place within an economy of pre-shared leisure experiences, signaled here by the billboards and our surrender to their logic of reproduction,

Chocolate replicas of the Empire State Building (Photo courtesy of
Martine's Chocolates)

the barn removes itself from the scene, becomes a spectral emanation
maintained solely by multiple tokens of its appearance; or, better, maintained by the ongoing enactment of *capturing those tokens;* by, that is,
the act of photographing itself. The resulting photographs, after all, offer
no particular interest beyond their having been created under the given
conditions. Since there is nothing to distinguish a photograph of the
Most Photographed Barn in America from a photograph of some other
barn in America, the participation in the transaction of photography is
the sole point.

The collective quality of this enactment is essential, "a kind of spiritual surrender" in which "we see only what the others see." The barn disappears within the energy of this collective hallucination, but so does the photograph. Indeed, we could go further: so does the experience. This is not, finally, an experience at all, just an enactment, a ritual participation, in a meaningless simulacral system absolutely typical of tourism.

But here we should perhaps be more careful, and more neutral. The experience of the Most Photographed Barn in America is not meaningless at all—such judgment is both moralistic and materialistic, suggesting a level of more essential experiences, or encounters with real things, that this situation purportedly lacks. But that Platonic cast of thought, with its presumption of deceitful illusions masquerading as realities, is part of the very scolding epistemological structure dismantled by the simulacral barn, with its self-canceling superlative. When the barn exists entirely as the sum total of attempted captures of its image, there is no appearance/reality logic left in play. Tourism is not false, it is spectral; and not meaningless for all that. Now we are pilgrims not to holy sites, or even to peak experiences; we are pilgrims on a circular journey that leads us only back to where we were, disappearing into our cameras, and hence ourselves. The surrender is the meaning. The surrender is everything.

The Empire State Building may be the most reproduced building in America. And if it doesn't quite disappear in the manner the barn does, it is nevertheless subject to its own kind of invisibility. Because of the blasé attitude typical of urban dwellers in general, and honed to a sharp edge by New Yorkers in particular, the sheer size of the Empire State posed an immediate problem: it was impossible for its immediate neighbors to look at it. I don't mean merely that they could not comprehend its volume and height, though this is indeed the case when, for example, one stands at the Fifth Avenue entrance and looks up. The wall shears away into the sky like a floating slab of ancient runic significance or heaven-bound limestone spaceship, spinning the viewer into vertigo. New Yorkers could not look at the tallest building in the world precisely because it was the tallest building in the world. Once again, the superlative became the point of the phenomenon but, with the same stroke, reduced the phenomenon to a specter.

There was also, just as influential, the Empire State's new and un-precedented version of the same destabilization found in all buildings, namely, the tension between its inside and its outside. The Empire State, I have said, was conceived and executed as an unprecedented demonstra-tion in the use of technology and materials, a tangible and lasting poem in praise of steel, stone, and glass. But it was also, and by the identical logic, an exercise in the efficient creation of efficient space. The flex-model floor designs and multitude of windows available to tenants made the Empire State an excellent early example of the user-friendly techniques now found in most office buildings, especially those with ridged or tesser-ated structures that increase the number of corner offices. In a Mies-style building, by contrast, there can be only four such offices per floor, raising the stakes for making partner or getting promoted to vice president.

The inside of the Empire State Building provides a giddy simu-lacrum of time travel. As building boosters never hasten to point out, the Empire State lacks the high-tech capabilities that made the World Trade Center's twin towers such a favorable location for brokerage firms and investment banks. The backbone of the Empire State tenantry has long been the garment trade, serving the nearby Garment District, north and a little west of the intersection of Thirty-fourth and Fifth, where one may still see an occasional rack of plastic-shrouded samples being hauled across a busy street. Of course, given the realities of a global labor market, many of these firms have since shifted their manufactur-ing operations to the Far East or Eastern Europe, or closed altogether; but it is still common to see such names as Garan, Bollman Hats, and Accessory Network in the building's list of tenants, with offices along the mazy corridors of worn-linoleum floors.

Other clients include lawyers, dentists, various charitable founda-tions and not-for-profits, plus a smattering of jewelry wholesalers and dubious holding companies whose lights are rarely on. The oldest living tenant is Jack Broad of Empire Diamond, who has been on the seventy-sixth floor since 1931, before the building was entirely finished. (His ninety-fifth birthday party, to be held in the eightieth-floor func-tion room, was the subject of much agonized conversation in the fall of 2004, not least over his plan to invite five times the room's capacity and have the guests rotate in shifts, and to cater the event himself entirely with peanuts and soda from a corner deli.) Altogether it is a building whose interior seems stuck in the same 1930s style-warp as its comic-book exterior. Wandering the empty hallways on the thirtieth or fifty-sixth floor, one would hardly be surprised to come across a painted-glass window of a shady private investigator or a fly-by-night pulp-fiction concern.

The literal backbone of the building, meanwhile, makes it unlikely that terrorists could succeed in attacking it as they did the World Trade Center—a prospect much on the minds of high-rise tenants, particularly in New York—even if we set to one side the telling point that no similar assault is expected from a group that rarely does the same thing twice. The Empire State's foundations are firmly planted in bedrock; its stairwells are encased in thick concrete, and its steel interior, married to the limestone cladding, is more like a vertical radiator than the spindly framework typical of newer towers. These newer structures are actually designed to sway, giving as much as seven horizontal feet for wind tolerance at the top, meaning that water would slosh all by itself in upper-level sinks and a plumb bob hung from a high office ceiling would swing almost continually. ("Why is that moving?" someone once asked a man who did this very thing in the World Trade Center. The answer is: It's not, but the building is.) The Empire State is a different creature altogether. If a jet plane ever struck the building, it is unlikely it would melt and collapse from the inside as the twin towers did.

Tenants of the building tell you these things, to reassure themselves no doubt but also to exhibit a fine-grained version of that mixture of charm, insouciance, and gallows humor that is so typical of the New York demeanor—what people often mistake for rudeness. The interior Empire State is as much a microcosm of New York culture as the exterior is the city's most potent and familiar image. It is unfortunate that the hundreds of thousands of tourists who visit the building and ascend to its observation deck—about 3.5 million a year, and 324,000 in one recent June alone—bypass the entire life of the working building. In fact, some tourists seem to think the whole thing is there just to support the view. One longtime tenant, descending to the lobby coatless one winter day, overheard a visitor say, "Hey, do you think there are offices in this building?" Well, yes. "I mean, it's not like the Eiffel Tower, where you can see that there's nothing there," the tenant said, shaking her head and laughing. "Do they think it's all an empty facade, with just a tourist shunt running people from bottom to top?"

In a sense, that is exactly what they think. Like the initiates of an ancient cult, they are ushered from street and light through a series of routinely minatory challenges of expense, boredom, and duration, an enforced (if mild) misery of unfreedom, until they can reemerge again into a new, higher light: the light of the sun, the panoramic vision, from which the space they quitted an hour or two (or, alas, three) before is revealed again, transformed into the *view*. Here the acquisition of the view, however briefly, is retroactive justification for the inconveniences and supplications just endured. Outside is traded for inside, and then for outside again; but a new and better, an elevated and transcendent, outside. The passage in between is thus rendered meaningless except as an enclosed, difficult, and opaque space *on the way to the outside vision*. It is an irony of the difficulty of this passage that initiates often feel compelled to spend more time at the summit than inclination dictates, to "make the most" or "get their money's worth" of the spectacle—really the *passage to* the spectacle.

Once you are at the top, after all, there is not that much to do. In his pamphlet *Above the Clouds,* Alfred Smith makes much of the fact that people find the view inexhaustible, enumerating various stories of visiting potentates and ambassadors staying two hours and more, missing important appointments and neglecting matters of state. He lists in detail the natural features and architectural landmarks of each side's vista: the Palisades, the Orange Mountains, the Hudson; the Woolworth, Chrysler, and Met Life buildings; the Queensboro, Williamsburg, Manhattan, and Brooklyn Bridges; Union Square, Madison Square, Central Park. He leans hard on the thrill of being here at the summit. "Anyone who has experienced any or all of the joys of mountain-climbing can testify to the thrill that such an experience brings," he says, looking, like a technological Kantian, for some analogue to the natural sublime. "Unfortunately we cannot all find the time or the money to go mountain-climbing, and we may not be sufficiently air-minded to trust our lives to aeroplanes from which fleeting glimpses of passing landscapes may be had. We can all go up, however, without danger or physical effort, twelve hundred and fifty feet to the top of that man-made mountain Empire State Building."

True, but perhaps not as thrilling as he implies, at least not anymore. There is, of course, a great deal to see; but the views are available *all at once* on each of the four sides, and not as time consuming as the hard sell implies. The shops here, meanwhile, are nothing to compare with the commercial cacophony left below. The tea room and the sweeping Deco-style cocktail bar, with its curved chrome rails and long-ago twenty-five-cent martinis, where formerly, in Smith's words, you could "obtain good things to eat and anything you want to drink," are long since closed. Especially in an age when "aeroplane" travel is so common and has offered so many spectacles of height to us casually "air-minded" people, many visitors find, oddly, that there is really little point in lingering more than a few minutes—a tiny fraction of the time spent acquiring that very access. Summit scalers at the Empire State are not invited, as the visitor to the Eiffel Tower is, to contemplate the radiating paradoxes of construction itself, to see engineering exposed to the naked gaze and so to make each of us *think like an engineer.*

To walk down the spiral stairs of the Eiffel Tower, said the architect Giedion, "gave the moving spectator a glimpse into four-dimensional experience"; it renders our experience of space explicit, in the time it takes us to walk, all that forced contemplation of struts and beams, the very rivets shivering with significance. The tower was, for him, the paradigm of modern architecture—or, in the words of Theodor Däubler, the "scaffold and skeleton of the future." It demands in every instant of its existence what only elaborate scale models of other buildings can, which is to say, a full awareness of its assembly and, thus, potential disassembly. Not architecture at all, thought the artist and photographer László Moholy-Nagy when it first went up; rather a *sculpture,* "a broken-through, completely perforated 'block.'" The tower enacts, in its distinctive lineaments, a battle with the forces of nature, a built hubris with a hollow center. Walter Gropius thought it indicated "the growing preponderance of voids over solids" in modern architecture, the shape of things to come.

Well, only up to a point. We have perhaps, in these first years of the new millennium, grown used to the idea of architecture as sculpture, with the grand public buildings of Libeskind and Gehry—the Jewish Museum, the Guggenheim Bilbao—taking their place as, in effect, monumental works of conceptual art. But solids are still very much with us, and the Eiffel Tower remains the exception rather than the rule. The Empire State Building plots a different logic, being a building that, in a sense, merely happens to serve as a tower. Though beautiful and distinctive, it does not intend to be sculptural even in the attenuated sense of the Eiffel Tower; it retains the standard architectural distribution of 90 percent space to 10 percent built form, but does not *display* its play of voids and solids. Thinking like an engineer is possible at the summit of the Empire State, but it is not obligatory, as it is with the Eiffel Tower, where simple contemplation necessarily becomes a structural exercise. The Empire State is still a building, with the structure itself invisible beneath our feet; the thought of its engineering requires imagination, not just sight, and so it can be avoided. We look out, but we do not look down. The floor beneath us is just a floor and, in its bland serviceability, conceals its own architectural triumph.

"The cohort of visitors which is enclosed by a monument and provisionally follows its internal meanders before coming back outside is quite like the neophyte who, in order to accede to the initiate's status, is obliged to traverse a dark and unfamiliar route within the initiatory edifice," Roland Barthes observes. "In the religious protocol as in the tourist enterprise, being enclosed is therefore a function of the rite." But in contrast to an initiation into museum, church, or gallery, initiation here actively negates the intermediate interior, renders it as pure passage. It must be traversed, but there is nothing to be decoded along the way except the task of passage itself—reduced, in this instance, to waiting in line for access to various cash nodes, security checkpoints, and elevators, like way stations on the road to a miniature Santiago de Compostela. It is a series of obstacles to be overcome, often with satisfaction and the application of invidious distinction. (One of my most cherished possessions ever has been the pass that allows me and five of my guests to jump those elevator queues—a pretty high-grade New York positional good, in both senses of the word.)

And so the pilgrim-tourists get no opportunity to hear the courtly joshing of the long-serving elevator guides in the tenant part of the building, uniformed figures offering fashion advice and stylized big-city greetings like something from a Cary Grant movie. They do not get to see the world-weary competence of the in-house electricity and plumbing departments that, with almost 900 tenants to serve, forestall a genuine office disaster, a flood or fire, at least once a day. The 250 staff people in the building, most of them of long unionized employment, offering services from engineering and locksmithing to printing and public relations. The business of these people is to allow other people to go about their business. In some cases, they may be new to the building but they nevertheless maintain the culture of nostalgic affection that suffuses the building.

That affection runs all the way from the marble lobby, with its list of service awards, including plumber's helper, to the clear shining air of the eighty-sixth floor, where it feels like you are atop the only tall building in the world. In between, people decorate their offices with King Kong posters, architectural drawings, kitschy figurines, and coeval New York icons: the 1939 World's Fair's famous sphere-and-obelisk pavilion, for example, or the incandescent glory of Coney Island's Luna Park on a hot, long-ago summer night. Guy de Maupassant may have wanted to lunch in the Eiffel Tower café in order not to look at what he regarded as a cast-iron monstrosity, but workers in the Empire State Building seem to want multiple images of their tower around them, toys and photos and paintings, perhaps because they are virtually the only New Yorkers who cannot look up, or out a window, and see it. They feel deprived, perhaps, of that sense of connection, the linked sightlines of the shared nodal view—I see it and see you seeing it too—that is offered to every other New Yorker. It may be that a model or a poster, held near, allays the sense of interior blindness, a felt invisibility of one's identity with the building when inside.

Such a species of shared love, organized around representation, can even be enough, sometimes, to overcome the usual surliness and suspicion of post-9/11 security personnel, working a neat inside-out logic. Not long ago, taking a wrapped thirty-inch model of the building into the elevator, the product of some inspired haggling in a tourist shop across Fifth Avenue, I was stopped. "The supervisor thinks that's a drill," the young guard said, pointing to his exposed X-ray view of the building's familiar pinnacle, which did indeed resemble a power tool if not quite a deadly weapon.

Standing there on the security threshold, off the street but not yet quite inside the building, I said, "It's the building." Meaning, of course, not that it was the building, since we were standing inside that, but a model of the building. Actually, an X-ray image of a model of the building. "Obviously it's the building," I said, pointing at the screen. Of course it was not obvious at all. It was the opposite of obvious.

"Obviously it's the building," the guard repeated, nodding in what he probably did not realize was agreement in a strange metaphysical bargain. "You have a nice day now."

All of this is of course generally invisible, and of no special concern, for those who experience the Empire State, if they experience it at all, from the outside in. Even tourists, those most likely to break the city's commandment and simply gaze at the building from the street, or wait in line for a chance to ride to the top, tend to do both with no thought for the thousands of people working in the vast space between sidewalk and summit. For them, the building's working life is another world, and not of much interest, just the incidental filling between the soaring walls and lofty views.

The combination of these factors makes the image-making of the Empire State especially important. As a series of commercial exchanges, often at the literal base of the tower-temple where we shop for pictures or models amid a clamor of price competition, as in a desert bazaar, we reaffirm a worldly economy in these routine exchanges of capital for memory: the purchase of the souvenir. We also place ourselves in the larger economy of representation and circulation, the proliferation of reflections. Place ourselves, and acquire place holders: chunks of memory, of depiction, which we in turn circulate back to our homes, our towns, our linked worlds. We might even say that the images allow us to look at the building *for the first time,* to gaze without being caught looking.

Many of the first appropriations of the building were, not surprisingly, comments on its size: the superlative quality expressed graphically, sometimes tortuously, in scalar comparisons. The Empire State stood next to the other skyscrapers of the midcentury, next to the Eiffel Tower or the Leaning Tower of Pisa. The *London Daily Mail* pointed out that it was nine times taller than Nelson's Column in Trafalgar Square. Illustrating the strength of a new two-hundred-inch telescope at Mount Wilson, the *Philadelphia Inquirer* noted that the "point of a needle, held some yards away from the lens, would appear as large as the great 102-story Empire State Building from a distance of a few blocks."

Modern Mechanics and Inventions informed its readers that if the thickness of a postage stamp represented the record of human history, the building would not be high enough to represent the rest of astronomical time—something to think about the next time you find yourself riding up to the observatory. Child's Restaurants estimated that two days' servings of its popular pancakes would make a stack as high as the building. Maybe most impressively, *Scribner's Magazine* informed the world that the copies of Margaret Mitchell's potboiler *Gone With the Wind* sold in 1933 would, if piled one on top of the other, form a stack 250 times taller than the Empire State Building—a claim so hard to imagine that it invites its own scalar repositioning, as for example in proximity to the moon.

Nor were all the comparisons driven by height. The building became, indeed, a kind of immediate yardstick of the very technological, materials-driven economy of which it was such a prescient expression. This had begun, indeed, with Smith and Raskob's construction-period publicity campaign, with the precise tallying of speed and materials serving the secondary purpose of grandiose comparison. "If all the materials which came to the corner of Fifth Avenue and Thirty-Fourth Street for the construction of Empire State had come in one shipment," one article began, "a train fifty-seven miles in length would have been needed. When the locomotive of such a train would have entered New York, the caboose on the rear end would have come to a halt in Bridgeport, Connecticut. Ten million bricks were used in building Empire State. A single workman, had he continued at it every day, would have had to work for 25 years before he could have finished mortaring these bricks." Such conversions abounded: wiring expressed in miles, marble in acres, plaster in the form of an imaginary sidewalk that Starrett Brothers estimated would run from central Manhattan to the Capitol Building in Washington, D.C.

Indeed, future versions of the grandiose comparison often turn on such acts of covering or plastering, enacting a new kind of cultural invisibility, as the building's materials are, as it were, redeployed from their real functional site into new forms of consumer durables or desired luxury items. Kelvinator officials estimated that the 6 million square feet of porcelain tile they used in 1933 would clad the Empire State seven times over. Once every eight hours Kellogg's Cereals used enough Waxtite paper to encase the building—a sort of Christo-inspired art installation before the fact. Clay Morgan, publicity director of the French Line, told his customers that all the fresh linens stocked aboard the cruise liner *Normandie,* sheets, tablecloths, and napkins included, would completely cover the building in snowy white material. Unfortunately, he was not able to report what Le Corbusier, who had arrived in New York on that very ship, thought of the idea.

We do know that the brilliant Le Corbusier, fan of the skyscraper as an idea, had not been much impressed by American versions thereof in the first decades of the century. He had mocked them in his modernist tour de force, *Vers une Architecture,* published in English translation the same year the Empire State was finished, warning, "Let us listen to the counsels of American engineers. But let us beware of American architects." An accompanying illustration shows the overdecorated summit of the Manhattan Company Building, clearly in Corb's view a disaster of stylistic excess. By 1935, when the *Normandie* sailed up the Hudson, bearing Le Corbusier to his New World destination, the tune had changed. "We saw the mystic city of the new world appear far away, rising up from Manhattan," he reported, the advocate of the City of Tomorrow chastened into reluctant awe. "It passed us at close range: a spectacle of brutality and savagery. In contrast to our hopes the skyscrapers were not made of glass, but of tiara-crowned masses of stone. They carry up a thousand feet in the sky, a completely new and prodigious architectural event; with one stroke Europe is thrust aside."

This excited, almost mythic scene must remind one of a similar resonant arrival, this one fictional and representing a vaster migration. Karl Rossmann, the young hero of Kafka's unfinished mythic novel *Amerika* (published by Max Brod in 1927 as *Der Verschollene,* or The Man Who Disappeared), arrives in New York harbor in a dazzle of eye-filling height. "So high!" he says to himself as he regards the Statue of Liberty—which in this case, Kafka never having seen it, sports a sword rather than a torch in her upraised hand. Karl is seeking a new life in New York after disgrace in the Old World (he has impregnated a family servant) and finds it, after a fashion, working as a uniformed lift-boy in a tall Manhattan hotel. "Karl's deepest disappointment was the discovery that a lift-boy had nothing to do with the machinery of the lift but to set it in motion by simply pressing a button, while all repairs were done exclusively by the mechanics belonging to the hotel." Karl's engagement with vertical speed is, like ours, nullified by success: the elevator works by not revealing its workings, by rendering them invisible.

The Empire State occupies the central place, the *nexus primus,* in the shift of epochal power so clearly measured by height. It was, and remains, the yardstick of New World achievement. The building even becomes, after the fashion of all perverse cultural physics, a mythic unit of energy, the way the *minihelen* functions as a unit of beauty (a face able to launch just one ship) or, as mentioned before, the *warhol* as a unit of fame equal to exactly fifteen minutes. "The energy women use in a year to wash clothes," a contemporary ad for Oxydol detergent said, "would move the Empire State Building a block if translated into moving power." The illustration shows a woman hauling the building along by a rope, expending her fraction of that high-order equation. A Sinclair gasoline ad from the same period shows the building being picked up by a crane: "Amazing as it may seem, there is enough energy stored up in a single gallon of the powerful new H-C gasoline, if it could be fully utilized, to hoist the world's tallest building 1¾ inches in the air." Such claims must echo, for those of us born after the Second World War, the awesome and terrifying physics of another equation, $e = mc^2$, whose power and scale were barely comprehensible in theory, and hardly welcome in practice.

Such imaginative equivalences, the stuff of a gee-whiz worldview ("amazing as it may seem"), were so neatly parodied by Dorothy Parker— "If all the young ladies who attended the Yale promenade dance were laid end to end, no one would be the least surprised"—that *we* would not be at all surprised if they were eligible for permanent retirement as a result. And yet, the logic of laying end-to-end retains a grip on the mind struggling to give expression to enormity, in both senses of the word (just as Parker's original assessment of the units of value at the Yale prom have been reassigned, variously, to the Harvard-Yale game and the entire undergraduate populations of Brandeis, Wellesley, and Vassar).

Even today, comparisons are a handy option for those in need of vivid illustration, though not as often in the can-do spirit of the postwar boom. In the documentary film *Super Size Me,* about the fast-food chain McDonald's, the filmmakers point out that the total volume of one day's worth of trash produced by McDonald's packaging would fill the total interior space of the Empire State Building. The scene making the point shows the building opening like a giant trash can as several thousand tons of crumpled burger cartons and spent soft drink containers are piled in.

The building was also a staple, as the Woolworth had been before it, in the early-century boom in picture postcards, many of them cheaply aquatinted lithographs or engravings and often sent, per the day's convention, with just the addressee's name and postal information—that is, with little or no accompanying message, perhaps just a scrawled line or two. The images were sent as signs of witness rather than as attempts at communication, often without a text to position or inform them: zero-degree images, in short, tourism tokens circulated through the hyperefficient postal service of the 1930s and '40s as signs of documented presence. They were, in effect, precursors to the shared imagistic economies of television and film, creating bonds of shared visual stimulus across geographical distances. "A picture-postcard is a symptom of loneliness," Graham Greene wrote. Postcards betray the same desire to allay one's solitude that, today, creates the categorical urban imperative: that no walk or drive, no matter how short, shall be undertaken without a cell-phone call or text message. But how much more poignant is the almost-lost gesture of selecting, writing, addressing, stamping, and depositing a token of my presence, here before this tourist attraction or atop this impressive edifice, and sending it to you?

A card from 1914 depicting the Woolworth Building, for example, sent to Mr. Levi S. Connor of Conboconk, New Hampshire, by someone identified only as R. S. C.—son? brother? friend?—on the power of a green one-cent Washington stamp. This chunk of mediated loneliness turns up nine decades later in a rural junk barn and provides a glimpse of the long-gone world of wonder that prompted it, the wispy relationships and separations of which it is the signifier. Published by the Union News Company of New York, it sports a pastel-tinted image by Photochrome G&S, also of New York, with a copyright to Littig and Company. The faded black ink on the front says, near the top of the tiered and backed building, "570 odd feet—55th story—Was up this last winter." On the back, the card is dated—Saturday morning, the 31st of July, 1914—and is brisk and dense with thick-and-thin italic penmanship. "Down here on a short trip," it says. "2nd time this summer. Come visit Fall River. Dandy sail and seas day-time. Going to Mountains first of next week to drive car down for folks. Trust you all are getting along bestest possible."

The Empire State inspired even more such penny-card images, quickly becoming the most reproduced building in America. Officials estimate that more than a billion postcards featuring its image are produced every year—a figure that invites doubt, though it is probably acceptable code for "uncountable number." These are supplemented by commemorative posters, pennants, place mats, and eventually, the billboard of the late century, T-shirts. Nowadays, characteristically, various artfully aged Empire State Building shirts join a long list of faded athletic gear and old-fashioned advertising imagery, much of it invented, as part of a retro-clothing fad peddled by such nostalgia-oriented retail outlets as American Eagle or Diesel. The various two-dimensional images were soon joined by every imaginable kind of souvenir object, from paperweights and ashtrays to piggy banks, snow globes, and thermometers. Such items are still to be found in the shops scattered around the base of the building, along with crystal, steel, plastic and rubber models of the building, ineffective pencil erasers in its image, and even pewter salt and pepper shakers in the shape of the respective summits of the Empire

State and the Chrysler buildings—a fitting counterpart to the sphere and obelisk shakers designed for the 1939 World's Fair. By the fiftieth anniversary of the building in 1981 it was estimated that some 80,000 miniatures of all kinds had been sold, making the building the most replicated structure of all time. By the seventy-fifth anniversary in 2006 the number will likely have reached 150,000 or more. (In contrast to the inflated postcard figure, this number actually seems rather low.)

Nor, over the years, have two-dimensional reproductions and souvenir miniatures proved sufficient to satisfy the desire to populate the cultural world with replicants of this wondrous construction. An anonymous man from Tacoma, Washington, used 135 decks of playing cards to construct a house of cards in the form of the Empire State. Another man carved a four-foot-high version out of soap. Students from Kelvedon Hatch Primary School in Brentwood, England, closed the distance between them and the New York landmark by constructing a seven-foot eight-inch model that used 3,212 matchboxes. T. B. Wu fashioned a ten-foot-high model out of plaster and powdered sugar. Models have been built at all scales from Lego blocks, carved out of cheese, chocolate, and butter, stitched into crochet samplers and embroidered onto jackets, made into abstract prints and decorative batik wall coverings. It has been mimicked in stacked champagne glasses in its own lobby, and there is at least one headstone carved in its likeness, marking the grave of a man who worked on its construction.

Only a few can claim that distinction, but anyone can build a likeness of the building. In the early 1980s, Perigee Books offered a plastic scale-model kit for those who craved construction as well as replication, and since 1991 the Milton-Bradley Company has enjoyed success with a three-foot, three-dimensional puzzle kit of the building consisting of 902 foam-backed pieces that fit together in a toddler-friendly homage to the original. The Thai company IDA-3D offers an exquisitely detailed laminated cardboard version of the puzzle, complete with wiring for interior lights, resulting in an excellent simulacrum about two and a half feet high—though I can say from experience that the instructions, in fifteen languages including "Vietnamesesese," are rather optimistic in suggesting this feat can be accomplished in "two to four hours depending on skill level."

The peculiar satisfaction of building these models is not really one of solving a puzzle; it is, rather, the age-old pleasure of fashioning, with one's own hands, a replica of something great—the very same atavistic drive to re-present, in miniature, that creates a wide spectrum of everything from the cave paintings at Lascaux to the precision scale aircraft models of youth, painstakingly constructed with glue, X-acto knife, and careful paint. The model's place in the human heart is permanent, and not restricted to the adolescent boy toiling alone in his makeshift workshop. How many architects, designers, and artists felt the first tug of longing to create while handling Lego blocks or cutting injection-molded polyurethane ailerons or fuselages away from a piece of sprue?

There is a wonderful scale model of the building in the lobby itself, of course, complete with lighting, that stands in a glass case next to the ground-floor information desk. Along the display cases to the right of it there stood, not long ago, the artist Robert Moskowitz's installation of multiple plywood-frame versions of the building, each covered with different materials: soft buildings and hard, spongy buildings and shiny ones. The New York Botanical Garden offered a train ride through grounds landscaped with waist-high topiary replicas of famous city landmarks, including St. Patrick's Cathedral and the Empire State, the stone and steel rendered in carefully pruned box, ivy, and rose. The artist Tony Lordi went a step further and constructed a series of six-foot-high images of the building, each entirely constructed of found objects, otherwise known as garbage: the transformation of detritus into representation, the discarded materials of the earth repurposed in the image of the Ur-building . . .

Michael Chabon's *Amazing Adventures of Kavalier and Clay* established a different sort of aesthetic relationship with the building. Chabon tells a sprawling story of midcentury immigrant New York by way of an escape artist from Prague, his tough Brooklynite cousin, and the hardscrabble living they make as purveyors of anti-Nazi comic books during the Second World War. The Empire State looms everywhere over their amazing adventures, from the graphic representation on the cover—an old postcard altered by the graphic designer James Wang to appear out-of-scale large, comic style—to the fictional world of their first title, the

Escapist, who lives in "Empire City, home of the needle-tipped Excelsior Building, tallest ever built." Like many a New Yorker, especially when set loose to wander in the angular nighttime shadows thrown near Madison Square by the Metropolitan Life Building, they felt the world split into inked-pulp frames and garish action, "walking along the trembling hem of reality that separated New York City from Empire City."

Fact and fiction collide throughout the novel. A bomb scare grips the Empire State Building in a scene that begins in the "souvenir-cluttered office on the thirty-second floor of the world's tallest building" belonging to Alfred E. Smith, president-for-life of the Empire State Building Corporation. It is October 25, 1940. The alleged bomb is in the offices of Empire Comics, on twenty-five, the new home of Kavalier and Clay and their employers, Empire Novelty Company, Inc., formerly of the Kramler Building on West Twenty-fifth Street near Madison Square. Smith and his real-life business associate James Haworth Love, building manager Chaplin L. Brown, and Captain M'Naughton of the building's in-house fire brigade all converge on the rooms of the young graphic novelists. The floor is being evacuated but one tenant, Joe Kavalier, won't leave because, he says, "he has too much work to do." Somehow, he has managed to snag the handcuffs belonging to one of the building's security captains and locked himself to his desk.

"The waiting room of Empire Comics was a cold expanse of marble and leather moderne, a black tundra frosted over with glass and chrome," Smith finds. "The effect was huge and intimidating and coldly splendid." Smith and Love do not persuade Kavalier to leave, but he convinces them the bomb threat is a hoax. The building is, in the book's words, "a kind of dream habitation," and so is the novel, where Salvador Dali, Orson Welles, Eleanor Roosevelt, and Max Ernst, among others, make cameo appearances, and the two young Jews fight off their bad memories by lining and inking their frames full of violent fantasy. The Empire State is both inside and outside to them, home and icon, site of a lightning-charged romantic summit during a summer thunderstorm, origin of signals carrying the radio broadcasts of the Escapist's amazing adventures, symbol of possibility in Empire City.

Or is it New York? Chabon beautifully captures the blending of apparition and actuality that visits supplicants to the layered richness of Manhattan, that palimpsest of dream narratives. "One of the sturdiest precepts of the study of human delusion is that every golden age is either past or in the offing," we read on page 340, just past the book's halfway point. "The months preceding the Japanese attack on Pearl Harbor offer a rare exception to this axiom. During 1941, in the wake of that outburst of gaudy hopefulness, the World's Fair, a sizable portion of the citizens of New York City had the odd experience of feeling for the time in which they were living, at the very moment they were living it, that strange blend of optimism and nostalgia which is the usual hallmark of the aetataureate delusion."

In a book published just twelve months before the 2001 attack on the World Trade Center, the sentiment acquires an eerie morbidity even amid the golden glow of its own optimistic-nostalgic delusion, the author's palpable, and winning, affection for his town. Here was another reminder of history's slaughter bench, another violent intimation of mortality for those momentarily distracted by the glowing neon and glittering chrome. Frenchmen and Britons—and Jews—were dying in Europe in 1941, but New York preserved, just as it did in 2000, a fantastic inwardness. We can hardly blame those who enjoyed the dream. In the middle of it stood—and stands—the tall lantern of limestone-clad ruggedness, beckoning, real and unreal, edifice and dream: the needle-topped Empire State, tallest in the city.

But just as history can be held off only for so long, the expanding paradoxes of image-making, the dividend of fantasy, must eventually be faced. So now we reach, only in the middle of our ambles around and into the building, the heart of the iconic matter: the logical quandaries of representation itself. Our own metaphysical ground zero.

All the multiple reproductions of the building, especially when keyed to size and greatness, which on the surface appear to constitute an extended exercise in type-token metaphysics and so affirm the superlative nature of the building, actually work to diminish, and then eliminate, the physical reality of the building. They and it are caught in a new, simulacral economy typical not only of the twentieth century's image-proliferating visual culture but also of the culture of tourism more generally. New York becomes suffused with visual memory, images and dreams entertained before. The Empire State is, in this sense, just one of a series of much-reproduced images that cycle through our collective experience, a thing whose materiality shimmers and goes out of focus with each added postcard or tchotchke.

Consider, for example, the variety of materials that put Edvard Munch's painting known as *The Scream* to commercial purposes—bastardized uses of the image in advertising, editorial cartoons, and urban design, not to mention various inflatable "Scream" figures, sound-effect pillows, and other assorted knick-knacks available for purchase at gallery shops the continent over. Here we see on view the all-too-familiar commercialization of our culture, which makes of everything, however serious and powerful, a possible image for coffee mugs and T-shirts. The more extensively replicated the image of anguish and dread becomes, especially as deflected from the "serious" context of contemplating a work of visual art, the more any significance in the image seems to leak away. So the first issue with Munch's *Scream,* as with any multiply reproduced image, is commodification, which we can think of as represented by the fairly familiar figure—you have probably seen them if you visited a gallery or novelty shop—of the inflatable doll in the shape of the original painting's main figure, the screamer himself (or herself?).

In his 1934 essay "The Work of Art in an Age of Mechanical Reproduction," Walter Benjamin went so far as to denounce what he called the fascism of aesthetic "aura." For Benjamin, writing at a time when reproduction looked more liberating than delimiting, the glorification of the individual, "authentic" artwork reduced it to a mute object before which we must stand in equally mute rapture, an experience which, far from liberating, made us no more than unwitting communicants in a ritual of observance that preserved the elitist structure of the gallery as a kind of secular cathedral of sophistication. (The muteness of this experience is particularly significant in the case of *The Scream,* since it is the very inarticulacy of the central figure, the frozen silence of his anguish, that opens up the painting's many associations in viewers—who nevertheless also remain silent.) Thus in Benjamin's view mechanical reproduction could have liberating, democratizing effects, if it broke this unnatural—and politically reactionary—connection between art and power.

Even attempts to deconstruct this cult of authenticity, such as Andy Warhol's celebrated multiple silk-screens and commodified objects—including images of *The Scream* itself—eventually surrender to it. That is, they cannot avoid becoming commodities themselves, tokens now of sophistication or hipness. As Benjamin's contemporaries Theodor Adorno and Max Horkheimer argued in countervalence, reproduction is most often politically nugatory, not liberating. Therefore the issue of the value of the copy in fact becomes more pressing, not less, as the means of reproduction become more sophisticated. The cult of authenticity takes on a more and more distant, atavistic aspect as we surrender to a world of near-flawless reproduction, falling under the influence of the assembly lines of the culture, which take our "authentic" selves, flatten them out, and sell them back to us as slick, often banal product. Thus does the supposed enlightenment of cultural experience become, in the words of Adorno and Horkheimer, no more than a "mass deception."

A complementary process entails that, at the same time as the aesthetic image is divorced from its original setting and made into a cheap commodity, the experience of viewing the work of art itself becomes all the more closed into the regimented, bourgeois, culturally safe context of the gallery experience or the tourist shuttle. The gallery shop and souvenir kiosk exist side by side with the ostensible object of our interest, the artwork or the view, features of the same process of commercialization. The irony here is structural: emasculation of the aesthetic experience's presumed power to move and inspire happens just to the extent that this two-pronged movement of commodification occurs—selling the image in knick-knacks even as we render the actual work little more than a piece of lifestyle wallpaper, a photo-op backdrop. We sell the sublime image in goofy forms such as fridge magnets or inflatables, and so we also sell comfort in the form of viewing what should, by rights, be provocative with the same deadened gaze we nightly direct toward the television screen.

Nor, of course, does the process of the culture industry stop there. Recombinant forces, such as those that fuse an iconic Che Guevara image with that of a gorilla or a *Star Wars* storm trooper to create a momentarily novel T-shirt, continue to exert themselves. We have not just *Scream* inflatables, then, but also Scream-based happy inflatables, the features of voiceless anguish replaced with the smiling yellow face of another ubiquitous bit of cultural flotsam. The body language of the torso is identical, including the wavy lines of Munch's brushwork, now in bright yellows and oranges rather than angst-ridden black and purple. The arms no longer clutch the face but now fling open in a friendly greeting or a dancing excess of joy. The archetypal vision of anguish is transformed into this jokey-banal vision of happiness. Or, as in a fast-fading example of recombination involving another much-reproduced work of art, the ordinary pretty face of fifteen-minute Monica Lewinsky is Photoshopped onto Leonardo's *Mona Lisa*—already a work more luminous in photos than in its bulletproof-glass encased, crowded-room reality at the Louvre—and rendered into a second-order but immediately parseable cultural sign: the presidential temptress as inscrutable maiden, keeping her counsel with a toothier smile and blander features. (Lewinsky's silence did not last very long, dissipating the aura in a cloud of banality, a problem paintings do not have.)

These may be an example of what the novelist David Foster Wallace called "reverent irony" in popular culture, though it is hard to tell for certain what is irony here, what reverence, and whether there is any combination of the two. What *is* clear is that we are now at least three conceptual steps away from Munch's original painting. This is not just a reproduction; nor is it even simply a commonplace or absurd reproduction; it is, in addition to those deflections from the authentic object, a debased quasi-reproduction. The smiley-face inflatable is thus a good example of *simulacral cultural experience*. A genuine image of anxiety, the one found in Munch's original paintings, is almost entirely drained of its power, first through reproduction and then through irony. Like the Most Photographed Barn in America, the painting disappears within the economy of its own success. The inflatables are not to be used as flotation devices, their warnings say; yet they bob along behind us wherever we go, buoying up the commercial imperatives and ironic distance of our cultural industry. The two toys, the anguished Munch screamer and his smiley-faced cousin, stand side by side in a little cultural diorama, the outstretched arms and big smile of the yellow one lurching toward, trying to enfold, the twisted and screaming original—who looks back in well-justified dread.

Such layerings are now so common on our city streets that it is almost not worth untangling them, since part of their appeal is the sense of depth offered by the images, images of images, and distortions of images of images. The Empire State Building, though not an artwork—not, that is, created first and foremost to be viewed with rapt attention—nevertheless has acquired such a status. The celebrated Lewis Hine photographs of its construction are a telling example, themselves now treasured iconic scenes of icon erection. The handsome, cheerful faces of those long-ago rivet catchers and line runners, rendered in mythopoeic black and white, activate a force field of urban nostalgia. They glow with mechanical pride and can-do resolve, generating a pre-facto affinity with the grim jauntiness of B-17 bomber crews and at-rest platoons on the way to combat. The brave toppers and beam lifters offer a de facto Jazz Age rainbow coalition of Italian craftsmen, Russian artisans, Mohawk bloods, and Irish hooligans. The images are immediately mythic, converting the building to iconic status even as it is being built, indeed as a function of its being built. Hine even captioned one vertiginous work "Icarus," an allusion its subject, a fearless laborer high above the earth, may not have appreciated; but Hine knew, as we do, that "Daedalus" would lack poetry. Like Margaret Bourke-White's equally treasured studies of the Chrysler Building, with its poised-hawk cornices and gleaming metal skin—her own presence there making her a kind of Leda, a prostrate feminine presence—Hine's photographs radiate a light greater than their gelatin silver materiality. Exhibiting the process of construction, they demonstrate a human-metal theorem of success, the booted, overalled agents of movement smoothly assimilated into the total system of assembly.

Always, the building is there only by implication, not yet finished, its hatching of I-beams and spider's web of wiring growing, as if organically, around the human figures scaling the quickly growing height. In these photographs we never see the building—neither do they—but it is there, always there, in its implied teleology, the logic of building working itself toward completion, the summit, the top. One of Hine's images is so iconic, indeed, that it has generated its own spin-off economy. Down in SoHo, where books and bags, T-shirts and timepieces, are for sale on every street corner, you can buy any size of Hine's image of a half dozen steelworkers blithely lunching on a cable-suspended beam, the distant city skyline framing them in the thin air. So much is obvious. You can also purchase papier-mâché renderings of the beam and the workers, or ceramic miniatures of the same scene of careless bravery: various hand-made images of images, art of a sort in the former stronghold of the New York art world, little kitschy connections to the celebrated celebrations of those who built the unbuilt building. The building's presence, over your shoulder in the uptown distance, renders this time-frozen scene of mundane courage sensible, a visual gesture in an overall dance of celebration. Then, perhaps inevitably, a further declension: the image is amiably appropriated in the "couch-opening" sequence of an episode of *The Simpsons,* with Homer and family astride the lowering beam, rendered in authentic black and white tones, and munching their meal now in front of the television. Homer lifts the remote and changes the channel . . . (There is yet another image from the series involving the Empire State: a shot of the family atop the building as if they had just scaled the exterior in the approved Kong manner.)

"As a commercial building, it has never stood out and has never made sense," a broker with Helmsley-Spear, the building's manager, told me, sitting at a desk on its twenty-ninth floor surrounded by images of the exterior we could not see. "It's more about being gorgeous to look at." In this way, the building takes its place centrally not as an edifice but as a node within a system of imagistic exchange, and is thus subject to the very same kinds of layered reproduction, distortion, and irony. Consider Madelon Vriesendorp's surrealist images of the building, for example, which render the straight and tall structure curvy and seductive and now lying in bed in a high apartment with another skyline outside. Or the recently fashionable T-shirt that features a highly stylized outline of the building along with the words "EMPIRE STATE BLDG" and "New York City" running above a borderline-nonsensical imperative appar-ently lifted from a Japanese fashion spread: "Your destiny is coming, are you ready?" Like the *Scream* inflatables or the Che Guevara T-shirts, these are doubled or tripled appropriations of an iconic original; they are possible only when all other, more conventional avenues of reproduction have reached a point of surfeit. Or, since this is about New York, we should perhaps say suffered a gridlock. The third-order appropriation is a function of mass-cultural market flood: when every possible picture or doodad is already available, we must find new and more attenuated imagistic maneuvers to capture the building.

Which, to be sure, simply stands there the whole time, a fact worth remembering. It was surely for this reason that Andy Warhol, responding to the twinned proliferation and invisibility of the image-laden building, shot his 1964 film *Empire* as a resolutely banal expanse of duration in which nothing happens. For eight hours, the sixteen-millimeter film offers a single telephoto shot of the building taken by Warhol and his associate Jonas Mekas from the office of the Rockefeller Foundation in the Time-Life Building. They actually shot the film at the standard movie speed of twenty-four frames per second, then slowed down its projection to sixteen—a deliberate distortion of time that makes the film not a simple capturing of the image but a sort of temporal abstraction of itself.

Empire, like Warhol's appropriation of pop-culture images more generally, is intended as an exercise in unstable recovery; or we might better say, as a lesson in the impossibility of recovery. One watches the film not to see the building at all but rather, as Warhol himself said, to watch time go by. (During the filming he was apparently more forthright, summing up the project as "an eight-hour hard-on.") The resulting artifact, now viewable only by borrowing a print from the Museum of Modern Art in New York or attending one of its rare screenings, has moments of both intentional and accidental drama. At about the six-and-a-half-hour mark, the floodlights illuminating the building are dimmed, and for the remaining ninety minutes of the film its ostensible subject is invisible. And where there is invisibility there is also visibility. On three occasions Warhol and Mekas, after changing film reels, forgot to switch the lights back off before they resumed filming. As a result there are three brief images of them, reflected in the window of the office, looking out toward the building.

Not everyone is willing to sit through the whole eight hours for these instants of drama, however. In 2004 a one-hour edit was released as part of a new Warhol-film DVD set, Four Silent Movies, produced by the Italian company Raro Video. A spokesperson from the Warhol Museum in Pittsburgh immediately denounced it as a bootleg, and we can perhaps sympathize with a kind of passion that goes beyond a mere copyright dispute: at anything less than its full length, *Empire* is not *Empire*. "It's conceptually important that it's eight hours long," Callie Angell, director of the Whitney Museum's Warhol Film Project, told the Web site of *New York* magazine. "Some people show it at the regular sound speed to make it go by faster, and I just think that's not the film." As one commentator said, this is the kind of thinking that "guaranteed from [1964] on that every film student would suffer at least one solid day of monotony."

The same writer wondered whether the notorious 1968 attempt on Warhol's life by Valerie Solanas, founder of the Society for Cutting up Men (SCUM), might have been driven to it by *Empire*. The male artist, according to the *SCUM Manifesto* of 1967, has "nothing to say" and so "resorts to symbolism and obscurity," conning the gullible "into believing that obscurity, evasiveness, incomprehensibility, indirectness, ambiguity and boredom are marks of depth and brilliance." Solanas cornered Warhol in his East Side studio and fired three gunshots at him, hitting him once in the abdomen. She also shot another man in the thigh. Warhol recovered but refused to testify at her trial, and she was sentenced to three years.

Empire is certainly boring, and while it may not be brilliant, it is surely challenging, as genuine boredom may often be—or so, at the risk of being one of those men with nothing to say, I believe. Boredom, says the psychoanalyst Adam Phillips, is "that state of suspended anticipation in which things are started and nothing begins, the mood of diffuse restlessness which contains that most absurd and paradoxical wish, the wish for a desire." As Arthur Schopenhauer knew before him, boredom "paints on the human countenance a real sign of despair," one pole in a constant exhausting swing from anxiety to enervation. *Empire*'s rich and unavoidable experience of boredom, its devilish bargain with time, offers a comment on the assumed economies of wanting; it is doubly unstable, and doubly revealing. Unstable, first, in the mechanical-reproduction sense already mentioned: the works of art created become new commodities in an art world forever flexible enough to extend its boundaries in the service of profit. But unstable also in that, in the apparent act of getting the building back by prolonged, intentionally boring exposure—*It's just a building,* the film seems to say, *just something standing there!*—Warhol succeeds not in rescuing the building from its iconic entrapment but in transforming the gaze and making the Empire State once more invisible, both literally and figuratively.

Any materialist impulse, the film seems to suggest—any desire to enfold or possess, or even just to acknowledge the alleged firmness of the physical—is foiled by its very own attempts at reification, and by the inevitable passage of time itself. The film forces us, among other things, to recall Peter Conrad's characterization of architecture as "time made manifest as space"—a living memorial to its moment, but also a species of force, making us deal with its prolonged presence as we try to move around it at whatever speed we possess. In the film's punishing long shots and actual-duration time lapses, the building becomes more spectral, not less. Held in the gaze so relentlessly and so long, its solid mass seems to sway and dissolve before our eyes, to go limp and, finally, disappear.

Nor does it really offer any direct experience of time as such—a logical impossibility in any event, as Thomas Mann exhibits so deftly in *The Magic Mountain.* Hans Castorp's three-week sojourn at the Sanatorium Berghof stretches imperceptibly into seven years measured not by clocks and calendars but by temperature checks and dwindling cigar supplies. We all know perfectly well what time is but, as Augustine said, find ourselves confounded when we try to say what it is. Its assumed linearity, its measured "flow"—these are quietly desperate metaphors, coping fictions that ward off temporal confusion with a meretricious precision. (The digital clock is a vivid example of Heidegger's point about the allure of technology, its carnival of mastery.) Time is inseparable from consciousness, what Mann called "a hope-filled and hopeless striving of life to comprehend itself, as if nature were rummaging to find itself in itself—ultimately to no avail, since nature cannot be reduced to comprehension, nor in the end can life listen to itself."

Human awareness may be the world becoming conscious of itself, but that awareness is limited by the very same fact of its temporal existence: consciousness is life turned against its own conditions, struggling vainly to comprehend them. We cannot understand our understanding, and if our minds were simple enough to understand, we would be too simple to understand them. Julian Jaynes compares consciousness to a flashlight: we are never in a position to illuminate the source of our own light. And so we construct narratives, or plots, to structure and order, however falsely, our mortal span: sketches of sense. As Murray tells Jack Gladney in *White Noise,* "Your whole life is a plot, a scheme, a diagram. It is a failed scheme but that's not the point." All schemes, all diagrams, fail because all plots lead deathward. And altering the medium does not alter the message. Film, especially an anti-narrative like Warhol's film, may appear to be a technology where space is negated and time turned back on itself, where time comes clear; but in truth film, even this film, is a dead object unless, as Mann says, it is "given back to the element of time as a series of blinking flashes." A film is really just multiple still-lifes in series until we add light and duration; it doesn't contain time, at best gestures toward it.

Some analysts claim to see *Empire,* with its scriptless duration and mundane subject, as a precursor to reality television. It is, in fact, much more. After eight hours of exposed erectness, it achieves not joyful release but rather a deflation, a sort of sad, impotent, post-metaphysical collapse.

By this stage, we may be growing impatient with talk about simulacra and specters and want to assert some straightforward claims about truth: the truth of the building, and even the truth of the simple image. We want to say: the representation we have before us, postcard or poster or plastic model, is an image of the building. As such, it may be true or false, accurate or inaccurate, scalar or otherwise. Let us decide.

I have numerous plastic, metal, glass, and ceramic models of the building grouped around me as I write this, including a gold-colored one in a murky Chinese-made snow globe, and a metal fragment measuring just three-quarters of an inch from base to spire, billed, in an inevitable inversion of superlatives, as "the world's smallest Empire State Building." These tchotchkes, for sale everywhere at the base of the building, in every imaginable size and material, are perhaps the most obvious violation of the copyright protection that Helmsley-Spear has vainly tried to enforce since 1999—an impossible task given that, as one employee noted, these models proliferate in Far East workshops faster than running shoes. Even the rule on images, which stipulates that any image depicting the building as more than 10 percent of the displayed New York skyline is a violation of trademark, is prima facie absurd. How can such a thing be calculated? And how policed? "The building belongs to everybody," the same employee said, making the obvious point. "You see it and you know it's New York City."

That is exactly what you know—or so we usually think, and let the matter rest. But there are other issues of knowledge raised by these models and images. Some of them, we notice immediately, seem more faithful than others to the contours of the actual building. This seems at first like a trivial issue, if we can even call it an issue. We look at a cluster of such models and think it will be no large chore to decide which of them is the most accurate. (Perhaps some of the variation is intentional, motivated by a desire to evade the trademark?) The security guard and I may enact a certain easy performance of metaphysical agreement when faced with an image of a model of the building—"Of course it's the building"—and lucky for me he thought so, too. But in fact there is a layered series of difficulties here, and deciding between tokens, which are so much part of our taken-for-granted relationship with the physical world, is actually far harder than it appears.

First, there lurk various familiar and oddly pleasant feelings of disorientation generated by scale representation itself. I mean those light-headed, semi-nauseous thoughts occasioned by looking at a model of the building inside the building. I look, and then I imagine myself there, looking at a model of the building, in which there is another, smaller version of myself sitting, lost in contemplation of *his* model of the building—and so on. Something about this easily purchased out-of-body experience is peculiarly satisfying, a sort of freebie *Twilight Zone* episode, whereby I might imagine picking up the model and feeling the building itself shudder and break free of its foundations. The desks and papers and computers now shift sickeningly across the tilted floors as the giant fingers grasp the central column and lift . . .

For some reason, such urban destruction fantasies are hard to quell when we are confronted by the collapsing scale of the model-within-the-model. On the fourth floor of the Shanghai Urban Planning Exhibition Center, for example, there is a vast and elaborate scale model of the planned new city that the Chinese government is acting quickly to realize in that sprawling river port of 20 million souls. You circumnavigate the model on a metal track, looking down and across floor-size stretches of white plaster and polystyrene mirroring the city outside. Little signs on the steel viewing platforms say "Don't Jump!" It may just be a perverse response to that absurd injunction, but I believe it is impossible not to, first, locate your own site on the 1:500 model, with its 6,500 square feet of miniature utopian ambition, and then second, to see yourself stomping through the little streets, crushing apartment blocks and office towers, maybe with deathbeams shooting out of your eyes.

Nor can we, typically, stop there. I recall from my youth a popular brand of Christmas candy whose painted tin container carried an image of the very tin it was, with the candy spilled out onto a table. The represented tin was likewise decorated with a picture of the tin, candy spilled out; and the tin on *its* side was, naturally, an identically painted tin, with candy spilled; and on and on, into a disappearing infinity of Zeno-style minute reductions in the size of the identical image, like Russian matrioshka dolls marching away to oblivion, the abyss of miniaturization and inner inscription: the mythic *mise en abyme,* in fact, that confounds any simple logic of representation, in Plato's homunculus regress in the *Theaetetus* as much as Jacques Derrida's deconstruction of that very Platonic urge to master images and reflections within a hierarchy of Forms. The tin arranged these downward shrinking meta-representations in such a way that they appeared to inscribe a spiral, what I would nowadays be able to notice was actually a Fibonacci-series nautilus curve, arranged, as in the classic proportions of landscape painting, according to the Golden Section. What I did in those days was, of course, try to spill my actual tin of candy such that the scene before me started in the so-called real world and corkscrewed inevitably into the so-called represented one with a hiccup at the boundary—if it really is a boundary!—between actual tin and represented one. I spent happy minutes enjoying the cheap thrill of riding the waves that ran in and out of this weird diorama of epistemological paradox.

Because I have more than one model here, however, our thoughts do not rest there, spooling and unspooling the nested images. Comparison is inevitable, and I see, for example, that an eight-inch-high plastic model of the building is elongated and flat when set next to a cast-metal representation half its size. Both give the impression of a different building altogether from the heavy twenty-inch model, complete with clambering King Kong figurine, standing next to them. And the small crystal image, at once cheesy and expensive, shimmers and glistens next to these in a silhouette more reminiscent of the slim Chrysler Building than the chunky Empire State we think we know. An older resin model, scavenged from a junk shop hundreds of miles from here, is the only one that seems to set up a scalar resonance with the largest model, the two of them playing the expected concerto of theme and repetition that we expect from representations.

A perhaps notable irony is that these two are the only ones in this semi-random grouping that were made in the United States. The others are products of those very Asian economies that are fast creating the skyscrapers of the future—some of them, indeed, the very buildings we might imagine toppling or hurling during the cathartic devastation of the Shanghai model. But this variance is more than a mere discrepancy of workmanship; it indicates the outlines of an economy of representation in which no image is really more accurate than another, where the idea of accuracy—indeed, you might even say the idea of representation—is comprehensively undermined.

Consider, for example, the small practical issue of how we would decide which of these models is "best." Suppose we are being challenged by a passing co-worker, a tenant of the building, who observes the cluster of buildings-within-the-building that stand here on the desk. How would we decide? The first thing we realize is that, thus situated, we have a fairly major cognitive deficit. Inside the building, the building is not available to us! That is, we cannot do what anyone outside the building might: hold up a given model in front of the building for a crude but effective dead-eye reckoning. Here on the twenty-ninth floor, where we might be considered closest to the building, we are, in this representational-model sense, farther away from it than almost anyone else in Manhattan. What to do?

Well, we might think that we should pursue what the eye does naturally: that is, compare the various models for clues internal to their relations. We lack any opportunity for what might be called transcendent evaluation—comparing the appearance to the reality—but perhaps we retain the chance of a kind of modular immanent critique, evaluation from the inside. If we try this—as indeed we must, given no other option—we notice two things almost immediately: first, the differences among the models, the fact that they are not all the same; and second, the apparent congruency of the largest model with one of the others. The tallest model is very like the chipped and battered but still recognizable old one. This, the only near-match of representations in our sample, stands out to the mind: in seeking truth, we are apparently sensitive, among other things, to similarity; it constitutes pattern, a hint of signal in the noise of difference. If *all* the models were different one from another, there would be no pattern to recognize and our task might well seem impossible. If there were another match, or even two more, we would be back at our starting point, since any two together is equal to all being different. Even with a much larger sample, the incidence of matches would not be definitive.

Nevertheless, here, with a small sample and just one match, it is at least suggestive. Why would there be any match at all unless there were some tracking of the truth going on? We might argue, for added inferential weight to the match indicating accuracy, that the smaller, near-matching model is also the oldest. With the added premise, not easy to prove but often thought valid, that craftsmanship even of silly tourist doodads was superior in the past, we could claim extra weight to the argument. And, at the risk of indulging national chauvinism, we could instance the common made-in-America fact of the two matching models, thereby lending still more credence to any claim of accuracy. These craftsmanship premises (oldest, most American) are not logically sound in themselves, not least because often counter-demonstrated, but they do carry some influence in general. We conclude that these two models, then—matching, American, and embracing both largest and oldest—must be the most accurate. The others, with their slim lines and disproportionate setbacks, fall away.

Even here, however, familiar problems remain. There are, for example, significant discrepancies between the two models. There are more floors depicted on the larger than on the smaller. Some quick work with a ruler shows that, though they look quite similar, in fact the larger one is slightly out of proportion with the smaller—not as much as both are out of whack with the others, and they with each other, but enough to see when one moves just a little beyond the naked-eye matching of before. The setbacks on the smaller model are more pronounced, the base on the larger squatter and more conspicuous. The link between the two, once a source of happiness, begins to dissolve. The closer we look, the more it begins to appear as if we are, in fact, in a state of representational disarray where all models are different one from the other.

Now, at this point we may have a number of conflicting feelings and desires. We might simply give up and decide that the issue of accuracy in models is irrelevant. Or we might decide that accuracy is still important in general but in this instance there is little to be gained by deciding among the candidates. We might decide that it's time to go get a cup of coffee or a drink. But suppose that this last option is debarred to us, since it also involves the possibility of carting the models down to street level and, a modest cab ride later, reaching a position from which an eyeball assessment of the models could be made. Suppose we are being held hostage, for example, and must decide the superiority of one model before we will be set free. Or, if that is too creepy, suppose we are just perverse and want to settle the issue before we have that coffee or that drink.

At such a stage we are in an unstable but not impossible position. The similarity of the two models is not perfect but it is not entirely notional, either—we did see something that suggested they were linked. Now what do we do? Well, typically, we invoke, first, a form of mental reconstruction: I have seen the building many times, not least just a little while ago as I approached it northbound on Fifth Avenue. Which of the models, we ask ourselves, *looks most like my memory?* It may seem an odd question, and indeed it is, rather, since memory does not "look like" anything; still, we have some sense of what we might call mental representations, pictures or images in the mind, and we try to compare these, whatever they may be, to the models before us.

The results are not terribly helpful. Whatever the importance we attach to these mental representations, we soon find that they are unreliable indicators of accuracy. We possess (if that is the right word!) various images and glimpses of, in this case, the building: I see a shot of the summit, apparently taken from a helicopter; I remember the sight of soaring planes of limestone when I paused very briefly to look up while crossing Thirty-third Street at lunchtime; I recall the last time I walked over the Brooklyn Bridge at night, after eating pizza in Park Slope, and noticed that the building's signature lights were not red, white, and blue, though I can't now remember what they were; I visualize the opening sequence of a popular television show, now in reruns, that uses a titled time-lapse image of the building against a cerulean sky; and so on . . . I may *think* I have a complete and coherent idea of the building in my mind, in other words, like a bird trapped in some epistemic aviary, or, varying the image, like a photograph filed away in a metal cabinet; but close examination shows that what I have, if I have anything, is a layered and sometimes confused gathering of partial exposures, half images, cropped aspects, sentimental associations, and other jetsam of consciousness, experience, and memory. Even to call them a gathering is to suggest that they were waiting somewhere, roughly ordered, waiting for someone—that is, me—to come along and flip through them. Instead, they were scattered here and there, random and disordered, sometimes only forcibly or painfully recalled, and surely, we must believe, at least a little bit unreliable. In fact, even saying they were *scattered* suggests a spatiality that memories do not possess. They could not enjoy even the lowly state of disorder because they cannot show either order or disorder; all of these are metaphors, images of spatial occupancy.

Sitting here, in the office on the twenty-ninth floor, we are all at sea. The various memories we have of the building do not, in themselves, add up to a coherent image of the entire edifice, still less do they equate with the real item and so give us a reliable basis for comparisons of the type before us, that is, among rival representations in the form of tourist models. The idea of the building we have, as it were, in mind is no more than another representation and, indeed, might be considered no less than an imperfect and fractured one at that.

We might think, at this point, to turn not to exploration of interior consciousness but to exploration of the physical interior. We ought to look inside the building itself. Surely there must be an image of the building somewhere handy that will settle the matter? And, to be sure, there are many such everywhere around—we don't even have to leave this floor—since, as I mentioned before, the inhabitants of the building appear to enjoy keeping nearby some rendering of the glorious structure they inhabit but, in doing so, cannot see. But these two-dimensional images offer no gain on their three-dimensional counterparts; indeed, they may induce a further declension of the central problem, since we cannot fail to notice that any two-dimensional representation of a three-dimensional object is even more abstract and notional than a tiny scale model.

We may invest such images with a great deal of significance, so focused are we in this office setting on the play of two-dimensional surfaces, the papers and pictures that together represent a reality we are attempting to influence; but deep down we know, don't we, that they only exist as part of a general mimetic suspension of disbelief that allows pictures to function at all. Any picture of the building involves a bargain with the possibility of representation, and that is just what we have been forced to question. We cannot use further representations of the same thing to demonstrate that one or another of those representations is better or more accurate than another, since in such a move we both assume and dispute the same premise at once. That is, we are assuming that there is a congruency among all possible representations (that they are "of the same thing") in order to deny the congruency of some actual representations (that some are "better" than others). The attempt to demonstrate accuracy via representation begs the question: in making it, we have assumed the very thing we need to prove. It would be, as Wittgenstein said, as if we attempted to prove the accuracy of a newspaper headline by dashing out and buying further copies of the same issue to add weight to its claim of fact.

But suppose we managed to discover, in our now frenzied rummaging through the office, a set of blueprints. We may think that now we will have an answer, but the thought is premature and destined to fail, for all the reasons that went before. The notion of a *definitive* two-dimensional representation is itself an assumption, or presupposition, in the larger assumed economy of representation. This two-dimensional document is marked by, we might say, a representational asterisk: it comes to us set off, by color and function, as authoritative. It is, we might say, the baseline representation, as close to the thing itself as any two-dimensional thing could be. It was, after all, the basis from which the building itself was constructed. But that claim to authority does not allow the blueprint to escape the tangles of representation, only to take a certain place within them. Indeed, the blueprint functions, precisely, to close the loops for good because it glues the connection of all two-dimensional representations to all three-dimensional ones by being the point of contact, or rather the threshold, between them.

In this sense, the blueprint is not a representation of the building at all; the *building* is a representation of the *blueprint*—which we now see is actually, as it were, a *pre*-presentation. If the blueprint re-presents anything, it represents those earlier pre-presentations, the initial diagrams and even the rough sketches that preceded them. These earlier images, we might want to say, in turn represent the even more *a priori* "idea" of the building, its notional existence. And yet, this language of *a priori* building-ideas is rather too transcendental, since the building is not, at least not to me sitting here right now, platonically more real as an idea than as something to enter or work in. We think: the building's actual coming-to-be is necessary for there to be a building at all. And that coming-to-be makes the building what it is, constrained and ordered by materials, physics, money, and labor, so that it may be realized in a form quite different from early ideas or even diagrams. There is no complete building lurking in anyone's mind, even the mind of god, before the building goes up, any more than there exists a fully formed, pre-linguistic *idea* of what I want to say before I construct a mental sentence.

Perhaps the sketched blueprint represents, in its own peculiar language of abstraction, the *intention* of the architects to realize the building? That is, maybe the blueprint functions as a conduit between their imaginations, themselves first represented by sketches and preliminary drawings, and the materials-based language of the contractors who erect the actual steel, stone, and glass? In that way, the blueprint would be a sort of underwriting in two dimensions of the discursive space, and collective practice, of architecture—architecture now understood as distinct from mere building, a world of *intentional* construction, not mere problem solving concerning shelter or the logic of handy materials. This is a refinement of the "pure idea" account that does not carry the same metaphysical cost. The importance of both architect's sketches and the blueprints that take them closer to possible actualization: they are pictures of the active imagination at work.

Is this language of "representing the imagination" really coherent, though? This account, too, assumes a preexisting picture in the mind, now of the architect, which is simply transcribed onto paper. In fact, the process of drawing, like the process of speaking or sculpting—or, indeed, of building itself—is one of constant recursion and occasional surprise. We go back over our work and erase or alter, to make things come clear; or we follow a lead we had not planned, to see how a line unspools or a space gets blocked out. In architecture, furthermore, such sketching is itself often a collaborative process whereby various people, perhaps a whole team, process ideas and sketches even before the thought of blueprints is raised. (This was certainly the case with the present building.) Whose imagination is being represented when a sketch is taken forward to the next stage of building, to become a blueprint? Whose intentions are reproduced thereby?

It is overhasty even to speak of architectural intention at all, I think, for two related reasons that take us, finally, beyond any notion of correspondence truth or representational accuracy. First, in contrast to the premodern age, where architecture might proceed without diagram, almost as a collective performance from common ideas—the great medieval cathedrals are the highest achievement of this type, created over generations by associated craftspeople and believers—the practice of architecture today offers many opportunities to design and draw buildings that will never get built. The highest aspiration of a young architect may be, in fact, to get a drawing published: as in conceptual art, *this* is now the sign of creative intervention, and any physical realization of the drawing is unnecessary, an afterthought; or even undesirable, a materialist declension into rude time and space. The practice is to extend the imagination entirely in the form of two-dimensional representations—or three-dimensional ones if a model is also built. *Representation* is likewise exactly the wrong word to use here, since there is nothing preexistent to these documents that is being presented again. They antedate, and so obviate, then obliterate, any possible building.

Second, even if we find such conceptualism unconvincing—*we want buildings, damn it!*—the deepest truth of all buildings is that none of them stand (or can stand) alone. In style, materials, techniques, and aspirations, they are expressions of all past buildings, a distilled response not merely to the immediate surround but to the collective history of building itself. And not just the past; also the future: any building, like any text or sentence, finds its meaning only in the shared field of expression stretching across time. Like a poem, a great building uses existing, even familiar tools to say something that has not yet been said, and so makes sayable in future things that have not yet found their sayers. A building is intertextual, a gesture in a game whose moves are slower and more lasting than speech but no less connected.

We can go even further. It is for reasons like this that radical architectural theorists such as Peter Eisenman argue for *postfunctionalism* or *antihumanism* in architecture. They suggest that, so far from being products of human intention, buildings are self-organizing systems that use human agency as part of their projects of self-realization. We think we are building buildings, but really *they* are building *us!* The cherished basic notions of classical architecture, the Palladian norms and proportions of Vitruvius, are rejected as anthropomorphic hubris. Scale becomes its own argument, rather than a reflection of, or accommodation to, the size of human bodies. Protagoras, Socrates tells us in Plato's *Theaetetus,* is supposed to have said, "Man is the measure of all things." Not so. Eisenman's postfunctionalism says *measure* is the measure of all things, itself first of all. Man is just along for the ride, trying to capture scale with units or numbers but in fact merely serving it as a drone attends his queen.

A prescient satire of this position can be found in Evelyn Waugh's 1928 novel *Decline and Fall,* where Professor Otto Friedrich Silenus, a heavily caricatured Corbusier clone, is hired to renovate an English country house. "The problem of architecture as I see it," he tells a reporter of his ferroconcrete and aluminum project, with its lifts and glass brick, "is the problem of all art—the elimination of the human element from the consideration of form. The only perfect building must be the factory, because that is built to house machines, not men." Later he ponders: "I suppose there must be a staircase. . . . Why can't the creatures stay in one place?" The line is echoed, maybe intentionally, by Eisenman, who, when told that staircases in one of his buildings were causing regular injuries, reportedly said, "Good. They will never take stairs for granted again."

There is indeed a sharp challenge to the taken-for-granted here. As with meme theory (whereby culture is understood as the transfer of isolable bits between human hosts, on the model of genetic heritance) or Heidegger's theory on language (language, he says, speaks us, not the other way around), postfunctionalism emphasizes the uncomfortable truth that the field of architecture is bigger than any individual user or even designer. We think we are in control of our actions, or our designs, but in fact we are mostly at their mercy. They have a logic, summed from all previous and future building, that renders us insignificant. We must submit to it and serve it. This is especially so in a building like the Empire State, with its close relation to materials and their preinscription in the total system of deployed commodities. If it expresses anything, it expresses the extended algorithm of its own construction.

The diagram is not so much a picture of a human idea as it is a sort of order issued by a future building. It is a pre-gestural gambit in the building's own coming-to-be. Eisenman suggests we abandon the noun "architect" in favor of a verb—"to architect"—to unsettle the assumed stable identity of the designer. But even that carries too strong a whiff of control, I think, as I sit here, the models gathered around me. Inside the building, struggling with the logic of representation, we cannot help but feel the pressure of the building's own logic, its mechanical movements, its overmastering solidity, its implacable will.

The search for the accurate representation takes us, finally, into the iconic heart of the matter. We approached the building via models and pictures of it, only to find that models and pictures of it exist, as it were, on the other side of the building. Both *a priori* and *a posteriori* images are linked in the same system of exchange, in this case by the building in which I still sit, so that they swirl around it in a flurry of proliferating two- and three-dimensional production-consumption cycles.

We think that the building itself, whatever that means, will settle any disputes arising from those images. But this is an error, because it drives us down a careering road where the only possible outcome is some sort of transcendental crash. Soon we reach the rather startling point that only a full-scale model of the building would be adequate to the task of representation, as in the Jorge Luis Borges tale of the county ordnance map so detailed it covered the entire county. Perhaps such thinking is what led the World Trade Center architects to their decision?

This fantastic urge is already present in the Empire State at the moment of its conception, of course. Richmond Shreve, the architect, had said that construction of the building was "like an assembly line placing the same materials in the same relationship over and over." He meant over and over on each floor, at each stage of the construction; but so perfect is the mechanical automatism of the building's design that, in theory, *the entire thing* could be built over and over. There would be no extra cost except in labor and materials. The Empire State was not only built using assembly-line principles, it was itself the product of an assembly line that, in the event, produced just one product. Construction is here reduced, or rationalized, to the point of simple assembly. The building is unique, yes, but only as a mere matter of fact: there could easily be other tokens of the exquisitely precise design erected elsewhere. These would not be models or copies, just late-model examples of the same. We cherish the building's uniqueness in part because, as we think more deeply, we realize how contingent it is! There could be any number of Empire State Buildings—how wonderful that there is only this one!

Of course any such desire for duplication is absurd, and misses the point. A second full-scale building, fancifully called a "model," would no more make the first "building" definitive than a six-inch-high model does. Neither edifice can escape the logic of their shared subjection to cycles of image-making. Like a Borgesian library of self-collapsing taxonomy, the entire set of feedback loops of the Empire State Building is just part of its relation to all other buildings, both those literally around its space and those surrounding it in time, themselves including both the precursors of the past, which are set into a different position and meaning by its greatness, and those that will come after it, unable to ignore that achievement.

We make a mistake when we assume, as we so often do, that the key to settling issues within a system of image productions is to get altogether outside, or above, it. This cannot be done; there is no such outside. Moreover, even if it could be done, the results would not reassure us. After all, an economy of proliferating preexisting buildings existing purely, and more accurately, in the minds of architects invites, as we have seen, a metaphysical burden most of us would be unlikely to shoulder. True, architects often feel disappointed with the concrete results of their work. But we can hardly instance that in discussions of accuracy without a collapse. For, by that token, all buildings, and hence all images of all buildings, would be rendered inaccurate. And that would not be very useful!

The point of this extended exercise in epistemology is not, as people often suppose, to deny the reality of the building. Such a thing could hardly be done when the building is, after all, right here; certainly it would be a good day for philosophical reflection if it were ever that powerful. No sane person denies the existence of the Empire State Building. On the contrary, its irrefutable existence is often considered proverbial: it is as unmissable as the nose on your face. That is one reason I write from a position of actually sitting in the building, touching the nose on my face you might say, so that the personal stakes could not be higher for me. Nor is it to undermine the workaday attempts to decide such things as whether one model is more useful than another, which surely proceed more or less successfully without any particular aid from philosophical reflection.

It is, rather, to pursue another and more important goal of such reflection. I mean shifting our desires away from the transcendental-representational model of truth that still holds us in thrall, and toward the sort of use-conscious sense of truth (I won't say "model," since that would merely recapitulate the problem) that reveals deeper connections of mind to world. The truth of the Empire State Building is not its material existence considered *apart from,* or *against,* its various representations. Nor is it, as some might be inclined to say, the sum total of its representations. The truth of the building lies in its entire universe of use and meaning: the webs of relation and work that spin through its webs of plumbing and wiring; the shunting workers and tourists who find themselves here today, or tomorrow, and carry away memories and postcards; the entire palimpsest of history, of events and moments over seventy-five years, which together embed the site, rising in layers with each passing year to a soaring height of lived reality equal to the physical span.

The truth of the building is me sitting here right now, thinking these thoughts, my models before me, experiencing the building as a place and not just a space—not just an orientation in three dimensions, in other words, but an orientation to how I walked here this morning, and who is nearby and what they said as I came in, and how I will leave, too soon, always too soon, and walk up Fifth Avenue to another Shreve, Lamb & Harmon creation, the brick-clad little brother at 500 Fifth, with its similar setbacks and funny family-resemblance familiarity, where I will stop in at the ground floor and buy some cigars at Nat Sherman, a shop that has been here since the year before the Empire State opened its doors, and then walk along Forty-second Street to Grand Central Terminal, where I will order a manhattan—because, today, what else?—and drink it looking over the Grand Concourse and think of those ethereal, iconic black-and-white pictures of the same place, from another era, with hatted men and gloved women.

6
Moving Pictures

But it's only here you can turn around 360 degrees

And everything is clear from here at the center

To every point along the circle of horizon

Here you can see for miles & miles & miles

Be born again daily, die nightly for a change of style

Hear clearly here; see with affection; bleakly cultivate compassion

Ted Berrigan, "Whitman in Black"

ay Wray, the actress and noted gorilla consort, paid her last visit to the Empire State Building in May 2004. She rode to the observatory summit in the company of Ray Harryhausen, the special-effects pioneer responsible for, among other things, the wonders of Claymation.

The 1933 version of *King Kong*, with its climactic scene of Kong climbing the building chased by machine-gunning biplanes, catapulted Wray to stardom from a position then not much above professional babe, and inspired Harryhausen to pursue his brilliant career creating both luminous Saturday matinee titles such as *The Seventh Voyage of Sinbad* (1958) and *Jason and the Argonauts* (1963), with its memorable sword-wielding skeletons and seven-armed demon, and bizarre stinkers like *Clash of the Titans* (1981). The two made an outwardly unlikely but somehow fitting pair, standing in the glassed-in section of the skyborne viewing level, Harryhausen in a checked jacket and tie, his hand on the arm of the ninety-four-year-old Wray, elegant as ever in a beige twinset.

Harryhausen was born thirteen years after Wray and was that age exactly when the original Kong climbed across the building, and his idiosyncratic career in the movies, with its lifelong devotion to wire-and-rubber monsters, is impossible to imagine without Kong. Special effects have long since outstripped his painstaking procedures of stop-action filming, but now, characteristically, the old ways have acquired a new, second-order value, like the obsolete turntables and tonearms of the pre-CD era. (Nick Park, the Oscar-winning clay-based animator of the Wallace and Gromit series, acknowledges Harryhausen as an influence.) Harryhausen was of course too young to have anything to do with the original *King Kong;* and, alas, when the time came for him to offer his own tribute to the giant-gorilla genre, the 1998 remake of *Mighty Joe Young* as an ecologically correct Charlize Theron vehicle, it was one of his duds, technically accomplished but offering little in the way of improvement over the 1949 original—itself a misfired attempt to surf the success of *Kong* fifteen years before. Harryhausen's efforts were dwarfed, but arguably not surpassed, by the 2005 remake of *King Kong* by Peter Jackson, famous for his successful *Lord of the Rings* films,

Mike Keefe, "Fay Wray," 2004 (Copyright Mike Keefe)

who constructed an entire miniature Manhattan, complete with accurate Empire State Building, for shooting in New Zealand.

That classic has itself suffered an earlier remake, of course, the tiresome 1976 semi-spoof with Jessica Lange in the Wray role and a long-haired, overweight Jeff Bridges as the safari photographer who brings the mighty Kong back to Manhattan, this time to cavort atop the World Trade Center chased by jet helicopters. When the actor Robert Armstrong, playing Carl Denham in the original, sums up Kong's tragedy with the words, "It wasn't the airplanes. It was beauty killed the beast," we actually believe him, and the story rises above its prima facie absurdity. When Jeff Bridges attempts the same thing after Lange's extended lovemaking scene sitting in Kong's hand, it only prompts justified scorn, as when Judith Crist, in the *Saturday Review,* noted that, here, "the one and original lovable monster is lost amid all the hydraulic manipulations in what now emerges as the story of a dumb blonde who falls for a huge plastic finger." No one who has not seen the original Merian C. Cooper *Kong,* with its Expressionist chiaroscuro photography, so reminiscent of Ernst Lubitsch or, indeed, Max Ernst, can appreciate the pathos of the monster's fall from primitive solitude to the excitations, and tragedies, of the city. It is a story of beauty and the beast, to be sure, but also a story of even greater mythic proportions—of innocence and experience, of love and loss, of wilderness and city.

The Empire State is its fitting site of climax, not simply in being, at the time, the tallest building in the city, and the world. It is far more: both the physical and the spiritual center of the island, and of the universe; the mythic tower around which the urban jungle arrays itself. Surely, we think, even the 1976 Kong would have known better than to scale the World Trade Center, stranded down there at the far end of Manhattan with nothing on two of its sides but open water. And there are *two* of them, for god's sake!

More than a hundred major films have been made featuring the Empire State Building, but not one of them is as famous as *King Kong*, and no single pair of characters is more closely related to the building than Kong and Fay Wray. (Few people other than film cognoscenti remember the name of her character, but everyone remembers hers—stardom in action.) But the relationships were not always happy ones. "He's our friend and our enemy," an Empire State spokesperson says of Kong, who is, indeed, the closest thing the building has to a permanent resident ghost. His image is never far from mind, whether in the jokey plastic models of the building or perspective-trick photographs available to tourists, or in various promotions and gags designed to take advantage of his sacred and profane memory.

A scheme to place an inflatable Kong on the building's side in 1983 collapsed when, larger and heavier than expected, the balloon Kong itself collapsed, hanging in deflated puffs and flaps off one side of the great building. In 1986, lawyers for Turner Broadcasting, which had acquired the rights to the original film, along with scores of other classics soon to be violated by deplorable "colorization," tried to stop the Empire State from using any Kong imagery in their promotions without first paying a permission fee—a move the building's lawyers countered by employing nameless gorillas in promotions whose taglines went conspicuously Kongless. The building's owners knew they could not lose in such a battle of icons, confident that tourists and consumers would reliably supply the suppressed premise of this media enthymeme: if there is a gorilla (or, rather, man in a gorilla suit) in or around the Empire State Building, then, name or no name—trademark or no trademark—that gorilla must be King Kong. It was as if Turner had tried to trademark the name of a bearded fat man in a red suit between Thanksgiving and New Year's Eve.

The building's promoters were less lucky with Fay Wray herself, who, though always a resolute fan of the building that helped make her famous, had a love-hate relationship with her gorilla friend—a not uncommon fate for a performer linked forever in the public imagination with a particular partner or bit of stage business. During the May 2004 visit to the building, Wray refused outright to be photographed next to one of the building's nameless gorillas—a rare moment of abruptness in an afternoon of sophisticated good manners and good feeling. And yet, when she lay dying just a few months later, on a sticky Sunday afternoon in August, she asked her companion and caretaker to put the film on her video recorder. She fell asleep watching it, and paid her second final visit to the top of the building, this time in the virtual reality of celluloid and magnetic tape.

Two days later, on the evening of August 10, 2004, the famous lights at the top of the Empire State, which had first flashed red, white, and blue for the 1976 American bicentennial and which had, since then, celebrated everything from Christmas, St. Patrick's Day, and the New York Marathon to the new blue M&Ms, were dimmed for fifteen minutes in tribute to this converging iconic personage, the human face of the building's first decades. The *New York Times* called this public act of mourning "the recognition of a deep and genuine tie between Wray and the building that helped make her famous." Which it surely was; but the pathos of the relation goes deeper than that rather bland assessment suggests. In 1969, Wray herself wrote, "When I'm in New York, I look at the Empire State Building and feel as though it belongs to me, or is it vice versa?"

Or is it vice versa. Wray knew, in her last moments, what she had long suspected and sought, now and then, to evade. If Kong was the building's ghost, she was its prisoner. And the two of them would be locked, forever, in an embrace more powerful than Kong's own, the grip of the cultural memory. Her final choice of Sunday viewing is not, as it might appear, an act of movie-star egotism; nor is it even the performance of some kind of iconic devotion. We observe, rather, a mixture of defiance and surrender—surrender to the inescapable cultural logic by which she had come to be, inextricably, tied to the building; and defiance of that very fact, an assertion of will in the face not just of death but also what is often far more painful, namely memory. She may have gone peacefully, in her quiet sleep, but Fay Wray did not go gently.

Of course, many people feel as though the Empire State belongs to them. It is, we might say, part of its iconic genius that the building, at once so forbidding and so familiar, becomes its own kind of monumental household possession, a shared treasure not just of all New Yorkers, but of anyone who has ever visited New York—in person or, sometimes more powerfully, only via the overwhelming imaginative medium of film. All of us alive at this moment get our sense of life's possibilities in part from the movies. It is the condition of the age that things experienced cinematically are frequently more influential, and emotionally more resonant, than things merely experienced.

Our mediated condition is especially acute when it comes to experiences of the distant metropolis, the mythic city where life is lived at a higher volume, with a greater degree of class and intensity, than anything available to us, wherever we may be. During the twentieth century, under Hollywood's cultural dominance, that mythic city has been, more often than not, New York. Or, rather, Manhattan—not the real Manhattan of actual streets and transactions and crimes, but the seamless Manhattan of the stylish black-and-white imagination, with its open vistas of possibility, seen for the first time from, as it might be, the concourse of Grand Central where in a bygone age you would have arrived to test your world-beating mettle against the city of cities.

As so often with shared cultural experiences, the phenomenon of cinematic mediation is further amplified by feedback. Influenced by the aspirated desires of the film world, in other words, we filter future experiences through the past expectations of what we might agree to call the *mytho-cinematic urban.* I mean the depicted and desired world of swanky nightclubs and luxurious ocean liners, of neon-washed streets, soaring architecture, and dim bars where beautiful people are drinking smart cocktails and making smarter conversation. Where anything is possible and there are ten million stories waiting to be told. Where the romance I have been waiting for is somewhere nearby, maybe just around the corner, waiting too, waiting for me to come along . . .

Obviously the appeal of these romantic—and often nostalgic—visions is not restricted to actual adolescents. Perhaps we have to acknowledge that the dream of urban sophistication speaks to the perpetual adolescent within us all, the whole tangle of feedback loops and mediated expectations an intersubjective form of arrested development. But such an assessment is, by itself, too harsh, for this economy of desire can also sometimes speak to the better part of ourselves, those often-thwarted longings for aesthetic purity, smooth civility, and easy success. Even longtime New Yorkers, priding themselves on their hard-nosed realism, are not immune. Indeed, they might even be the most devoted acolytes of the mytho-cinematic pantheon, keeping well hidden but nevertheless enjoying the feeling they get while walking along Park Avenue in a superb suit, on their way to a date at Gramercy Tavern or the Rainbow Room.

Or, less lovely, they might indulge those crippling perpetual desires for the generalized other—that imaginary better boyfriend or date—that also belong to the city. These longings are depicted but also fueled by such schizo-romantic fantasies as *Sex and the City,* a television show that seemed to oscillate deliberately between sweetness and softcore, making it, like so much actual sex in the city, the disease for which it purports to be the cure. Not surprisingly, the title sequence of the show features a pretty shot of the Empire State Building—also of its girlfriend the Chrysler—and seeing it we know, as surely as if we had heard the words "Once upon a time . . . ," that we are in mytho-cinematic New York, land of martinis and mojitos, of orgasm and agony.

We all hold a stock of such images in memory, and indeed layer them in with our memories of actual events such that they begin to form a semi-solid mass of desires and aspirations that may shape many future actions and choices. Marketers speak of aspirational discourses, such as those found in fashion or home-decorating magazines, which feed off the omnipresent desire in socialized humans to alter the material conditions of their existence, to dress, eat, and live differently. At an extreme—an extreme that is everywhere obvious—this issues in mere lifestyle pornography, the shameless excitation of desires that are understood to be beyond fulfillment, and can lead only to further titillation of the same kind. The evil truth at the heart of all aspirational magazines and television shows is that you cannot shop your way to happiness but you can be made to think you can, if only briefly. We all know this. We all likewise know that knowing it makes little difference to our behavior.

That is why attempts to escape the reach of market desire are usually ineffective. We find, when we try to flee or resist, that our resistance has already been commodified and waits, packaged and soundtracked, for us to come and purchase it. No matter what form of escape we seek, the way is already blocked: the signs of revolt reduced to fashion, the markers of aesthetic differentiation prescaled as invidious distinction and positional goods. Everywhere we go, we meet a suitable-for-purchase version of ourselves. We might say that this is Veblen's leisure-class analysis made ubiquitous by the false democratization of the capital market, where everything appears available but is, in fact, strictly regulated by the social distribution of money itself.

Thus does an entire lifeworld come to exhibit the cynic's predilection for knowing the price of everything and the value of nothing. Repeated experiences of this structural always-alreadyness in the cultural marketplace are enervating and, eventually, depressing: there is nowhere to run, nowhere to hide. As with the materials of the Empire State Building, our desires are preinscribed in a total system of commodity deployment. Working like a jiujitsu master, the market uses our own energy against us, finally sapping any will to get outside of it. For its central message is precisely this: that there is no outside.

These seemingly inevitable *reductios* may be enough in themselves to convince us that resistance is futile, and we may simply, perhaps after long struggle, succumb to the general social imperative to cultivate the virtues of the good consumer, justifying self-indulgence under cover of "helping the economy" or "creating wealth through spending." Such glib post-facto justifications are themselves always handy, waiting there for our use; they are certainly effective in sustaining the current arrangement. But there is another, deeper reason why seeking escape is not the right response—and it gives us some glimmer of how desire can be turned to the more important task of identity formation, the very thing that, in its perverse way, marketing exploits. In a strict sense, per definition *all* human desires are aspirational, and every one of us, no matter how fond or otherwise of shopping, is engaged in a constant project of recursive narrative formation. We all must, that is, tell a story about ourselves by moving into the future while necessarily facing the past, using the bits and pieces of memory and everyday life to, as it were, curate our personal exhibitions.

The materials we use to construct this tale often include, like it or not, bits and pieces of cultural detritus that, however apparently superficial, help us become who we are. The city of New York, and the Empire State Building as its symbolic lighthouse, its soaring beacon, figure prominently in the process, and this takes our analysis to a new level. For this is not New York itself, but what is in some ways far more influential and therefore more real, namely, the oneiric New York, the New York of our dreams.

Our task is not really to diagnose ourselves, and our culture, as if they were diseases to be cured; it is rather, in the words of the critic Marjorie Garber, "to read culture as if it were structured like a dream, a network of representations that encodes wishes and fears, projections and identifications, all of whose elements are overdetermined and contingent." And there is no dream more fertile than the one that swirls around the grid-embedded, upthrusting Empire State Building.

Nicky Ferante is a ladies' man, a famous playboy, a man about town so well known that his engagement to heiress Lois Clark, the implicit retirement of a notorious "big dame hunter" into the safety of marriage, is television news, "a romance that has captured the imagination of the whole world." This would hardly be surprising if Nicky were a movie star or a champion athlete. He is, in fact, a painter.

Terry McKay is a former nightclub singer from the not very glamorous city of Boston, a beautiful redhead with a heart of gold and a devoted fiancé, Ken, waiting for her in New York. She meets Nicky on board their shared cruise liner when, avoiding the prying attentions of a celebrity-hound eager to bag a lion, he pretends they are friends.

Which they soon are. She's heard about him, of course, and is wary. But he is charming—charming as only a man played by Cary Grant can be, with his enviable wardrobe, perfect manners, and easy banter working their magic on Deborah Kerr's sweet-sexy Terry. They really don't write them like this anymore, with all the playful smart call-and-response of old-fashioned sophisticated flirtation. There is a definite spark between the two accidental shipmates, then a retreat—they are becoming gossip. Nicky tears up a photo of them together, but another one gets by him and into the papers. They can no longer dine together. They share a stolen kiss on a gangway and pretend not to know where the other might be.

Then they visit Nicky's relatives at one of the ship's ports of call and all barriers fall away. A glimpse of the real Nicky, his multivalent talents and lack of real love, his sincerity and well-masked unhappiness. His beloved female ancestor senses something is different this time; she gives Terry a lace shawl as the ship's horn calls them back on board. But the two are still engaged to other people, and the meeting off the ship in New York is dire: cameras and reporters for Lois Clark and her beau, earnest dopey Ken for unknown Terry. The spell of transit, that electrifying freedom of the in-between place, is instantly broken.

Nicky and Terry have a pact, though. In six months' time, on July 1, they will meet at 5 p.m.—if, that is, they really do love each other. Coming up the Hudson to dock, Nicky suggests, maybe half joking, the top of the Empire State Building, unmissable in front of them, the 102nd floor. "Perfect," Terry says, delighted. "It's the nearest thing to heaven we have in New York!" Another mythic place, after all, a tower of possibility. If they can make it, they will come; and if not, there must be a very good reason.

Well, we all know what happens next. The six months pass and Nicky, dressed superbly as always, rides the elevators to their rendezvous. Terry, rushing along the street after shopping for something to wear, afraid she will be late, makes a fatal New York mistake: *she looks up at the building.* We hear but don't see the car: the sudden horn, the screeching tires, the sound of impact. (Actually, in a manipulative narrative twist, we learn about the accident only later, so that for a time we are left as mystified as Nicky.) Not only is she going to miss the appointment with him, she is going to miss a lot more because now she can't even walk!

The rest is vintage cheese, pure 1950s Hollywood weepie, but still pretty great for all that. After waiting until midnight, thinking each arriving elevator car might be the one that holds her, Nicky puts on his hat and returns to earth, walking off in the summer thunderstorm. He is so dejected he goes off to paint for six months, returning just before Christmas with what are, in fact, egregiously awful pictures even for a fiction like this one. There is, naturally, a sentimental portrait of Terry wearing his mother's lace shawl. Meanwhile she has returned to the care of gentle Ken, who lives in witless hope but is loyal beyond his own interests; after they see Nicky by chance at a show, he nevertheless urges Terry to tell him what happened. No, she says, "unless I can walk to him, and by walk I mean run, then no." There is some other claptrap about how Nicky would think it was his responsibility to help her, and he can't afford it, being just a humble painter and all (albeit with thousand-dollar suits).

But Nicky tracks her down, and the final scene of the movie is an excruciating confrontation hinged on dramatic irony: we know she can't walk but he doesn't because she's lying on a couch. First, *he* pretends to be the one who failed to keep the appointment, voicing his pain by indirection. Then he tells her about his six months of traveling, making and keeping all kinds of high appointments with willing women: "the tops of pyramids, the domes of cathedrals, the Eiffel Tower." Then he cracks. "I thought everything was fine until I saw you last night," he says. We have to watch all this with the usual frustration. Tell him! Why won't she tell him? We all know they're going to end up together!

Finally, Nicky tells her about the painting, and how at first he couldn't sell it. But he decided to give it away, because his dealer told him someone had loved it and that someone had been cruelly afflicted . . . wait! Can it be? Is it . . . ? Is she . . . ? He shoulders into the bedroom and we see it reflected in the mirror. The music swells as Nicky's eyes well up. He rushes back to Terry, also crying, on the couch.

"It was nobody's fault but my own," she tells him. "I was looking up. It was the nearest thing to heaven. *You* were there!"

An Affair to Remember, from 1957, has proved the aptness of its title, not least because of the archetypal goofiness of its story. So many implausibilities, so little time! One contemporary critic, Paul Dehn, diagnosed the film, accurately enough, as "ninety masterly minutes of entrancing light comedy and twenty-five beastly minutes of melodramatic, pseudo-tragic guff." But let us just note, first, the laughable narrative conceit of the possibly curable crippling accident that must remain a secret from the one person, besides the victim herself, it affects most. Of course; exactly; makes perfect sense. And second, one of those excellent movie lacunae that, like some kinds of metaphysical speculation, make absence more real than presence. The long shot of Cary Grant waiting for Deborah Kerr, looking anxiously at every elevator as the hours pass, paradoxically obscures the fact that the two *never meet at the top of the building.* Like the words "Play it again, Sam" in *Casablanca* (or indeed "I think, therefore I am" in Descartes's *Meditations*), neither of which actually occur, the film becomes famous for something that does not happen. For five decades romantic couples have cited the film while planning rendezvous at the building's summit, apparently overlooking the fact that the whole point of the story is that the rendezvous never takes place.

(A related film footnote concerning another thwarted assignation: in a signature scene from *Bell, Book, and Candle* in 1958, sexy witch Kim Novak and the spellbound publisher played by James Stewart kiss atop not the Empire State but the Flatiron Building at Twenty-third Street and Broadway. "We had no luck at the Empire State Building," says Novak, explaining to the enchanted Stewart why they are there. "Not at six a.m.," he agrees.)

Every generation varies the central romantic trajectory to suit its tastes, and *An Affair to Remember*'s Technicolor lushness is as apposite to its time as the sprightly twinkle-toed comedies of Fred Astaire and Ginger Rogers, with their pitch-perfect silver-screen Deco styling of chromium trim and curved interior contours, were to theirs a generation, and a world war, earlier. Such cultural products are not merely representations or straightforward expressions of their cultural circumstance, for, as we have seen, they cannot be that without inviting insuperable paradox; they are also, every now and then, shapers of that circumstance, rising from the vast and usually mediocre flow of cultural product to achieve a definitive or classic status, style makers as well as style carriers.

Cary Grant is one of those Hollywood stars whose image is itself iconic, an enduring model of manners and dress who endows virtually every one of his films with a decided aura of glamour. In *An Affair to Remember,* just as in, say, *The Philadelphia Story* and *North by Northwest*—to take two quietly disparate examples, a comedy and a thriller—Grant appears very much to be playing himself. That is, his smoothly flirtatious character and perfect necktie-and-pocket-square charm are identical in all three, the same perfectly straight hair-parting and knowing half smile; likewise the same winning combination of confidence and vulnerability, Grant's particular style of masculine grace. His iconic power comes from this ability to navigate emotion without ever losing his male control and sense of fun. That is why his character is so often, regardless of outer circumstances, a playboy on the verge of reform, a role he sustained long past what would be considered possible in today's ruthless, youth-devouring film world. He is a man of the world, adept at its challenges and fond of its pleasures, but nevertheless open to the love of a good woman. He is willing to be moved, even to cry, if the occasion warrants. He will allow his pain to show, even if only indirectly or via ironies that might be lost on a less literate audience. (Fifty years later, in the first decade of the twenty-first century, the polarity has been reversed. It is now so obligatory that a male character should weep that the surprising thing would be a non-comic-book film hero who refuses to get all busted up.)

In so many of Grant's iconic films, there is a scene in which the playboy banter dissolves in emotion and the bond with the good woman is sealed. Nicky Ferante weeps alongside crippled Terry McKay. C. K. Dexter Haven chides and mocks Tracy Lord until, discussing their yacht *The True Love,* she sees the devotion beneath his sharp tongue. Roger Thornhill lets Eve Kendall feel his anger and jealousy when he thinks she has been playing him sexually. These mannequins of style—a fashionable painter, an idler, a shallow advertising executive—become real men under the pressure of a mature femininity, embodied so differently in each case. Deborah Kerr's soft humor, Katharine Hepburn's brittle intelligence, Eva Marie Saint's distant allure, all work their magic on a virtually identical Grant character. Or perhaps we should put it the other way. Remaining the same, the still point in a revolving circle of film possibility, Grant's playboy persona convinces all three, and thus, by inference, all women period.

Both sides of this diptych are fantasies, to be sure, reflections of a shared delusion: by men, who believed they could, or should, be suave ladies' men yet open to commitment; and by women, who believed they, at long last, would offer the kind of attraction to make a man commit. It is a measure of the power of this delusion that the Grant icon is nevertheless so easily recognizable and attractive. In each film there is at least one scene that becomes a synecdoche for romance, shared by successive generations of viewers as an embodied gesture of tenderness. The scramble on Mount Rushmore, with the groping desperate hands reaching for Saint, which become a pull up to a railway-car sleeper. The bantering, emotional scene by the pool in Philadelphia and that Hepburn cry, "My, she was yar!" And, in *An Affair to Remember*, it has to be Cary at the 102nd floor, waiting, and waiting, hat in hand for the love who will not come. In that cinematic moment, two icons fuse and become one: Grant and the building, the solid man solidly held, but inside crumbling, crumbling with mounting disappointment and grief. Though the scene is of the inside of the building, we may always find ourselves remembering it from the outside as well, looking up, as Terry McKay did, dangerously, and thinking, it is near to heaven simply because he is there.

Nowadays, things are not so glamorous, or so romantic. Lacking cruise ships and grown-up banter—not to mention tap dancing—to urge them giddily along, romantic comedies find themselves becalmed in cultural doldrums of irony and allusion, where the only romance is one of referring back to earlier romances. Or, worse, they become stuck in a bog of ham-fisted moralizing and contradictory imperatives. The playboy of yesteryear is today more likely to be considered an aging adolescent suffering arrested development or latent homosexuality. He is a candidate for censure and even, as for example in *About a Boy* (2002), where a feckless Hugh Grant is finagled into a kind of parenthood, simply not allowed *not* to be a father. The good woman of the past, meanwhile, is now either a hungry career girl trying to navigate her own sexual smorgasbord while still yearning for marriage, or a deranged harpy angry at the world as her childbearing years melt away to leave her stranded in a house full of cats. Thus has romantic comedy, once a genre of sweetness and light, largely become a battlefield of gender crimes, bitter recrimination, and passive-aggressive maneuvering.

Variety magazine called *Sleepless in Seattle,* the 1993 Tom Hanks and Meg Ryan hit that riffs on *An Affair to Remember,* "shameless," which it surely is, despite the intermittent cleverness of Nora Ephron's script. (The same adjective might easily be applied to its effective sequel from 1998, *You've Got Mail,* another glib crowd-pleaser with the identical leads and scriptwriter, heavily plagiarized from both Ernst Lubitsch's *Shop Around the Corner* and the 1959 entry *Pillow Talk,* the first of several lumbering romantic comedies featuring Rock Hudson and Doris Day.) It is not just a matter of having to trade Cary Grant and Deborah Kerr for Hanks and Ryan, a net loss by any reckoning, but also that the gimmick here is even more preposterous, a kid-centered fantasy for the heartwarming postboom 1990s. Kid and father lose mom and wife to unspecified illness. Kid mourns for his mourning dad, calls radio phone-in show and intrigues the nation—including curious journalist engaged to dull professor. She begins a conversation. They begin to fall for each other, uttering, as *New Yorker* film critic Anthony Lane put it, "the last word in romantic common sense," namely "safe love." And so a meeting is planned at, where else, the top of the Empire State Building at midnight on Valentine's Day. (And good luck to them getting up there without waiting in line for three or four hours first—they never show that part.)

"What if someone you never met, someone you never saw, someone you never knew, was the only someone for you?" What if, as the ever-acute cultural critic Lisa Simpson once informed her naive mother, Marge, "romance is dead. It was acquired in a hostile takeover by Hallmark and Disney, homogenized, and then sold off piece by piece." Well, we needn't go so far, but it is a shame that romance here becomes a parable of political correctness and resolved male-female hostility rather than a delicious meeting of two adult minds. The Meg Ryan character is irritated by her male co-workers' joking that a woman over thirty is more likely to get hit by a car than to get married. ("That isn't true," a female friend says, sharply. "But it feels true.") She is engaged to a safe and nebbishy man, an academic and so by definition nonthreatening, to avoid a presumed descent into fatal spinsterhood. The Hanks character, meanwhile, can no longer possibly be anything like a playboy or man of the world. He has to be a widower-father because that shows, first, commitment (married young, didn't fool around, willing parent) and, second, goodness (it's not his fault his wife died; it's not like he *left* her).

He is also an architect, but absolutely not in the black-Armani and thick spectacles mode of the style-conscious East, a look presumably out of place in grunge-inflected Seattle. Hanks, like Cary Grant, tends to play himself in films of disparate style and circumstance. His semi-rumpled, not-quite-handsome face is perfectly similar, a visage of everyday goodness and solid appeal, in *Sleepless in Seattle, Philadelphia, Cast Away,* and *Saving Private Ryan* (to name just the biggest box-office successes). Whether playing sad dad, AIDS victim, shipwrecked courier, or fatherly Ranger captain—it doesn't matter. He is always Hanks the Hollywood Everyman. To say this is not to disparage his acting ability, exactly, which is perfectly pitched to the prevailing bland tastes of American filmgoers, but rather to analyze why Hanks—and in the present case co-star Ryan—never manage to rise to the status of icons.

Partly this seems a matter of style in the simple sense. There is no glamour here, only pathos (and unfortunately bathos, especially in the scenes where the son is telling the nation about his plight). Ryan is perky but never luscious, Hanks endearing but never charismatic. She dresses like an ordinary office drone, with no hint of the slinky evening wear and Givenchy polish Kerr gives to Terry McKay. He is a disheveled doofus from the Pacific Northwest in workmanlike flannel and dungarees, apparently one step away from joining the Pearl Jam fan base. *Sleepless in Seattle* includes a discussion of *An Affair to Remember* but also a clip, which is surely a mistake. "For one thing," as Lane said, "any Cary Grant film always looks better than what you're watching. And for another, what does it say about a movie that its funniest and most delicious moment comes from the fond remembrance of cinema? Maybe Ephron is so cushioned by celluloid that she can't conceive of any adventures still waiting out there in the fresh air."

Glamour eludes Hanks and Ryan, then, but not just for reasons of style; they are encompassed by an economy of image-making in which they are, by definition, of at best the second order. Their glamour, such as it is, remains borrowed, allusive, and simulacral. In *Ways of Seeing,* his influential short treatise on visual culture, the critic John Berger defined glamour as the light that shines forth as a result of reflected envy. The glamorous is the desirable because it is already the desired; we respond not to some inner light but to an economy of wishing of which the glamorous person is the focal point. Grant himself captured this nuance neatly when he said, "All men want to look like Cary Grant. *I* want to look like Cary Grant." The comment goes beyond the usual I-am-not-him actor's defense; Grant is here acknowledging the way iconic glamour functions, by drawing into its space—here a space of personal style—an entire spectrum of aspiration and anticipation. Grant and Kerr are desirable company aboard ship, and they are desirable company for the audience. We look at them and want, in some fashion, to be them—though maybe without the crippling accident or without the, in another sense, crippling painting style. If we do not have these desires, the film does not work, either as a romance or as a piece of Hollywood glam—which are, indeed, the same thing when film romance is working at its best.

The Hanks and Ryan characters are unable to generate this desire. We watch them from the outside, never identifying sufficiently to find their story romantic. We may want them to meet, not least so the whining half-orphaned kid can get a new mom and we can at least leave the theater; we may even feel some sense of genuine sympathy; but at no point do we experience the vertiginous tug of cool that Grant and Kerr generate, that sense of easy movement through a world fraught with temptations, previous commitments, and prying eyes. In *Sleepless in Seattle,* the romance dies on the screen, and the culminating scene, where the two characters finally meet, is painfully anticlimactic, almost managing to reduce the exalted site to a cliché. Whereas Cary Grant elevates and illuminates the building, a star shining from within as he fruitlessly waits, Hanks and Ryan diminish it, make it trite. We almost wish they had chosen another rendezvous.

They could not, of course, since part of the romance here is one of cinematic reference to the past. The film confesses its futility by trying to overcome its second-rate romance by encompassing a first-rate one. This, it seems, cannot be done. A more thoroughly ironic appropriation of *An Affair to Remember* might achieve that, but *Sleepless in Seattle*, typically for its time, wants it both ways. It craves the air of currency that comes with cultural embeddedness, the hipness of allusion, but it also wishes to be sincere and moving. In fact, it is merely manipulative and superficial, a lesson in confusing two narrative approaches while leeching off the energy of another.

We often forget that *An Affair to Remember* was itself a remake, by the same director, Leo McCarey, of his own very successful 1939 romance, *Love Affair,* nominated for Best Picture of that year. Charles Boyer and Irene Dunne are the cruise ship companions this time, a European man of the world and a New York ingenue, and the resulting comedy is altogether more whimsical and physical, if less lush and sad, than the Grant-Kerr outing of two decades later, but this does constitute one of the few examples where a director has revisited the same story twice with success. (Contrast it, for instance, with Alfred Hitchcock's disastrous second try at *The Man Who Knew Too Much,* the original serviceable film noir reduced, in the bizarre James Stewart and Doris Day remake, to an inexplicable comedy-musical-thriller with no thrills.) For no good reason anyone can see, *Love Affair* was even remade again, this time with Warren Beatty and Annette Bening in the starring roles, in a film that *Screen International* called, perhaps rather prematurely, "the nadir of Hollywood's obsession with re-makes."

There is no novelty in observing that Hollywood, especially of late, cannot do novelty. Mass-culture film audiences are of regrettably short memory, and good stories are in regrettably short supply, so an economy of make and remake is probably inevitable. What worked with a theater full of people two, or five, decades ago might just fetch them again. Or, as with Beatty (who also produced and co-wrote his version of *Love Affair*), there is sometimes an obsession to see today's stars taking on the roles that defined yesterday's. And yet, the overwhelming evidence is that appeal does not time-travel well, and allure is not a transferable quality. Most remakes flop, and for fairly obvious reasons: the times have actually changed, and the universal appeal of, say, a boy-meets-girl tale is more than offset by the stylistic peculiarities of decades past failing to match our own—whatever they may be.

Actually, there is an answer to that question. It is a function of a culture in retreat to trade so obviously in the backward look, to focus on successive waves of "retro" style and claims for rehabilitated looks or fashions. Thus did millennial North America indulge a series of "rediscoveries" that continues still, an extended rummaging in the cultural attic structured by the false but useful categories supplied by "decadism." Not decadence, decadism: though, yes, the roots are identical. The original decadents were millennial harbingers of a previous century, absinthe-sipping Symbolist poets and dissolute aesthetes indulging end-of-days tastes. Decadism is not so much decadent, morally bankrupt in the eyes of a shocked bourgeoisie, as merely bankrupt in its own terms. It structures cultural experience into notional brief periods with preassigned characters—'60s rebellion, '70s anarchy, '80s affluence, '90s retreat—and shuffles them through the machinery of the culture industry as needed. Important nuances are rubbed smooth and misapplications tolerated even as the process continues. At the moment of this writing, for example, teenage girls loudly disdain what they call "eighties style," usually meaning something either later or earlier, and submit without demur to the return of leg warmers as a fashion accessory.

The grains of truth in these decade labels sustain them for use, and the usefulness of tagging style likewise, such that no original thought is ever needed to pursue the project of self-presentation or identity formation. Nor, for that matter, is there much call for originality even in the purveyors of fashionable materials, who simply recombine existing elements in momentarily novel conjunctions. Fashion, as Roland Barthes said, is always a system structured by novelty whereby the small range of vertical-axis categories, from hair to shoes, are kept alive by an incessant parade of horizontal-axis options; but here we see its final reductio, an absolutely content-free, or rather always already filled, grid of ever-recycled newness.

Was it ever thus? Perhaps. But there is a quality of nostalgia suffusing these constant claims of novelty that gives the decadist remake culture a particularly mournful mien. The style here is not even the alleged cheerfulness of postmodernism, playfully eclectic; it is, rather, a slick surface of borrowed elements absent their context, what we might call Late Capitalist Pan-Modernism. I mean that jumble of materials and gestures so characteristic of our day whereby the formerly revolutionary steel-tube furniture and sleek neocubist lines of the early twentieth century, say, are rendered as mere backdrops to catalogue fashion shoots; where modernist architecture is shorn of all utopian pretensions and made into a playground of the very rich, always surrounded by the forever revivified glow of transient glamour. Our ongoing tangle in these elements of the past, denatured and made into props and stage business, is the future: a future where all departure lounges and hotel lobbies feature the same brushed steel and polished hardwood; where all buildings feature unacknowledged and unwanted sub-Corbusian debts; where the link once forged between style and political change melts away as laughable, uncool, even deranged.

"Publicity is, in essence, nostalgic," John Berger wrote in the long-ago year of 1972. "It has to sell the past to the future." Nostalgia is no simple longing for the past, however, not least because we can be made to feel it for experiences we did not, and could not, have ourselves enjoyed. Nostalgia literally means—from the Greek, *nostos algos*—a painful longing for one's home harbor, and Odysseus may be considered by this token the most celebrated nostalgic in history or literature. It is a paradoxical pain even in its simplest form, since there is the pain of return as well as the pain felt as return is successively thwarted: you really can't go home again, because when you get there it is not the same as when you left. Then there are those yearnings for the unreal and unavailable, the cozy past or the bright future, the perfect Christmas and the just society. Nostalgia may be felt for both past and future, in fact: not just for a past to which we might return in future, but for a future we envisioned during past moments.

Viewers of the retro silver-screen hero Sky Captain, for example, who battles global villains in a 2004 Hollywood film, were delighted with the opening scenes, a long dizzying sequence showing some Hindenburgclass dirigible docking at the summit of the Empire State Building during a snowstorm—an operation in reality never completed, indeed eventually judged impossible by U.S. Navy engineers after the now familiar docking tower was completed in 1932, at a cost of $750,000. William Lamb objected to the mast, which spoiled his original flattop design, but it was good publicity for a flight-mad era, when dirigibles and propeller aircraft were still rare enough to seem heavenly; it would also decisively end the skyscraper race, putting a solid two hundred feet between the Empire State's summit and the top of the Chrysler's vertex. Lamb had described the latter as belonging to "the Little Nemo school of architecture" but he submitted to John Raskob's demands—"What this building needs is a hat!" the latter said—and designed the now indispensable (and inescapably phallic) steel tower, with its winged supports arranged in flying buttress style. His draftsmen, knowing his real views, gave him a cartoon of a gargoyle perched on a column and saying, in a thought bubble, "Hear no dirigible—See no dirigible—Who said anything about a dirigible!"

Al Smith, for one. "The directors of Empire State, Inc., have come to the conclusion that in a comparatively short time Zeppelin airships will establish trans-Atlantic, trans-Pacific, transcontinental and, possibly, South American routes from New York," he said in a 1930 speech. "Building with an eye to the future, we have determined to build a mooring tower 200 feet high on top of the new Empire State Building. The roof of the building itself will be 1,100 feet from the sidewalk. That will mean the Zeppelin would be anchored more than 1,300 feet in the air, with elevator facilities through the tower to land passengers downstairs seven minutes after the ship is anchored." Alternatively, they could stop for refreshments at the observatory café before hitting the elevators and the street below. What Smith failed to say was how the pilots would manage in the swirling winds of midtown Manhattan well enough to make a fixed point docking, let alone offload passengers safely. Or what they would do with the dumped ballast water usually falling harmlessly on a grassy airfield.

The film version of the fantasy was beautiful in a way only the imaginary can be. (Even a seasoned veteran of Empire State Building film cameos, not easily impressed, was delighted with this luminous moment of postmodern image appropriation.) The film is billed as *Sky Captain and the World of Tomorrow* but it is, of course, as with all late-century Deco appreciation, really an elaborate bit of nostalgia: the world of yesterday looking to tomorrow as imagined by today. (Other films that exhibit the same stylistic premise, so prominent in Late Capitalist Pan-Modernism, include *Brazil, Gattaca,* and *Dark City;* in all of them, men in hats wield fountain pens and pneumatic tubes against a foggy urban backdrop of hulking skyscrapers and floating jet-cars. Even Ridley Scott's much-praised *Blade Runner,* while outwardly distinct, partakes of the same design conceit.) The further irony is that these marvelous appreciations of 1930s technology are possible only because of the computer-generated imagery produced by twenty-first-century technology. They offer one of those moments, like the companion spectacle of technology advanced enough to depict the destruction of technology—as when a massive shock wave obliterates Manhattan in another 2004 film, *The Day After Tomorrow*—that are typical of our peculiar postmodern condition.

And yet, this bit of stylish decade-collapsing appropriation of the Empire State is more than just irony. Like all nostalgia, it speaks to desire, however confused and spectacle-gripped, and therefore completes a bit of unfinished cultural business with a momentarily satisfactory flourish. Wouldn't it have been incredible, after all, to alight from a Berlin-sent airship and descend a gangway to the sleek Tea Room lounge for a re-storative cocktail? The wonder here is the same we feel when viewing drawings of the notional skyscrapers that would lift whole detached-house plots, complete with garden, into the sky; or when listening to Le Corbusier describe the Celestial City with its electric cars and bucolic parkland spoked by glass towers. These swanky visions of the future-past are, in turn, sustained and bridged by intermediate moments of techno-optimism, as when 1950s engineers and big-science boosters pursued the project of jet-age improvement of everyday life. Then, as before, the vision and optimism are eventually tempered by life's reality principle, the failure of machines, and the forces of planned obsolescence; but their power is still considerable.

The narrator of Nicholson Baker's *The Mezzanine,* himself a nos-talgic object-fetishist of considerable passion, dwelling at length on the chunky beauty of old-fashioned staplers or the gasoline-pump lines of spring-loaded cigarette vending machines, confesses a moment of disillusion with the self-promoting text on a men's-room Warm Air Hand Dryer. "I disapprove of this text now," he says, "but when I was little it bespoke the awesome oracular intentionality of prophets whose courage and confidence allowed them to scrap the old ways and start fresh: urban renewal architects; engineers of traffic flow; foretellers of monorails, paper clothing, food in capsule form, programmed learning, and domes over Hong Kong and Manhattan." Nothing so clearly illustrates the libidinal economy of techno-nostalgia as that conjunction of the phrases "when I was little" with "monorails and dome cities." In the year 2000, poking fun at these desires, the *New York Times Magazine* ran a feature on technology that included every boy's frustrated demand: "Where the hell is my jetpack?" A student complained to me not long ago, using that new ironic form of sincerity, that the millennium had passed and she was disappointed to find she still had to cook her own food.

Nostalgia is not restricted to mix-and-match futurism and a longing for an idealized past, then. Even the sincere utopian dream confesses its own kind of nostalgic preoccupation, now for a sleek and perfect future that seems always to be slipping out of reach. Behind the full-scale utopian vision, furthermore, typically lurks an often unexamined belief in the perfectibility of humanity: the possibility of a return to (or, what is much the same thing, first achievement of) a state of innocent grace. This persistent Edenic wish is the ultimate nostalgia, we might say, with the transcendent dreams of the religious and mythopoeic past now transported not just to an unexplored new world (as in Sir Thomas More or H. G. Wells, who mapped new continents and new planets, respectively) but to that forever foreign country, the future. The scent of the garden is never far from these visions even if their source, and their scene of action, is urban. The sincere utopian most often desires not the manmade wonders of technology but the natural wonders of rustic simplicity. Thus the rapt bucolic vision of Karl Marx's classless society, say, where we will all be careful craftsmen and exquisite connoisseurs of country leisure; or the bizarre lemonade oceans and cheerful glee-club competitions between

Charles Fourier's semimonastic anarcho-syndicalist phalansteries. If technology is foregrounded at all in these schemes it tends to be, as in Corbusier's radiant city schemes or the stacked Futurist conurbations, a physical representation of a spiritual truth, like the cruciform floor plans and flying buttresses of medieval cathedrals.

We are perhaps too quick in our dismissals of these utopian visions. Their political ambitions may indeed prove unrealistic, foolish—even dangerous—but their desires remain, we must acknowledge, recognizably our own. For a just social order; for a life free of conflict and full of creativity; for an authentic self that realizes its true nature fully. Without this aspiration, even when coupled to a hardheaded awareness of its dangers, we are not quite ourselves. "A map of the world that does not include Utopia," Oscar Wilde remarked, "is not even worth glancing at."

And thus does the hokey, sometimes, rise above itself, in fictions both grand and small. The 2003 film *Elf* is the story of Buddy (Will Ferrell), a human who grows up as a misfit in Santa's North Pole workshop—he can't make the toys fast enough and all the furniture is too small—then sets out on a quest for his biological father. Santa gives him, as a combined talisman and map, a snow globe of the Manhattan skyline: a piece of magic souvenir merchandise, just like the one that inspired resentment and even hatred in the man whose story I mentioned before. Here, however, the magic of the snow globe is more straightforward: it is a directional icon, a kind of map. Santa tells Buddy that his biological father, played by James Caan, works in the tall building right in the middle. As so often, the Empire State Building functions here as the beacon of New York. Buddy finds his way through "the seven layers of the candy-cane forest" and "the land of swirly-twirly gumdrops" to reach the Lincoln Tunnel and, finally, the mythic city of dreams. He walks along Fifth Avenue just below Thirty-fourth Street and, as so many of us have done, dares to look up. The building in the sky is the building in the snow globe: kitsch souvenir returns to its site of type-token origin, just as Buddy has returned to his point of biological origin.

There are difficulties, of course, hurdles to clear. Buddy's anxious workaholic father, a children's book publisher, is not entirely pleased to find he has another son, and one who seems to suffer from crippling delusions. The tale is standard Christmas hooey, a predictable riff on the lost-child-home narrative, but enlivened by Ferrell's inspired goofiness, much of it predicated on the contrast between childish naïveté and the bustle of New York. He presses all the buttons in an Empire State elevator car, exclaiming, "Doesn't it look like a Christmas tree?" to the disgusted passengers. He gets sick playing in a revolving door, sprays countertop perfume into his mouth, and battles a scary escalator. He also insults a department-store Santa ("You sit on a throne of lies!") and, naturally, gets hit by a taxi. "Be careful," he later warns his half-brother. "The yellow ones don't stop."

His encounters with the Empire State Building, meanwhile, include getting manhandled by lobby security and, once his father allows him to come to work for him, an exile to the basement mailroom, where a gang of apparent ex-cons are lazily shoving packages into pneumatic tubes—a nice steampunk touch—while getting high. "This is just like Santa's workshop," Buddy enthuses, "except it smells like mushrooms and everyone looks like they want to hurt me." Buddy high is not much different from Buddy straight, and soon the whole mailroom is joining him in rounds of Greek dancing on top of the piled mailbags.

The film culminates in the long-signaled visit of the real Santa to New York, his sleigh hampered by a malfunction in the jet-assist engine that runs on "Christmas spirit" and crash-landed in Central Park. Chased by four menacing mounted park police—a weird apocalyptic touch from director Jon Favreau—Santa manages, with Buddy's help, to lift off and complete his rounds. But not before Buddy's father is converted to genuine Christmas feeling, Buddy finds a girlfriend in winsome Zooey Deschanel (who also sings), and the whole family comes together as one. Hurrah. The final sequence of the film has Santa's sleigh careering loopily through the streets of Manhattan, down Fifth Avenue and up past the Empire State Building, its summit lit with the traditional red and green lights of Christmas. *Elf* is a billet-doux to New York as much as it is a celebration of Christmas or family; we might even say it collapses three mythologies into one, under the gentle pressure of a traditional quest form. Its final shot fades from action to another still image of the building, the snow globe that got us all here—that got us all *home*.

Any truly monumental building has a tendency to disappear from view, to become spectral or invisible, even if its material reality persists. This is true figuratively: over time the reality of the building wavers and fades, through familiarity, through reproduction, through cultural appropriation. But it is also true, as it were, merely literally; for there is no single vantage, whether from street or air, from bridge or balcony, where the building as a whole can be seen. The Empire State Building is as inescapable and as lasting as any feature of a city, and probably more than most; and yet we find, over and over, how little we are able actually to see it. Its thick presence makes it all the more remarkable how often, and how variously, the Empire State Building has, like Poe's purloined letter, ceased to be seen precisely because it is so obviously, unremarkably, and (we might say) merely there. The basic truth about the Empire State Building is that, although it is so forcefully actual, *you cannot see it*.

It is likewise important to dwell on how, and when, a building reappears. The gruesome attacks of September 11, 2001, ushered in a new moment of appreciation for those tall buildings of New York that were still standing. In part because the World Trade Center was unique in style, and uniquely doubled (so to speak), its violent removal from the skyline threw the entire city into a different light. New attention was paid to the classic skyscrapers of Manhattan; and so the otherwise impregnable fact of New York walking, that one must not look up, seemed for a time suspended, bracketed by desire and yearning. It surely counts as one of the minor consequences of that horrific day that the skyscrapers of Manhattan suddenly appeared at once more real and more fragile, vulnerable fingers stretched skyward in hope but all too susceptible to being broken.

In his intimate, lyrical celebration of the city, *Here Is New York*, E. B. White closes with a passage that falls sadly, and strangely, on the reader now used to White's gentle praise of his astonishing hometown. The shadow of possible war falls across the island of Manhattan, White says, a war of such destructive power that even New York's vibrant concentration of life and love may be simply erased, deconstructed, like

Marty Lederhandler, "The twin towers of the World Trade Center burn behind the Empire State Building in New York," September 11, 2001 (AP/Wide World Photos)

those Chinese cities bulldozed into oblivion to make way for the Yangtze River dam project or the streets of Dresden, obliterated by Allied carpet firebombing. These pages are more than a reminder of the nuclear anxiety that gripped every part of American society in the 1950s; they are an intimation of general mortality, an urban memento mori as necessary, and as caustic, as the skulls or rotting fruit rendered in the lush oils of eighteenth-century *vanitas* still-lifes. All beauty and grandeur must pass! The special illusion of the built environment is that, because it appears ready to outlast me, it seems it will outlast time itself. But of course it is not so.

We recall that, in the four corners of the ground floor of the Empire

State Building, near the names of the celebrated craftsmen, are the wall-mounted medallions that commemorate what the builders clearly considered essential features of their work: concrete, machines, elevators, decoration. In light of architectural debates both then and since, this is an odd list. Decoration was the very thing that Loos considered criminal, a sign of stylistic nullity—a judgment that, as we know, has continued to orient much design from that moment to this, whether overtly modernist or not. As early as Kant's *Critique of Judgment,* certainly at the center of all twentieth-century minimalism, architectural and otherwise, "decoration" is a term of abuse, denoting the aesthetically unmotivated, that which is merely present, without justification. Indeed, the very word suggests to modern ears an unwarranted excrescence, a useless curlicue or superfluous spandrel pasted on otherwise robust structures, as with the swirling plaster and marble excesses of the rococo church.

Elevators, meanwhile, were instrumental in allowing a building this tall to be also functional, as we know, but they are not usually isolated as features to be celebrated, still less as one corner in a foursquare toast to a great building's main pillars. Nowadays, elevators are so taken for granted by most of us that it hardly seems worth taking the time or attention to laud them. With new tensile strengths available in steel cable, rare is the building so tall that it must resort to the staggered series of shafts needed to ascend to the summit of the Empire State—though this experience does serve to remind the upward traveler of his constant, and contingent, suspension. There is nothing like having to change elevators three times to remind you that cable does not stretch infinitely far. (Also, perhaps, that it is the only thing keeping you up there!) But the experience is rare. Most of us, most of the time, can simply take the elevator for granted, the seamless space-change its inventor imagined. I enter a small room; the doors close; when they open again, I am somewhere else. The taken-for-granted elevator is perhaps the closest thing we have to the *Star Trek* transporter device, and it is so ordinary we hardly even think to think about it.

Concrete and machines are more to our current taste, more appropriate badges of the age. Even here we rarely pause to give concrete its due, a wonderful material too often subjected to brutalist abuse. And when we think of machines we are perhaps more likely to picture computers or video terminals than the mechanical winches and gear-in-gear arrangements of the pre-electronic age. The joy of these machines, as in the everyday mechanical devices celebrated by such enthusiasts as Nicholson Baker or Henry Petroski—the stapler, the nail clipper, the pencil—is the visible perfection of the contrivance. We admire, maybe only subconsciously, the way such a device *speaks its functionality aloud,* offering its utilitarian beauty for all to see. The mechanical wonders do not hide their workings, the way electronic devices, computers, and televisions do. If mechanical machines are democratic, electronic ones are tyrannical. They present just a bland, opaque face, a black box (sometimes literally), that is relieved only by the fiction of liquid crystal display or graphic user interface, the simulacral "desktop" with its alleged "folders" and "files." The movement of the machine, its logic, is not available to the mere user, here presumed to be inadequate to its genius.

For the Empire State builders, "machine" means an even more robust and dangerous creature, a macro-scaled ordering of steel parts and physical relations that could *get something done* in the unforgiving world of three-dimensional space, something improbable and fantastic, like lifting tons of steel, stone, and glass into the air. The machines used in the building were intricate and sometimes massive variants of basic mechanics, the ancient roll call of lever, pulley, and inclined plane. The triumph of construction—a building that stands tall, and lasts, that doesn't fall down or crumble—also makes for a kind of *total machine,* the implausible but ever renewed success of the infrastructure over time. The building takes its place in the system, itself supporting a vast array of uses. Now, three dimensions are rendered into four, because space becomes time. We live with the building and it lives with us. Time will outstretch even this success, yes, but for the time being it is here, *the building is here,* incontrovertibly here. And we all built it. We build it again and again, each day of the city's life.

The medallion for machines, it seems to me, means to trumpet the entire conceptual and practical realm of applied physics, the passed-on knowledge that allows humans to move and arrange heavy objects. It puts me in mind of those oddly moving opening sections of Wittgenstein's *Philosophical Investigations,* where he suggests that the origin of language—and hence the idea that "meaning is use"—lies in the need to coordinate the physical actions of building. "Slab!" Wittgenstein's primitive language-user cries out, communicating in a word the entire process of classification and order that makes "block," "slab," "pillar," and "beam" the constituents of a language, and of a building, the vocabulary of construction. This is language made to order the parts and tasks of building itself, responding to new needs and new materials, and so offering finer and finer grades of meaning-use, the beautiful architectural naming-of-parts: finials, cladding, aedicules, dentils, annulets, modillions, mutules.

Construction of what? In the *Philosophical Investigations* we don't know, we never learn, because the focus is seeing *that* language is used, not *for what;* but the project at hand is clearly a task of construction, a matter of coordinated action. I like to imagine it is the erection of a temple, a primitive cathedral, the first communal duty, the rendering in stone of our shared existence—and its brevity.

The events of September 11, 2001, did not signal merely a renewed awareness of the Empire State Building, a new moment of cherished visibility. They also began a painful, and in its way violent, period of self-examination. The coincidence of New York's state nickname, and hence the building's proper name, acquired a new resonance as America struggled with the realities of being an empire. Among many other things, no doubt, this brings to mind a less benign or celebratory sense of "machine."

An uncomfortable spectrum of kinship joins the total commodity mobilization of the Empire State Building's construction with the emergent war machine of the late 1930s. Primary sources from the period of the building's debut remind us of a fact sometimes lost, namely that the Great Depression was perceived by many as an economic trough that only war, and hence wartime production, could overcome. Raskob and his partners had tried, unsuccessfully, to rally the markets in September 1929. They risked massive investment in a construction project that made economic sense only in the local sense: cheap labor to build an unrentable megastructure floated on rhetoric of achievement and aspiration.

The stakes were high. Millions of men were suddenly out of work as a result of the 1929 crash. Banks closed by the dozen, then by the hundred. Automobile plants slashed their workforces by 80 percent, steel plants by 90. By July 1932 the Dow Jones Industrial Average had fallen from the September 1929 high of 452 to a mere 58. Social unrest was widespread, calls for violence or forcible nationalization of industry common. Cities from New York, Newark, and Washington to Cleveland and Detroit witnessed breadlines and riots. The socialist shudders that ran through Britain in the general strikes of 1919 and 1926, and even Canada, with its Winnipeg general strike of 1921, came late but inevitably to the United States.

One small but perhaps representative example. Writing from her family's summer cottage in Laguna Beach, California, M. F. K. Fisher, who would later become famous for her essays on food and cooking, recorded the following journal entry on September 13, 1933. ("Rex" is her father.) "Tonight Father and Denny talked at each other for an hour or so," Fisher writes, "sometimes one at a time, sometimes together and trying to drown each other out. From the talk I gather that they both think the N.R.A. [National Recovery Act] doomed, Denny a Democrat and Rex Republican. D. says it is too complex. Rex, scornful of a handful of economists controlling a nation's industries, thinks immediate war the only alternative to chaos and revolution, and one that Roosevelt will choose rather than see his plan a too-obvious failure. He says the national press is primed now to such an extent that war with Japan (or, second choice, Latin America) will be accepted as natural and inevitable by the people whenever it is declared." Rex, she goes on to say, gives the nation a year or even eight months before war comes.

As we know, it was more than eight years, not eight months, before that war came; and Latin America played no part. The passage, and Rex's analysis, nevertheless possess a weird prescience—not just for that war but for ones more lately engaged. The national press is primed; war will be accepted as natural and inevitable. It took the devastating surprise attack on Pearl Harbor to engage those forces of naturalism and inevitability, just as it took the destruction of the World Trade Center to motivate a "war on terror" that led the United States deep into Iraq, a country conspicuously lacking either a connection to the heinous events of September 11 or the weapons of mass destruction offered as justification for the war. What was certainly present was the largest military buildup in the history of the United States, defense budgets so large that a single line item might be more costly than the entire gross domestic product of a potential foe.

Whatever we may say about the strange mixture of isolationism and imperial power that characterizes twenty-first-century America, we can certainly offer the historical perspective that it could all be seen coming from a point some decades before even the first Persian Gulf War. America's dependency on oil, combined with its massive consumption of goods both labor- and capital-intensive, means that it cannot avoid a foreign policy de facto organized around Middle East aggression. This truth may not be reflected in the dominant rhetoric of the nation, to be sure. If the nation itself is seen as a machine that runs beneath the rhetorical superstructure, however, then it becomes clear that the energy needed to run the machine must be continually secured, often at some great cost in people and value. A president or a columnist may help himself to a rhetoric of liberation, suggesting that people around the world are eagerly awaiting the arrival of troops armed with both M-16s and ballot boxes, but this is mostly a sideshow.

The deeper truth is that the United States is locked in a condition subordinate not to any other nation, but to itself: the ceaseless demands, from the inside, for the very energy that must be expended, along with flesh and blood, to keep the machine running. And the entailment of that dependency is that the grossest damage done by this new-century empire is not to the target nations of its aggression, that list of alleged connection that leads from Afghanistan to Iraq to Iran; it is, rather, to its own citizens. Paul Virilio speaks of the condition of "endocolonization," when an imperial power begins to consume itself, eating up its own resources and citizens in a war set in motion theoretically to protect those very commodities. The machine of war is such that only total mobilization, which is to say eventual total self-consumption, is sufficient to the logic at hand.

There are further changes to be rung on the theme of machine, more metaphorical but also more relevant. The *social machine,* or line of control, embodies those forces of expectation or organization that define the limits of the acceptable or appropriate, especially in times of perceived crisis. These machines work to structure everyday life, sometimes merely pragmatically but often in the service of limitation or command. We may know that a society is firmly in the grip of a social machine when citizens utter the sentiment, so often heard of late, that if you have nothing to hide, you have nothing to fear. The presupposition of this sentiment is as much a part of the surveillance society as is any actual camera or agent, perhaps more so because it is beneath view, tucked away inside each one of us: an internalized sense of innocence that exempts the individual from a responsibility to anyone other than himself, presuming guilt for the alien other.

Of course, sometimes the security machine is the actual device through which we obediently pass our shoes or handbags (or models), meek before the social power that could prevent, as it might be, building access or homebound flight. But the security machine's reach is far more expansive and spectral than this, embracing every corner of a society where people must think twice before expressing spontaneity or resistance. Just as a prison guard does not need to be present in order to control the prisoner so long as the prisoner believes he is, the social machine functions best not when it is obvious but when it is taken for granted, internalized in the form of common sense, a set of expectations about "how things are done." This pervasive soft control should excite a gnawing worry in anyone actually, as distinct from merely rhetorically, concerned about liberty.

Buildings are symbols as well as constructions, vehicles of meaning as well as places to shelter and work. And sometimes the shelter becomes a target, its meaning the enemy's motive. There is a manifest insanity in the act, so indiscriminate and evil, of destroying the innocent in the name of a god and holy war; but there is, too, a kind of deranged rationality, isolating an iconic structure, a cluster of symbolized messages, in this case about finance and global influence, and marking it down for destruction.

The Empire State Building does not stand so clearly for the empire of postmodern political realism as did the World Trade Center. As I have tried to show, its position in America the culture (as distinct from America the nation-state) is more layered, and more romantic. The building has an unstable relation to its site. It is not as manifestly symbolic as the Statue of Liberty, that poetic expression of welcome; but it is not, at the same time, as crudely related to ideas of wealth and free markets as the blocky World Trade Center, whose very architectural blandness expressed a devotion to the business of business. Here are two ideas of freedom, one might say, two linked versions of the American dream: freedom itself and free markets. What do people do with their freedom, after all? What do they expect to get from the lady's promise of liberty, extended as they enter New York harbor? They work to make themselves better, which is to say better off. This linkage of freedom (the big idea) with freedom (the kind that comes with money) sustains all versions of the American dream, wherever they fall on the spectrum running from pure symbol to pure greed.

The building is neither a technical symbol of freedom nor a coded sign of financial might. Its durable elegance speaks clearly of its period, but the reality of that depressed moment is easily overlooked. It scrapes the sky, yet is solidly rooted in the workaday virtues of bustling Manhattan. It is more iconic of New York than of America more generally, despite the small coincidence of naming. Hence, it becomes a controversial property: a monument to the American dream erected on the backs of cheap workers, a symbol of magnificence in a reluctant empire, an office building that mostly fails to make economic sense. As early as 1932, the critic Elmer Davis, writing in the *New Republic,* decried the empty ambitions of its makers. "So there they stand," Davis wrote of the heaven-seeking Manhattan skyline, "those magnificent monuments to the faith of the nineteen-twenties—a perpetual inspiration to the beholder, provided he never invested any money in them. What is to become of them? The setback skyscrapers of Babylon have crumbled into hills of mud, but steel and concrete do not melt so easily. Of the faith that built the cathedrals of Île-de-France, enough has survived to keep those buildings in repair; but the faith that built the Empire State and the Chrysler buildings may presently be as dead as Bel and Marduk."

This view, though doubtless resonant in its moment, is mistaken; for the faith that built the Empire State and the Chrysler not only endures, bedrock into which new shafts of dreaming are weekly driven, but also shifts. New forms of cultural and ideological logic work the building over, make it their own, transform it. Nostalgia comes and clings; retro fashions and art appreciations swirl around and through; always, images and representations multiply and procreate. In the midst of it all, three-quarters of a century on, the building stands, invisible but necessary. Despite all its appropriations—in a way, because of them, because it is there to generate them—the Empire State itself is the fullest and best imaginable hymn to reality-based thought. One might even say that its successful construction and endurance are extended demonstrations of *how things work,* what happens when we take reality seriously and work with it, not invent it. Real human triumph resides in a building that lasts, not in a gesture of power that destroys and alienates.

Any building is also a part of the larger machine that is the engine of power, including the coded and practical forms of instrumental reason we call technology. The Empire State endures, and appeals, as a dominant technological wonder, an exceptional machine, constructed in the brief interregnum of America's growing dominance; and thus as an expression of the formidable nation between more violent engagements. Nor is that all. Its stature as a tower also makes it, as with all towers, a potential site of observation, an instrument of visual dominance—which is to say, part of the overarching social machine of surveillance, the security system. From this vantage high above the ground, we look down on those whose view we command. We survey and master. The grid beneath our view resolves itself, from this skyward position, into a system of Cartesian intersections, making individuals always localizable, always theoretically visible. They can run but they cannot hide.

More subtly, the building takes its place in a powerful economy of desire, a pervasive nostalgic futurism. Here, in this ever renewed dreamland of the city, the comic-book shadows and cinematic styles of 1930s Manhattan are always present, always available, beckoning us to a mythical past. Like all nostalgia, this bundle of desires and emotions can blind us to the concrete circumstances of the present, rendering the current arrangement of power invisible. Rem Koolhaas, one of the most persuasive analysts of Manhattan's dream logic, abruptly shifts his view of the city, and the building, in the new millennium. "From now on," he says, "the most important city in the world is dominated by a tower from which once dangled an ape." Koolhaas wants to ask: What is the connection between zero tolerance and the cult of Ground Zero? The answer, he suggests, is counterintuitive and bleak. "New Yorkers surrender to empathy. The tragedy of 9/11 inspires a mood of collective tenderness that is almost exhilarating, almost a relief: hype's spell is broken and the city can recover its own reality principle, emerge with new thinking about the unthinkable. But politics interfere [and] the transnational metropolis is enlisted in a national crusade. New York becomes a city (re)captured by Washington. Through the alchemy of 9/11, the authoritarian morphs imperceptibly into the totalitarian."

Nostalgia and reverie, always proximate temptations in life on the grid, give way to a violent assertion of the reality principle. The city is shaken out of its oneiric preoccupation. And yet, almost without pause, a new and higher-order pleasure principle swiftly closes in. The logic of avoidance is immediately reasserted through the twinned ideologies of security and nationalism. Thus, finally, a third irony of our analysis, this one specific to the building; namely, that its increased visibility in the wake of recent horrors, the new love openly expressed for its solid Art Deco perfection, may serve to render the conditions of its making, still more those of the city and country below it, invisible.

And yet, that conclusion is too simple, and too reductive. The best icons—the icons with staying power—tend, as I argued at the beginning, to enfold multiple, sometimes contradictory meanings in their layered reality. They change and shift, like the different plays of light and dark that cast lines across the building as the sun sinks and, eventually, sets. If the Empire State is an icon of technology, of surveillance, of nostalgia, it is also one of liberation, of possibility, of precisely the lines of flight

Gilles Deleuze celebrated. As with the grid of Manhattan itself, it sets us free precisely by appearing to constrain and yet not doing so. The grid is a free space, an unpainted canvas, and we each carve our pathways across, dancing through intersections and along streets, idiosyncratic contributors to the whole. The building, likewise, seems fixed and immobile, a monolith; in fact, though, it is fluid and airy, many things to many people.

The relationship between city and building is essential, and coeval. We ascend to its summit to observe the scene of our meander, not to control subjects or fix points, but to arouse ourselves, to feel that peculiar vertiginous rush of pleasure when we see where we have just come from, where we will return. The promise of the city viewed is that promise of life itself, of the unknown or surprising: not utopia, perhaps, but the heterotopia celebrated by Foucault, the hidden space, the space of otherness, that each one of us seeks in the right-angled heaven that is New York. The view from the top, the nearest thing to heaven, is not up to the skies, with some promise of perfection or salvation, or even an ideal city; it is down, to the ground, soon to be beneath our feet again, where the only dreams that matter, the ones we live, are made real.

Cary Grant's lonely wait reminds us that all is not always well. Sometimes our lover does not come. Sometimes we look down, as Deleuze himself did, in his final line of flight, and feel a desire to return more forcibly, and finally. That, too, is part of the building's meaning for us. Suicide, said Albert Camus, is the only truly serious philosophical problem. If we choose to live, then we must shoulder the responsibilities, as well as the joys, of doing so. The return to the ground is a return, for most of us, to tasks and burdens, of attempts to make sense of our being here. Exhilaration must sometimes compete with weariness, even despair.

The observatory is where things are observed: a laboratory of sight, a workbench of looking.

It is another cold day, a weekday in the last sunny dregs of fall, the city gathering itself for the giddy push of the holidays and the long wet months of the new year. The lobby prep space and ticketing zone are filled and jostling, the lines at each way station of the elevated pilgrimage long, and long-suffering. You are yourself impatient to get to the top, for you have only a little time. Not for you the bovine sluggishness of the sight-seeking tourist, that slowing of the soul that comes, and finds its gait, with the gallery shuffle, the cathedral crawl. You have just left the jaywalked grid, the laced and scored streetscape, and still have the knifing urge to cut through the crowd.

You get to the top faster than ever, faster than anyone. And here there is a small crowd, as usual, and you are surprised, as usual, to remember how small it is here, really. Just a balcony, a gift shop, the dimensions of a not so grand apartment, especially in this city of grand apartments.

A pause while the crowd rolls and transfers its bulk from inside to outside, the turnover of visitation. Now a space opens on the south side, your favorite, and you sidle into it, next to a young couple hugging each other in the chill. They are speaking German. Around you, other voices, in French and Italian, Czech and Japanese. A babble, in fact, and the tower has drawn them here, gathered them together—not for a dream of unity, perhaps, but surely by a kind of dream logic, an algorithm of desire. We all gaze south, pointing out, sometimes in words, the absence that still shimmers there despite the passage of years, years that feel like months, even weeks. Really so long ago?

You stand and look and listen. The voices of the twenty-first century. Graffiti in three languages, none English, festoon the wall in front of you. The urge to commemorate a presence, a visit. You think of that far-off rock formation in Wales, where they say Llewelyn hid, and the Victorian names and dates scratched into the wall. Everywhere, every time: I was here.

Downtown, off to the right, your old neighborhood, your former home. You can make out the intersection, not quite the building, and so complete, again, the kooky triangulation of the tower: I was there, looking here; now I am here, looking there. The lines of sight spun out and meeting, canceling or maybe reinforcing, sketching the Pythagorean notion across the span of the island, the city of spires and tall masts.

Nowadays, it is a temporal triangle, too, a plot into the past. Not just for you. Any high vantage is always a looking down, and hence, too, a looking back: a reflection. The person who has labored to the observatory observes more than just the external scene. You are that person; we are all that person. Struggling up, trying to get a look. The scene forces on you an inwardness as well, a critical reflection on who you are, what you have brought there, that which you have left below, and to which you will return.

In this space out of space, lifted high and near to heaven, gazing out and down, thinking of yourself soon to be returned to the street, resuming the life that you have chosen, the commerce of the streets, the shared space of citizenship, what do you see?

Bibliographic Essay

To keep the book as readable as possible, I have avoided footnotes and other forms of direct reference. The following essay indicates the main research sources, roughly in the order they appear in each chapter. Works not specifically cited but present as general background are found in the sections on the first and last chapters.

1
Palace of Dreams

F. Scott Fitzgerald's "My Lost City" appears in *My Lost City: Personal Essays, 1920–1940* (Cambridge, 2005).

There is a vast ephemeral literature on the Empire State Building, which I will not attempt to cite here, but book-length examinations are relatively rare. The best is certainly John Tauranac's comprehensive study, *The Empire State Building: The Making of a Landmark* (Scribner, 1995), which really obviated any other books on the building until the crucial shift in context created by the terrorist attacks of September 11, 2001. Since that date, there has been a very well produced large-format picture book, with abbreviated history, by Geraldine B. Wagner called *Thirteen Months to Go: The Creation of the Empire State Building* (Quintet, 2003). Tauranac and Wagner both mention but do not focus on the building's iconicity, the central concern of the present book.

Theodore James, Jr.'s *The Empire State Building* (Harper & Row, 1975) is an earlier, less thorough and more popular history of the building than Tauranac's. The architectural historians Carol Willis and Donald Friedman published their volume *Building the Empire State* (Norton, 1998) largely in order to reproduce the original contractor's "Notes on Construction of Empire State Building," together with expository essays by the authors. Not surprisingly, there are also many books about the building intended for children, of which the best I know is *Joe and the Skyscraper* (Prestel, n.d.), a sentimental but detailed picture book that includes various aquatinted postcard reproductions of Manhattan buildings and some excellent Lewis Hine photographs. Those photographs, and Margaret Bourke-White's studies of the Chrysler Building, are well known and widely reproduced. Many lesser known images of New York in the 1920s and '30s can be found in David Stravitz's wonderful book *New York, Empire City: 1920–1945* (Abrams, 2004), which includes many architectural and cultural photographs relevant to the concerns of my discussion.

Among more general studies, Neal Bascomb's page-turning *Higher: A Historic Race to the Sky and the Making of a City* (Broadway, 2003) also examines the Chrysler Building and the Manhattan Company Building in great detail. I have benefited enormously from the careful narratives offered in these volumes, of the Empire State specifically and of the general political and architectural culture of New York in the 1920s and '30s. Bascomb in particular has a deft eye for colorful detail and his work offers, among other things, a comprehensive bibliography of contemporary newspaper accounts of the skyscraper race, to which I would direct any interested reader. Several quotations in this chapter are taken from Bascomb's account.

May Day was established in 1889 at the first congress of the new socialist parties associated with the Second International, successor to Marx's First International. The one-day strike was established to commemorate the 1886 strikes across North America in which workers mobilized for an eight-hour work day; in Chicago the strike sparked riots and battles between workers and scabs the next day, during which police shot at labor organizers. On May 3 a protest rally in the city's Haymarket Square ended in violence when a bomb was thrown into the police ranks and they returned fire into the crowd. Eight anarchist leaders were arrested, tried, and sentenced to death. (Three were later pardoned.) While still observed in many European countries over a century later, the radical May Day was displaced in North America by Grover Cleveland's 1894 resolution, supported by the anarchy-shy American Federation of Labor, to observe Labor Day on the first Monday of September. It is virtually certain, however, that many of the workers engaged in the Empire State construction, being immigrants from Italy, Spain, and Sweden, would have noted the irony of the building's opening-day celebration.

A good discussion of Lamb's architectural vision, together with extensive excerpts from his own essays on the building, can be found in Rem Koolhaas,

Delirious New York: A Retroactive Manifesto for Manhattan (Monacelli, 1994; orig. Oxford, 1978), which offers an insightful, if typically offbeat, assessment of the Empire State Building's place in the theory of "Manhattanism," at pp. 132–51. Wittgenstein's references to hidden obviousness are in *Philosophical Investigations*, G. E. M. Anscombe, trans. (Macmillan, 1953). Roland Barthes's pregnant and, to me, highly influential essay on the Eiffel Tower has been much reprinted; I rely on the translation offered in Neal Leach's excellent anthology of writing on the built environment, *Rethinking Architecture: A Reader in Cultural Theory* (Routledge, 1997), pp. 172–81. Aldo Rossi, working with his own version of a structuralist architectural theory indebted in part to Barthes, discusses monumentality in his provocative book *Architecture of the City* (MIT, 1982); this work can be usefully contrasted with Kevin Lynch's analysis of "imageability" in cities, including monuments and other landmarks, in *The Image of the City* (MIT, 1960).

Koolhaas's complicating idea of the automonument first surfaces in his student-era collage, "The Berlin Wall as Architecture," and continues in, for example, his anti-skyscraper design for the CCTV Building in Beijing. For a good discussion of Koolhaas's place in the current economy of architecture, see Daniel Zalewski, "Intelligent Design: Can Rem Koolhaas Kill the Skyscraper?" *New Yorker* (March 14, 2005), pp. 111–25; also, for more scholarly discussions, see Aaron Betsky, "Rem Koolhaas: The Fire of Manhattanism Inside the Iceberg of Modernism," and Okwui Enwezor, "Terminal Modernity: Rem Koolhaas's Discourse on Entropy," both included in *What Is OMA? Considering Rem Koolhaas and the Office for Metropolitan Architecture* (NAi, 2003), at pp. 25–39 and 110–19, respectively.

2

Image and Icon

The most sustained and important analysis of American architecture in its iconic and simulacral aspects is of course Robert Venturi, *Learning from Las Vegas* (MIT, 1972; rev. 1977), a city which, perhaps inevitably, includes a miniature Empire State Building as part of the squashed New York skyline of one of its massive casinos. Le Corbusier struggles with functionalism and modernism in the circa-1923 journal essays gathered together as *Vers une Architecture* and translated into English as *Towards a New Architecture,* Frederick Etchells, trans. (Dover, 1986). These are, despite repetitions and tensions, a tour de force of architectural writing.

Mies van der Rohe and Giedion are discussed, along with numerous general arguments about modernism in architecture and otherwise, in Peter Conrad's enjoyable survey of early-twentieth-century art and design, *Modern Times, Modern Places* (Knopf, 1999). Adam Goodheart's poignant discussion, "The Skyscraper and the Airplane," was published in a special issue of *American Scholar* (January 2002) commemorating September 11, 2001.

Adolf Loos's celebrated essay "Ornament and Crime" has been reprinted in many places, including *Spoken into the Void: Collected Essays by Adolf Loos,* Jane O. Newman and John H. Smith, trans. (MIT, 1982). A good series of critical appraisals of the post-Loos moment is contained in Bernie Miller and Melony Ward, eds., *Ornament and Crime: The Arts and Popular Culture in the Shadow of Adolf Loos* (YYZ, 2002), which also includes a reprint of the original essay. See also Loos, *Sämtliche Schriften,* Franz Glück, ed. (Brenner, 1962).

C. S. Peirce, a pioneer of linguistics and semiotics, makes the powerful tripartite distinction among indexical, symbolic, and iconic signs in various places; for a full discussion, see Charles Hartshorne and Paul Weiss, eds., *The Collected Papers of Charles Sanders Peirce,* 8 vols. (Harvard, 1931–58). Roland Barthes's general theory of semiosis is outlined and defended in the long essay "Myth Today," which closes his classic volume of cultural-critical excavations, *Mythologies,* Annette Lavers, trans. (Paladin, 1973). Barthes discusses there his relation to Ferdinand de Saussure's general structuralist linguistics, first outlined in *Cours de Linguistique Générale* (Payot, 1916). Similar cultural applications of structuralist theory are evident in Dick Hebdige, *Subculture, the Meaning of Style* (Routledge, 1979), and Gilbert Adair, *Myths and Memories* (Fontana, 1986). Jean-François Lyotard's discussion of Samuel Beckett's eighty-year-old face is in Geoff Bennington and Rachel Bowlby, trans., *The Inhuman: Reflections on Time* (Cambridge, 1991).

Erwin Panofsky's studies in iconology are various. I have relied primarily on insights culled from his *Three Essays on Style* (MIT, 1993), which usefully extends iconological analysis from painting to film and architecture. The Michael Frayn novel *Headlong* (Faber, 1999) contains an excellent incidental discussion of the iconography-iconology distinction as part of a black comedy concerning art forgery. Michel de Certeau's evocative "Walking in the City," which starts at the top of the World Trade Center and descends to the streets below, is the first part of *The Practice of Everyday Life,* Stephen Rendall, trans. (California, 1984). Draftsman Matteo Pericoli offers a very different but equally gorgeous survey of New York with *Manhattan Unfurled* (Random House, 2001), including an essay by the critic Paul Goldberger called "Delicacy and Grandeur." Both works, image and text, are pinned to the World Trade Center in ways that now resonate with a sense of loss.

Utopian architecture and the utopian impulse more generally are made vivid and compelling in Ruth Eaton's superb *Ideal Cities: Utopianism and the (Un)Built Environment* (Thames & Hudson, 2001), which includes lavish illustrations of everything from ancient Babel-tower conceptions to contemporary and even science-fictional design for house-highrises and radiant cities. General issues of style in architecture, including an effective analysis of one block in Manhattan (the south side of Bryant Park, near the Public Library), are discussed in Witold Rybczynski, *The Look of Architecture* (Oxford, 2001). An idiosyncratic but illuminating treatment of virtuality and materiality in the built environment is given by Elizabeth Grosz in her collection of essays, *Architecture from the Outside: Essays on Virtual and Real Space* (MIT, 2001). Grosz covers some of the same ground as designer Jessica Helfand in her collection *Screen: Essays on Graphic Design, New Media, and Virtual Culture* (Princeton Architectural, 2001), and Hal Foster, *Design and Crime* (Versos, 2002). Helfand's essay on the proliferation of manifestos, "Me, the Undersigned" (pp. 17–28), is particularly good, as is Foster's dismantling of Bruce Mau's aesthetic pretensions; see also, on the last, Mark Kingwell, "Interior Decoration," *Harper's Magazine* (June 2001), pp. 72–75, and reprinted in *Practical Judgments: Essays in Culture, Politics, and Interpretation* (Toronto, 2002), pp. 212–26.

For more on what I call "monumental conceptual" architecture, see Jayne Merkel, "The Museum as Artifact," *Wilson Quarterly* (Winter 2002), pp. 66–79; also Mark Kingwell, "Monumental/Conceptual Architecture," *Harvard Design Magazine* 19 (Fall 2003/Winter 2004), online edition; "Redesigning Toronto: The $195-Million Scribble," *Toronto Life* (June 2004), pp. 70–75; "Stop," *Bite Magazine* (Summer 2004), pp. 13–15; and "The City of Tomorrow: Searching for the Future of Architecture in Shanghai," *Harper's Magazine* (February

2005), pp. 62–71. I try to survey the challenges and failures of modernism in architecture in "Meganarratives of Supermodernism: The Spectre of the Public Sphere," *Span* (Winter 2006), reprinted in Pascal Gin et al., eds., *Modernity in Transit: Twenty-five Years After the Postmodern Condition* (Les Éditions du GREF, 2006). Much of this work is incorporated into *Finding Your Way: Reflections on Cities and Consciousness* (Viking, 2007), a theoretical companion volume to the present work.

3
Scrape the Sky

Saul Bellow's *More Die of Heartbreak* (Morrow, 1987) is set mostly in Chicago, not New York, but for me it complements his great Manhattan novel *Seize the Day* (Penguin, 1976). *Above the Clouds,* by Alfred E. Smith, was a souvenir first published in 1934 by Empire State, Inc., and rendered in facsimile by Helmsley-Spear, Inc., for the May 1, 1996, celebration of the building's sixty-fifth anniversary. Paul Virilio's insights on speed and technology, especially the idea of dromofascism, are outlined in *Speed and Politics: An Essay on Dromology,* Mark Polizzotti, trans. (Semiotext(e), 1986; orig. 1977). Jed Perl's wonderful essay "The Adolescent City" appeared in the *New Republic* (January 22, 2001). The Everyman Library volume *Poems of New York,* Elizabeth Schmidt, ed. (Knopf, 2002), contains all of the poems quoted in this study, as well as the two cover images of the Empire State, one daytime, one night. (The cover designer for this revived Everyman series, Barbara de Wilde, deserves a credit too.)

The two main Futurist manifestos, from 1909 and 1912, both penned by Marinetti, are widely available, as are the various subsequent versions of Futurist declamation (see http://www.futurism.org.uk/futurism.htm for a comprehensive array). Bruce Mau's "Manifesto for Incomplete Growth" was published in several design magazines during the late 1990s and appears in his studio book *Life Style* (Phaidon, 2000); the Unabomber manifesto can be found at http://www .unabombertrial.com/manifesto/. Waugh's satires of manifestos and other tics of modernism are in *Vile Bodies* (Penguin, 1938; orig. 1930) and *Put Out More Flags* (Penguin, 1943; orig. 1942), among other places. Ayn Rand's *The Fountainhead* (Bobbs-Merrill, 1943) is hardly a great novel, but its influence is inescapable.

One small but perhaps telling example: Art Garfunkel, explaining his early career choice to attend architecture school, credited Rand's novel.

Information and quotations from Wright, Hulme, et al. are found in Conrad, *Modern Times, Modern Places,* cited above. The Ferriss setback schemes, especially the evocative charcoal sketches, are discussed at length in Koolhaas, *Delirious New York,* cited above (Tauranac also notes their influence). Michel Foucault surveys the surveillance society and the utilitarian panopticon in *Discipline and Punish,* Alan Sheridan, trans. (Pantheon, 1978), which retains more of its resonance in the original, *Surveiller et Punir* (Gallimard, 1975). Don DeLillo's extraordinary novel *Cosmopolis* (Scribner, 2003) is set on a single day in April 2000, as a hyperwealthy young financier goes across Manhattan in search of a haircut. The dreams of Psilopolis, extraordinary in a different way, can be viewed at http://www.eng.qmul.ac.uk/MEngProjects/Psi/, which includes schematics, charts, and rationales that do not entirely resolve one's sense that this is an extravagant, and brilliant, joke.

4
System and Structure

Hans-Georg Gadamer does not mention architecture in his volume *The Relevance of the Beautiful,* Nicholas Walker, trans. (Cambridge, 1986), but his claims concerning the centrality of "the gesture" in art are important for understanding the idea of a gestural building. K. Michael Hayes, in a paper delivered in Toronto in 2004, argued persuasively that the Seagram Building is a pure gestural building, and I am grateful for that stimulus.

Charles Tomlinson's line about the Chrysler's "Aztec pinnacle" is in the poem "All Afternoon," in *Poems of New York,* cited above.

Fredric Jameson discusses the importance, and limits, of postmodern architecture in his foreword to Jean-François Lyotard, *The Postmodern Condition: A Report on Knowledge,* Geoff Bennington and Brian Massumi, trans. (Minnesota, 1984; orig. 1979). Jürgen Habermas offers a somewhat less negative view in his "Modern and Postmodern Architecture," in *Critical Theory and Public Life,* John Forester, ed. (MIT, 1985). These two pieces are usefully read alongside a radically different position, such as the one defended by Georges

Bataille and effectively outlined in Denis Hollier, *Against Architecture: The Writings of Georges Bataille* (MIT, 1989). Charles Jencks's studies *The Language of Post-Modern Architecture* (Rizzoli, 1987; orig. 1977) and *Heteropolis: Los Angeles, the Riots, and the Strange Beauty of Hetero-architecture* (Academy, 1993) are also worth consulting.

For a good critical assessment of *post*-postmodern developments in architecture, see Hans Ibelings, *Supermodernism: Architecture in the Age of Globalization* (NAi, 1998), which makes a strong case that not all of these designs are (as often charged) grandiose and arrogant; nor is "globalization"—that floating signifier—always to be considered "the enemy." See also Marc Augé, *Non-places: Introduction to an Anthropology of Supermodernity* (Verso, 1995); and Neil Denari, *Gyroscopic Horizons* (Princeton Architectural, 1999). Daniel Libeskind's bits of autobiography and self-promotion, plus some insights about architecture, are found in *Breaking Ground: Adventures in Life and Architecture* (Riverhead, 2004), a book that never really settles the controversy with David Childs over Ground Zero; neither, for that matter, did the various "celebrity starchitect" profiles of Libeskind, of which the best was by the astute critic Paul Goldberger in the *New Yorker* (September 15, 2003).

Arthur Danto discusses and defends the third aesthetic realm, the one between the so-called fine arts and natural beauty—i.e., everything that counts as applied art, from fashion to architecture—in *The Abuse of Beauty: Aesthetics and the Concept of Art* (Open Court, 2003), especially chapters 3, 4, and 6. See also, for Danto's general "institutional" (really discursive) theory of art, *Beyond the Brillo Box: The Visual Arts in Post-Historical Perspective* (California, 1992). Theodor Adorno reacts to Husserl, and by implication Le Corbusier, in "Functionalism Today," *Oppositions* 17 (Summer 1979), pp. 31–41. See also Albrecht Wellmer, "Architecture and Territory," David Midgley, trans., in *Endgames: The Irreconcilable Nature of Modernity* (MIT, 1998). Husserlian phenomenological method is applied to issues of built form most assiduously and successfully by Edward S. Casey, especially in *Getting Back into Place: Toward a Renewed Understanding of the Place-World* (Indiana, 1993) and *The Fate of Place: A Philosophical History* (California, 1997). Husserl's own views about the space-place distinction of which Casey makes so much may be found in, among other places, *The Crisis of the European Sciences,* David Carr, trans. (Northwestern, 1970).

Georg Simmel's brilliant evocation of the stimulus-heavy urban attitude is the now-classic essay "The Metropolis and Mental Life," reprinted in Leach, *Rethinking Architecture*, cited above, at pp. 69–85. Simmel anticipates all later discussion about "cool." Hannah Arendt's too-brief remarks about the politics of the built environment, in particular its temporal persistence relative to human mortality, are found in *The Human Condition* (Chicago, 1998); architect-theoretician George Baird expands and applies these insights in a very important series of essays and interventions collected as *The Space of Appearance* (MIT, 1995). I try to pursue this line of argument in *Finding Your Way*, cited above, and in an earlier discussion of public space, *The World We Want* (Rowman & Littlefield, 2001), ch. 5. See also Kenneth Frampton, "The Status of Man and the Status of His Objects: A Reading of *The Human Condition*," in *Hannah Arendt: The Recovery of the Public World*, Melvyn A. Hill, ed. (St. Martin's, 1979); and J. H. van den Berg, *Things: Four Metabletic Reflections* (Duquesne, 1970).

Thorstein Veblen's definitive account of positional goods is, of course, *The Theory of the Leisure Class* (Penguin, 1979; orig. 1908). Lewis Mumford's massive work *The City in History* (Harcourt, 1961) is studded with important insights, including the one about measuring time (see also Virilio on the point). Obituaries of Philip Johnson were mixed in tone, but Mark Stevens's op-ed column in the *New York Times*, "Form Follows Fascism" (January 31, 2005), offered the unpleasant facts quoted. Quotations from Speer and Trotsky can be found in *Modern Times, Modern Places*, cited above.

A word about Heidegger, technology, and fascism. In the lecture "The Question Concerning Technology," delivered in 1950 (see William Lovitt, trans., *The Question Concerning Technology and Other Essays* [Harper, 1977]), Heidegger offers a profound response to the devastations of the Second World War. He sounds, indeed, what might be considered the plaintive keynote of the entire century, suggesting that the urge to "get" technology "spiritually in hand," whether by flight or by constraint, betrays a confusion, or extension of the original problem.

"The will to mastery becomes all the more urgent the more technology threatens to slip from human control," Heidegger notes. The obvious irony is that such attempts at spiritual control of technology quickly succumb to the self-same logic of control to which they purport to be the solution. The less obvious, and deeper one, is that the truth of technology is not instrumentality at all but the indebtedness and responsibility carried in all making, or *techné*, poetic and practical alike. Technology's essence is a bringing-forth, he says, a revealing; it is, as suggested by the Greek word *alétheia*, a revelation or clearing—in short, truth.

These insights had already been foreshadowed in an earlier essay, "Die Zeit des Weltbildes" (translated as "The Age of the World Picture" and included in Lovitt, *The Question Concerning Technology,* cited above). First delivered in 1938, this lecture discusses, among other things, the dangers of Cartesian abstraction and the rise of "giganticism" as an American response, not yet metaphysical, to the modern conception of space. Heidegger also refers in passing to the influential essay by Ernst Jünger "Die Totale Mobilmachung," published in 1931—the year the Empire State opened—and later part of Jünger's massive work *Die Arbeiter* [The Worker] (Hanseatische Verlaganstalt, 1932). Based on his observations of "total war" in the 1914–18 conflict, Jünger understands modern society as a system of "total mobilization" geared toward war, such that technology and labor alike are colonized and deployed as instruments of state-sanctioned violence. Indeed, the man-becomes-machine images of the First World War—fighter planes, tanks, gas-masked infantry—offer haunting figures of a new cyborg universe. Later Jünger would expand the view to suggest that all technological activity is a form of such mobilization: an insight given material force in the construction of the Empire State Building, that ultimate statement of ordnance delivery!

There are ironies of a different kind in Heidegger's subtle post-facto indictment of instrumental reason. We cannot ignore the fact that the thinking here, in 1950, is linked in complicated ways with Heidegger's notorious association with the Nazi Party as Rector-Führer of Freiburg University during 1933–34, just a couple of years after the Empire State Building was completed. Heidegger's speeches and memos from the period demonstrate the depth of his belief that only a radical antimodern nationalism could resist the perceived depredations of global liberalism. The gruesome irony is that the Nazis were eventually as beholden as anyone else to deadly technology and the power of bureaucratic rationalization, not least in the death camps.

Disturbing manifestations of human submission to instrumentalism still lay in humankind's future in 1931, to be sure. Carpet bombing, the split atom, and the weapon of mass destruction were no more than gleams in a military scientist's eye. But already in the interbellum period the contours of a fraught relationship are clear. Indeed, Heidegger's point is that this is by no means a distinctively modern problem, though it is true that the modern version is especially acute, given the swiftness of change and improvement and the relentlessness of the spiraling logic of control. Heidegger, too, thrilled to the siren song of fascism, though it can be argued that his philosophical reasons for heeding the call are quite different, and certainly there is no indication of the conceptual dropout that seems to have afflicted Johnson and other disillusioned modernists. Heidegger's calls for an architecture restorative of Being, which would allow *dwelling* in "the fourfold" of earth, sky, mortals, and gods (and hence real thinking, in the clearing of truth) was arguably part of his own kind of Romantic idyll, a sort of anti-utopian conservative utopianism.

Heidegger's fetishizing of a simple hut in the Black Forest stands as the easily parodied signifier of a nostalgic wish to return to a premodern condition. Heidegger would use such atavistic evasion again when attempting to explain his relations with the Nazis. "The inner truth and greatness of the National Socialist movement," he told the newspaper *Der Spiegel* in 1976, lay in its response to "the encounter between global technology and modern man." It failed to live up to its promise, mired in the wrong kind of radicalism. Significantly, Heidegger failed to acknowledge the death camps even at this late, and arguably costless, stage. "Only a god can save us," he said instead, surrendering his critical philosophy to the very onto-theological impulse he had tried so hard to challenge. This, for Hans Jonas and many others, was the "unforgivable" coda to Heidegger's intricate, and tragic, flirtation with politics.

5
Still Life

Don DeLillo's novel *White Noise* (Viking, 1985) contains many moments of acute cultural criticism, of which the best is the one quoted. The insights about tourism from Barthes are drawn, once more, from his essay on the Eiffel Tower. A useful broader discussion is Dean MacCannell, *The Tourist* (Schocken, 1976).

Statistics and comparisons discussed in this chapter are found in Tauranac, *The Empire State Building,* and Bascomb, *Higher,* both cited above, and in various bits of promotional material published by the building's owners. Graham Greene's remark about postcards is in *Stamboul Train* (Penguin, 1963; orig. 1932). Michael Chabon's novel *The Amazing Adventures of Kavalier and Clay* (Random House, 2000) deservedly won a Pulitzer Prize for its loving depiction of midcentury immigrants to New York and the intoxicating fantasies of the comic-book industry; it features an unforgettable image of the Empire State on its cover; as do, in quite different tenors, Salman Rushdie's *Fury* (Knopf, 2001) and Thomas Kelly's *Empire Rising* (Farrar, Straus & Giroux, 2005). The last is a shot from within the Chrysler, framing the Empire State in one of the trademark triangular windows of the distinctive apex.

Walter Benjamin's essay "The Work of Art in the Age of Mechanical Reproduction," which has been much discussed and much misunderstood, can be found in Harry Zohn, trans., *Illuminations: Essays and Reflections* (Schocken, 1968), pp. 217–52. On the issue of recombinant culture, Benjamin's analysis is usefully complemented by Theodor Adorno and Max Horkheimer, "The Culture Industry: Enlightenment as Mass Deception," in (among other places) *The Cultural Studies Reader,* Simon During, ed. (Routledge, 1993).

For years I labored under the belief that the story about the 1:1 scale map was by Lewis Carroll, until not long ago I read in Rebecca Solnit's *A Field Guide to Getting Lost* (Viking, 2005) that it is in fact by Borges. That confusion may itself offer a kind of Borgesian fable, one might think, since the existence of the latter story would not obviate the existence of the former, or more precisely my belief in its existence, and might even *emphasize* its reality in the form of influence from one genius of the literary-philosophical puzzle on another. The fable grows more intricate still when one consults Solnit's oddly selective bibliographic notes—and finds no citation for Borges.

I can say without hesitation that David Foster Wallace's discussion of reverent irony is "E Unibus Pluram: Television and U.S. Fiction," in *Review of Contemporary Fiction* (1993) and reprinted in *A Supposedly Fun Thing I'll Never Do Again* (Little, Brown, 1997), pp. 21–82. And details of Andy Warhol's death and near-death experience, together with excerpts from the SCUM Manifesto, can be found at www.rotten.com/library/bio/artists/andy-warhol/. The essay "On Being Bored" is included in Adam Phillips's excellent collection

On Kissing, Tickling, and Being Bored (Faber, 1933). Schopenhauer's views on boredom can be found throughout *The World as Will and Representation* (orig. *Die Welt als Wille und Vorstellung*, 1815) and, more vividly, *Parerga and Paralipomena* (1850). R. J. Hollingdales's English translation of the latter (*Essays and Aphorisms*, 1970) is the source work for a recent accessible selection of Schopenhauer's writings, *On the Suffering of the World* (Penguin, 2004).

Thomas Mann's *The Magic Mountain* (orig. *Die Zauberberg*, 1924) is all about time, really. Time, and cigars. And disease. Time, cigars, and disease. I have used H. T. Lowe-Porter's translation (Vintage, 1969), at pp. 66 and 104. Saint Augustine's famous discussion of time is found in his *Confessions* (orig. 400). Julian Jaynes's memorable flashlight metaphor is given in the classic, controversial text, *The Origin of Consciousness in the Breakdown of the Bicameral Mind* (Houghton Mifflin, 1976). Platonic type-token metaphysics are everywhere present in the Greek philosopher's dialogues but perhaps most obviously, certainly most influentially, in *Republic,* especially Books 4 and 10.

Peter Eisenman's theory of "post-functionalism" is defended in Charles Jencks and Karl Knopf, eds., *Theories and Manifestoes of Contemporary Architecture* (Wiley, 1997). See also the illuminating article by Jacques Derrida, in the Leach collection *Rethinking Architecture* cited above, called (with deliberate echo of Nietzsche's mad egotism) "Why Peter Eisenman Writes Such Good Books," which describes a collaboration between these two masters of wit and will.

6
Moving Pictures

Some details about the films discussed, including review quotations, are taken from John Walker, ed., *Halliwell's Film and Video Guide* (HarperCollins, 2000). Anthony Lane's *New Yorker* review of *Sleepless in Seattle* is reprinted in *Nobody's Perfect: Writings from the New Yorker* (Knopf, 2002), pp. 11–15. The quotation from Marjorie Garber is in the introduction to the superb collection *Symptoms of Culture* (Routledge, 1998). John Berger's *Ways of Seeing* (Penguin, 1972), a classic piece of tendentious art criticism, contains the seminal discussion about nostalgia in advertising and visual culture more generally. Barthes's well-known structuralist dissection in *The Fashion System* (Hill and Wang, 1983) has not been improved on. Nor, when it comes to books set entirely during a single escalator ride, has Nicholson Baker's *The Mezzanine* (Vintage, 1990), not least because it is the only known exemplar.

Charles Fourier's kooky utopian vision is best expressed in *The Theory of the Four Movements,* Ian Patterson, trans. (Cambridge, 1996; orig. 1808), which includes discussion of phalanstery organization, singing contests, and the eventual change of the saltwater oceans into potable lemonade.

In yet another anxiety-of-influence moment, the quotation I attribute to Oscar Wilde, about maps and utopia, has also been credited to Lewis Mumford. For a fuller discussion, see the Eaton volume cited on p. 209 and also Peter Turchi, *Maps of the Imagination: The Writer as Cartographer* (Trinity, 2004). The graphic design collection *You Are Here: Personal Geographies and Other Maps of the Imagination,* Katharine Harmon, ed. (Princeton Architectural, 2004), is a brilliant visual exploration of the mapmaking urge, its joys and limits. The book also contains (p. 135) a circa-1932 drawing by the Futurist engineer Barosi (first name not used) for "Fire in the Mouth," the Futurist cocktail that features cherries rolled in cayenne pepper and layers of whisky, honey, strega, and vermouth. The cocktail was included in Marinetti's *Futurist Cookbook* (Trefoil, 1989; orig. 1932), which also featured another Barosi concoction called Dolceforte (Sweetstrong) that calls for bread to be covered with bananas, butter, anchovies, and mustard.

7

Empire

E. B. White, *Here Is New York* (Harper, 1949), is one of the best essays ever written about New York's inimitable mix of flavors, including that oddly moving worry about political violence visiting the skies over Manhattan. It also contains the most accurate assessment I know of New York's peculiar gift, in the midst of overwhelming possibilities, the freedom "not to attend." This is Simmel's urban attitude raised to the level of theory, and it contrasts poignantly with the need, among citizens of smaller places, to attend everything that comes along, lest they never get the chance again.

Richard Sennett's essay "Plate Glass," *Raritan* (Winter 1987), is a nice complement to my discussion of concrete and indeed illuminates a good deal of architectural practice in the twentieth century. Preceding the advent of the glass-curtain wall, the Empire State builders celebrate a quadrumvirate of technical wonders that is still, from our point of view today, transitional from premodern to modern. For more on concrete in particular, see Mark Kingwell, "Concrete's Softer Side," *Saturday Night* (June 3, 2000), pp. 64–67, where, among other things, I note that concrete "doesn't want to be a flat wall all the time, as if it were hemmed in at some fundamental level, like the hard edges of bricks or those erector-set cubes fashioned from I-beam steel and sheet glass. Concrete wants to be, as well, an eye-filling groundswell, an organic, emergent property of the landscape. It wants to be a rock, a stone, a hump of matter pressing up out of the ground. Concrete is a material capable of cambers and blobs more primeval, more deeply rooted, than the angles and boxes we will make later. Straight lines are wonderful, but sometimes curves are better, and concrete gives us both. Its brutalism tamed, concrete opens up a profound connection to the earth. You might even say, it is the world itself coming into being." Like many people, I had to revise my view of bricks when I saw, at Case Western Reserve University near Cleveland, a curving brick wall, the textured wave of orange-red solidity fashioned by Frank Gehry for the business school.

Immanuel Kant distinguishes interest and disinterest, beauty and decoration, in *Critique of Judgment* (orig. *Kritik der Urteilskraft,* 1790), of which there are many translations; I rely on J. H. Bernard (Haffner, 1951). Gilles Deleuze and Félix Guattari illustrate what they mean by machine—a system of control and flight, a social structure—in *A Thousand Plateaus: Capitalism and Schizophrenia,* Brian Massumi, trans. (Minnesota, 1987). See also Gilles Deleuze, *Negotiations,* Martin Joughin, trans. (Columbia, 1995; orig. *Pourparlers,* 1990). Paul Virilio's notion of endocolonization is explored with Sylvère Lotringer in *Pure War* (Semiotext(e), 1997; orig. 1983). The quotation from M. F. K. Fisher's journal is found in *Stay Me, Oh Comfort Me: Journals and Stories, 1933–1941* (Pantheon, 1993), p. 9.

Rem Koolhaas's important revision of his views on New York, "White Briefs Against Filth: The Waning Power of New York," first appeared in *Wired* magazine (June 2003) and is reprinted, among other places, in Rem Koolhaas, ed., *Content* (Taschen, 2004), pp. 236–39. This volume also contains Koolhaas's instantly influential essay "Junk Space" (pp. 162–71) and a celebration of the CCTV design, "Dissecting the Iconic Exosymbiont: The CCTV Headquarters, Beijing, as Built Organism" (pp. 490–91).

It is not clear how much of Koolhaas's late-model disdain of New York is personal pique as opposed to critique. (He has, after all, thrown his lot in with Beijing, authoritarian repressions and all.) But there is good reason to think that the American empire that has made New York a simultaneous symbol and unanswerable argument is both postmodern and dangerous. Speaking to *New York Times* reporter Ron Suskind on the eve of the 2004 U.S. election, a Bush Administration aide explained the new postmodern condition to the liberal intellectuals of the Eastern Seaboard (and whoever else may be presumed to read the *New York Times*). Such people belong to "what we call the reality-based community," the aide said, where people "believe that solutions emerge from your judicious study of discernible reality." This was a view of things for which he clearly felt some pity, so deluded did these people remain. "That's not the way the world really works anymore. We're an empire now, and when we act, we create our own reality. And while you're studying that reality—judiciously, as you will—we'll act again, creating our new realities, which you can study too, and that's how things will sort out. We're history's actors . . . and you, all of you, will be left to just study what we do."

But the American empire is not only postmodern, achieving a degree of unchallenged power undreamed-of even by the most extravagant relativist, it is also *allegedly liberal*. That is, in contrast to previous empires, which were more straightforward in their designs on domination, or found quasi-moral justifications thereof, as in the case of Britain assuming what Rudyard Kipling called the white man's burden, the current example clings to a position of exceptionalism and even isolation. A rhetoric of liberation and human dignity masks any clear admission of aggression. The violence is real and undeniable but rendered always inexplicit, hidden behind claims of national security or distant oppression. This empire will not acknowledge any moral authority outside itself, yet it appears untroubled by internal contradictions in its own moral position, such as the recourse to lies and false justifications for exercising power.

As the political scientist Greg Grandin put it, this "easy acceptance of brutality in pursuit of an elusive liberal empire bears more than a passing resemblance to an earlier willingness of Soviet apparatchiks to justify repression in the name of a distant utopia." The contradiction is not news, because it is a matter of conflicting values. Hannah Arendt, in *The Origins of Totalitarianism* (HBJ, 1973; orig. 1951), made the very same point of an earlier generation of imperialists. British politicians who believed they could maintain a liberal imperial regime without recourse to racist violence were, she said, "quixotic fools of imperialism." Empire means violence, the imposition of will. It is not, and cannot be, a program of liberation, no matter what any given inaugural address might say.

American conservatives, meanwhile, who might have been thought sympathetic to the Christian moralism underlying this project of liberation, have reacted to recent imperialism with a mixture of concern and bitterness, making strange bedfellows with old-fashioned American leftists. The imperial policies of the first years of the twenty-first century seemed to violate the central promise of American politics, namely that it would put Americans first. One commentator, writing in *The American Conservative,* summed up the linked ironies this way: "The launching of an invasion against a country that posed no threat to the U.S., the doling out of war profits and concessions to politically favored corporations, the financing of the war by ballooning the deficit to be passed on to the nation's children, the ceaseless drive to cut taxes for those outside the middle class and working poor: it is as if [the Bush Administration] sought to resurrect every false 1960s-era left-wing cliché about predatory imperialism and turn it into administration policy." Which is, of course, just what the left wing itself was thinking, though perhaps less wryly.

The clearest symbol of the new postmodern imperium, meanwhile, is not a new figure but rather one whose features Marinetti sketched almost a century ago, celebrating what he called the New Man of Futurism. This exemplar of fast power will communicate, Marinetti says, by "brutally destroying the syntax of his speech. He wastes no time in building sentences. Punctuation and the right adjectives will mean nothing to him. He will despise subtleties and nuances of language." His thinking is cubist, jazz-age, fractured by fastness; it will show a "dread of slowness, pettiness, analysis, and detailed explanations. Love of speed, abbreviation, and the summary. 'Quick, give me the whole thing in two words!'"

Mission accomplished.

Index